THE AEGEAN

A SEA-GUIDE TO ITS COASTS
AND ISLANDS

By the same author

THE ADRIATIC
THE TYRRHENIAN SEA
THE IONIAN ISLANDS TO THE ANATOLIAN COAST

DARDANELLES : A Midshipman's Diary

© *H. M. Denham 1963, 1970, 1975, 1979, 1983*
First published 1963
Second Edition 1970
Third Edition 1975
Fourth Edition 1979
Fifth Edition 1983

Printed in Great Britain by The Camelot Press, Southampton
for John Murray (Publishers) Ltd, 50 Albemarle Street, London W1X 4BD

British Library Cataloguing in Publication Data
Denham, H. M.
The Aegean. — 5th ed.
1. Aegean Sea region — Description and travel
— Guide-books
I. Title
914.99′047024797   D972
ISBN 0–7195–3980–3

THE AEGEAN

A Sea-Guide to its Coasts and Islands

H. M. DENHAM

JOHN MURRAY

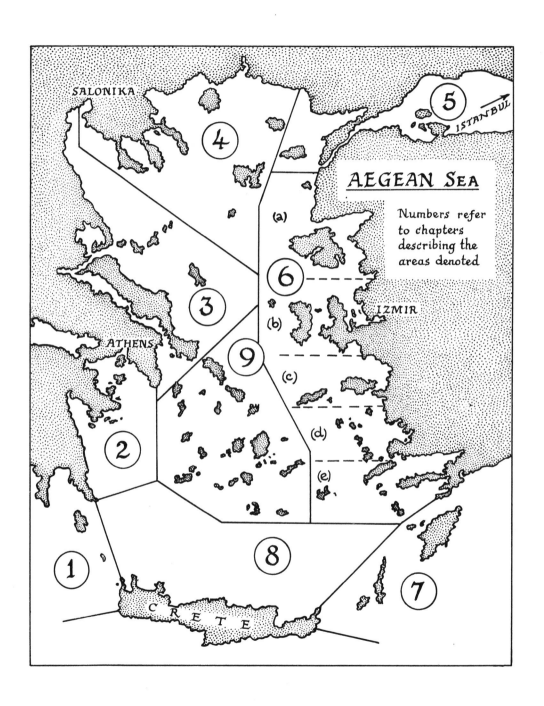

SALONIKA

⑤

ISTANBUL

④

AEGEAN SEA

Numbers refer
to chapters
describing the
areas denoted

(a)

⑥ - - - -

⑥

IZMIR

(b)

③

ATHENS

⑨

- - - - -

(c)

- - - - -

(d)

② - - - - -

(e)

①

⑧

⑦

C R E T E

Contents

Illustrations

SOURCES OF ILLUSTRATIONS

Sketch maps by Aydua Scott-Elliot, c.v.o. Drawings by Madge Denham. Title-page drawing by David Knight. Photographs: 1, 3, 5, 9, 10, 11, 12, the Author; 2, 4, 7, 19, J. Allan Cash Ltd; 6, National Tourist Organisation of Greece; 8, 23, Spyros Meletzis, Athens; 13, 14, Turkish Tourism Information Office; 15, 16, Mustafa Kapkin, Izmir; 17, T. Amorghianos; 18, 22, Yannis Scouroyannis, Athens; 20, Syndication International; 24, Voula Papaïoannou, Athens.

Preface to Fifth Edition

I have, as before, received helpful information from a number of sailing friends confirming or updating information for this latest edition. I should like to thank especially Mrs Jehane West, who has recently completed an extensive survey of Thrace and Crete as well as covering some of the islands; also Wing Commander N. T. Bulpitt, RAF, Mr Anthony Butler, Mr Robert Carter (USA), Commander J. S. Guard, RN, Mr Colin Hunter, Mr Walter Ingham (Elba), Mr Kenneth Marsh, Mr John Paton (War Graves Commission), Mrs Janet Sanso, Colonel Sheepshanks, Mr Van Marle (The Netherlands), Mr and Mrs Eric Williams, and the National Tourist Organisation of Greece and the Turkish Tourism Information Office for their co-operation.

In this edition the appendix with illustrations of local craft has been omitted, there being no longer any of these attractive vessels under sail in Greek waters.

This book is not intended to be a substitute for British Admiralty Charts and *Sailing Directions* and neither author nor publisher accepts responsibility for any consequences of the material being used instead of such official publications.

H.M.D.

1982

The grand object of travelling
is to see the shores of the Mediterranean.
On these shores were the four great empires of
the world – the Assyrian, the Persian, the Greek and the
Roman. All our religion, almost all our arts,
almost all that sets us above savages
has come to us from the shores
of the Mediterranean.

DR SAMUEL JOHNSON

Introduction to Greek Waters

GENERAL CRUISING INFORMATION

Spelling of Greek and Turkish Names. In the last twenty years the Greeks have changed many place names, either to eliminate names that were of Turkish or Venetian origin, or to commemorate some historical event or personage; moreover they have in many cases simplified or standardised the spelling of old names. The Turks, too, have substituted Turkish for older Greek or Venetian names. British *Sailing Directions* and all but the oldest Admiralty charts now follow their modern Greek and Turkish counterparts. Throughout this book I have observed the following system: such well-known places as Athens, Rhodes, Crete, Salonika, I have written according to our English custom, but to make sure that every place may be easily found in the Index I have in most cases inserted alternative names. For the less well-known places, I have followed the latest British Admiralty chart or *Sailing Directions*.

A guide to the pronunciation is given in the Index where the accented syllables have been indicated.

Port Officials are not mentioned at each place, since at every small Greek port there is normally both a Customs Office and a Port Authority. In very small places the local policeman sometimes acts on their behalf. The harbour officials dress like the Navy, though they are not sailors, nor are they administered by the Admiralty. On a yacht's arrival from a foreign port a transit log is issued at the Port of Entry (see list on page xxii) on presentation of the Ship's Papers. For the remainder of the yacht's stay only this log and a crew list, indicating the last and next port of call, are required by the authorities. Dues have recently been imposed on yachts at most harbours. (Formalities on entering and leaving Turkey are described on pp. 88–9.)

SUPPLIES

Fuel and Water

As they are an important concern for a small cruising yacht, the Tourist Organisation issues a list of 'Supply Ports' where these commodities can be obtained. At most of these places water and fuel have been obtainable at a section of the quay marked by blue and white zebra stripes, but in 1980 fuel was seldom available except by a bidon from a lorry; in the Cyclades water, too, was lacking at many of the quays.

Gas. Campingaz cylinders are easily exchanged in Greece. British Calor gas cylinders have fittings unlike those of any Continental country; it is never possible to exchange them, but in large towns they can sometimes be refilled.

Food and Drink

As the enjoyment of cruising in Greece can be so easily marred by stomach troubles, a few notes on the local food and drink are necessary.

In all the small restaurants it is quite in order for the customer to enter the kitchen and choose his dish from the wide copper pans spread out on the charcoal stove – generally there are chicken, lamb stew, stuffed tomatoes, savoury rice, and fish soup etc., all looking most inviting, as well as the Greek dishes such as *dolmádes* (meat and rice in vine leaves), *moussaká* (a sort of shepherds' pie with cheese and aubergine) and *pastízio* (baked macaroni with meat and cheese). Usually there is a charcoal grill, and lamb cutlets or fish cooked on this is a safe bet; but be sure to say 'without oil' (*óhee Ládhi*) when ordering or you will find cold olive oil has been poured over your grill. Fish is almost invariably good and fresh, but nowadays sometimes in short supply, except at fishing ports. Nearly all restaurants have little dishes of *yogurt*, and also delicious *baklavá* (honey-cakes with almonds). Never order your whole meal at one time, or you will find that the dishes will be brought all together, and by the time you have eaten your first course the second will be congealed. [For Turkish food see pp. 89–90].

Fish and Meat. The following are usually available:

Fish

Gilthead bream	*Tsipoúra*	Whitebait	*Marídes*
Sea bream	*Sinagrída*	Anchovy	*Antsoúya*
Common bream	*Lithríni*	Mackerel	*Skoumbrí*
Red mullet	*Barboúnia*	Spanish mackerel	*Koliós*
Grey mullet	*Kéfalos*	Prawns	*Garídes*
Sole	*Glóssa*	Squid	*Calamári*
Bass	*Lavráki*	Lobster	*Astakós*

Meat

Lamb } usually good	*Arnáki*	Steak (fillet)	*Bon Filet*
Pork }	*Hirinó*	Veal	*Moskári*
Chops	*Brizóles*	Kidney – usually good	*Nefró*

Butter is obtainable at most of the towns frequented by tourists.

Fruit and Vegetables. Early in the season are:

Apples, oranges, cherries, loquats, beans and peas, courgettes, artichokes and lettuces.
Some of these begin to go out of season in May and are followed by tomatoes, cucumbers, aubergines, peaches, apricots and figs. Later there are melons and grapes.
Anything eaten raw should be washed.

Wines and Spirits. Wine is obtainable everywhere in bottles or in small demijohns. A great many places have local draught wine (always the best), otherwise bottled retsinas and unresinated wines can always be found.

Local vermouth and brandy are passable aperitifs. *Oúzo* (a form of *rakí*), the local spirit, is obtainable everywhere on draught.

'Fix' beer and other brands can be bought nearly everywhere and are excellent.

Bottled soft drinks, either with water or as concentrate, are exceptionally good.

'Duty Free' drinks and tobacco are readily available at Piraeus for yachts over 40 tons net registered. Elsewhere their acquisition is too slow and involved to be interesting.

GENERAL INFORMATION

Health. The incidence of typhoid and tetanus varies from year to year in Greece, but there is always some, and it is sensible to be inoculated. Practically all the well-known medicines and drugs can be bought in Athens and possibly in the few big towns, but nowhere else, so it is advisable to have a well-stocked medicine chest. The *Yachting World* diary gives an excellent and comprehensive list which covers most eventualities. Two useful additions are Sulphamezathine and Lomotil, as, inoculated or not, many people in the Mediterranean become afflicted with some form of colic, particularly if eating ashore.

Malaria appears to be completely stamped out.

Nowadays in Greece there is no trouble in finding a doctor on the larger islands and even in the smaller places there is generally a qualified medical practitioner, a chemist and, at the worst, probably a midwife.

In Turkey medical facilities outside the large towns fall short of the Greek standard. Although three-quarters of the Turkish population live in the country towns and villages, the great majority of the doctors and dentists practise in the cities of Istanbul, Izmir, Ankara, Bodrum, Datça and Marmaris.

Shooting. Shooting cruises in Greece, usually in British yachts, continued until nearly the beginning of the First World War. Large schooners sailed from

England in January or February, collected the owner and guests in Italy or Malta and then mostly proceeded to the Albanian coast and north Greece. There they found an abundance of duck, partridge, quail and woodcock. Those who entered the Aegean were limited to red-legged partridges,★ hares and rabbits on the Islands, wild goat at Anti-Milos, and duck shooting on the Vardar marshes near Salonika. With the exception of the wild goat, all these still exist, but a special permit for shooting is required.

Fishing. At sea a variety of fish (listed on page xv) are caught by day and, during the dark of the moon, by night.

Night Fishing. Five 'ducklings' (*grigriá*) are each manned by one man and fitted with enormous gas-lamps over the stern. They are towed out of harbour to the fishing ground by the mother-ship, a *trehandiri*, fitted with winches and line-reels, followed by the net-boat, astern of which come the five little 'ducklings'. They usually have a long night on the fishing grounds and are seldom back in harbour until well after sunrise. The Turks occasionally use the same method of fishing, their craft being called *gugurru*.

The waters off the Anatolian coast, which receive the flow from a number of small rivers, yield the most fish, and are frequently poached by the Greek fishermen. By far the best fishing was in the Bosporus, but owing to pollution fish are now caught a few miles below in the Sea of Marmara.

★ Being non-migratory they are always to be found on most islands; woodcock, snipe, quail, geese and duck only come in spring and autumn.

Fish, generally, are becoming scarce, and consequently expensive. The reason for this scarcity is both because of the small-mesh net and the use of dynamite. Crayfish, though plentiful in Turkey, are nearly fished out in Greece.

Diving with deep-sea diving apparatus including use of oxygen is forbidden, also spear fishing with underwater lighting.

Pollution. In Greek and Turkish waters there still appears to be less pollution than in other parts of the Mediterranean. The effects of untreated sewage and oil pollution in Greece may be considered to have the most harmful effect in two main areas: the Saronic Gulf (Piraeus) and the Thermaikos Gulf (Salonika).

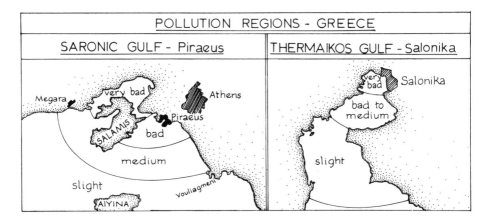

Saronic Gulf. It is not surprising that the Bay of Eleusis at the head of the gulf heads the contamination league. This bay is almost enclosed and receives most of the untreated outfall from factories, little of which can circulate and get away through the narrow exits. The bay, largely taken up by the Navy and laid-up ships, has a contamination twelve times that of the open waters of the gulf; but except when proceeding to refit at one of the Perama yards these highly polluted waters need not concern a visiting yacht.

Passing seawards by Salamis and beyond, the situation improves; but the waters on the west side of the gulf are slightly more contaminated than on the eastern. This may be due to surface wind-induced currents carrying much of the untreated sewage from the large populated cities of Athens and Piraeus to the west, possibly augmented by a small outflow from Eleusis Bay. The water here has normally half the contamination of Eleusis, while on the eastern side, with its marinas and bathing beaches, the situation is slightly better. Towards Vouliagmeni the cleanliness improves perceptibly.

For many years the Greek government took no action to improve these conditions, but in 1977 Captain McMullen (commodore of the Royal Cruising Club and a marine consultant) was invited to make a study of existing conditions and to prepare a detailed report with recommendations on how to improve matters. This he has done in a document of seventy-six pages, but it is a very complicated problem and no doubt further study is needed.

Thermaikos Gulf. Only the general situation is known as illustrated in the diagram.

In Turkey the area around Izmir is polluted and also parts of the Sea of Marmara, but details are lacking. Pollution is reported to have had an ill effect on the breeding of bonito and mackerel.

In all polluted areas one should think twice before eating the local fish.

Anti-Pollution Measures by Yachts. A Greek law has been passed forbidding vessels in ports and bays, or sailing within Greek waters, to jettison any liquid or solid waste materials. This law is strictly enforced in Zea Marina where vessels should be fitted to retain waste matter on board, or to ensure that during their stay in port toilet outlets are not used. Garbage should be packed in nylon bags and handed to the Garbage Disposal Service or put in cans provided.

Aegean Communications. There is a regular local steamer and car-ferry service from Piraeus to almost all the Greek islands, detailed schedules being obtainable from travel agencies. Air communication has been established between Athens and many of the islands and mainland ports.

There is a good bus service all over Greece – the buses often crossing to many of the islands by ferry; the bus stations can be recognized by the letters K.T.E.L.

There is almost no communication between Greek and Turkish ports; only in summer small tourist boats ply between certain of the Dodecanese and the Anatolian coast: Samos – Kusadasi; Khios – Çeşme; Kos – Bodrum; Rhodes – Marmaris; Mitilini-Ayvalik.

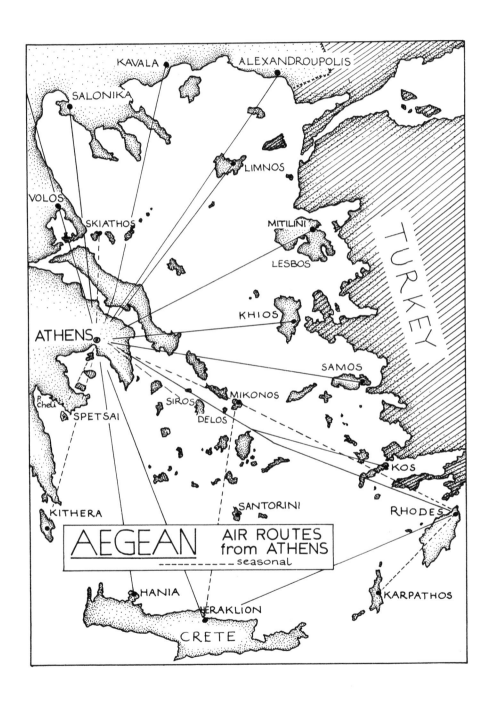

KAVALA ALEXANDROUPOLIS

SALONIKA

LIMNOS

VOLOS

SKIATHOS

MITILINI

LESBOS

KHIOS

ATHENS

SAMOS

MIKONOS

P.Cheli SIROS

SPETSAI DELOS

KOS

KITHERA SANTORINI RHODES

AEGEAN AIR ROUTES
from ATHENS
————————— seasonal

TURKEY

KARPATHOS

HANIA

IERAKLION

CRETE

PILOTAGE

Calm as a slumbering babe
Tremendous Ocean lies

ODYSSEY

The vagaries of the winds prevent the Aegean being classed as an ideal sailing ground; yet the appeal of the small sheltered ports and anchorages together with scenery of bold and striking contrasts more than compensate, and make the Aegean the most attractive part of the Mediterranean.

The winds, described on pp. xxiv–xxv, though largely predictable, may come up suddenly and without warning; but as the Aegean Sea is relatively small and well spaced with islands shelter is reasonably close at hand.

The coast, both of the mainland and the islands, is mostly hilly or mountainous, and with the exception of the islands lying a long way from the mainland and of part of Anatolia, the country is green and often wooded. The fascinating small ports, full of local colour, are often tucked round secluded corners, and reveal themselves quite unexpectedly.

When making an extensive cruise it is prudent to make use of the prevailing north wind and plan accordingly: i.e., during the Variables of May and June, it is recommended to make as far north as possible, and then, with the beginning of the Meltemi in early July, start cruising southwards with a fresh to strong fair wind behind one by day, and a calm at night. Similarly a yacht may expect to have a fair wind when coasting along the northern shore of Crete in an easterly direction.

The Mediterranean Pilot, Vol. IV (*Sailing Directions*), is the volume often referred to in this work. It is a mine of accurate information, and when further details of a place are required if not in sufficient detail in this book, *Sailing Directions* should always be consulted.

In the last century a number of British yachts, large by today's standards and without auxiliary power, visited the Aegean and sometimes published accounts of their cruises. Although they described ports and anchorages, this information is of limited value today, for their requirements were necessarily on a larger scale and moreover most harbours have changed considerably. Only reports or narratives by certain of H.M. survey vessels can be of interest in modern times.

British Admiralty chart numbers are quoted in this book, but when ordering a new chart it is wise to quote the title of the chart, as the Admiralty from time to time are apt to change the numbers.

Entering the Aegean. The Western Approaches (p. 3), Corinth Canal (p. 28) and Eastern Gateway (p. 200) are the passages into the Aegean and unless a yacht has already entered Greece she must do so at one of the following Ports of Entry: Piraeus (Zea), Vouliagmeni, Nauplion, Lavrion, Volos, Thessaloniki, Kavala, Alexandroupolis; the island ports of Limnos (Kastro Mirini), Mitilini, Khios, Samos, Syros (Syra), Rhodes; the Cretan ports of Hania, Heraklion (Iraklion) and Ay. Nikolaos. [Turkish Ports of Entry are listed on p. 89.]

If entering via Corinth Canal, Patras or Itea may be useful as Ports of Entry.

Prohibited Areas are, or should be, marked on the chart. They have been extended in the last few years, particularly in Crete. Those whose charts have not been kept corrected and who are already in Greece can obtain the necessary information at Room 410, 2 Filellinon Street, Piraeus, where charts can also be bought.

In addition to the prohibited areas, there are also exercise areas where from time to time, firing and bombing practice takes place. Warning of this is given at short notice by radio:

Athens   728 kHz at 0233, 0833, 1233, 1633, 2033 G.M.T.
Corfu   1007 kHz at 0233, 0833, 1233, 1633, 2033 G.M.T.
Patras   1511 kHz at 0233, 0833, 1233, 1633, 2033 G.M.T.
Hania   1511 kHz at 0333, 0833, 1333, 1733, 2133 G.M.T.
Rhodes   1493 kHz at 0333, 0833, 1333, 1733, 2133 G.M.T.

Special forecasts of dangerous weather changes are broadcast on 2182 kHz at 3 minutes past the hour and half hour.

The Weather and its Implications. Few countries as small as Greece have such a variation in climate. In some years at the end of March you may find summer at Kalamata and Rhodes, yet it is still winter in Arcady, Epirus and Macedonia. However, throughout the Aegean the latter part of April, May and June are usually good months for cruising. By mid-June the temperature has begun to rise sharply and it can be oppressive in July and August. The latter part of September and October are usually also pleasant sailing months.

Weather Forecasts

First Programme 728 kHz (412 m) at 1340 G.M.T (whole of the Mediterranean) in Greek. Forecasts in English, French and German at 0430 G.M.T. and twice subsequently at times that vary from year to year. In winter these are sometimes only in Greek and English.

Coastal Radio Telephone Station

Athens ⎫
Heraklion ⎬ On 2182 kHz at 0345, 0945, 1545 and 2145 G.M.T.
Khios ⎪
Limnos ⎭

Glossary of Areas in Forecasts for Aegean, etc.

North Aegean	Voreion Aegeon
N.W. Aegean	Voreiothitiko
N.E. Aegean	Vorioanatoliko
Central Aegean	Kentrikon Aegeon
South Aegean	Notion Aegeon
S.E. Aegean	Notionanatolikon Aegeon
S.W. Aegean	Notiothitikon Aegeon
Samos Sea	Thalassa Samou
Ikarian Sea	Thalassa Ikarias
Karpathian Sea	Thalassa Karpathion
Cretan Sea	Kritikon
Kithera Sea	Thalassa Kithyron
Libyan Sea	Livikon
Ierapetra Sea	Thalassa Ierapetras

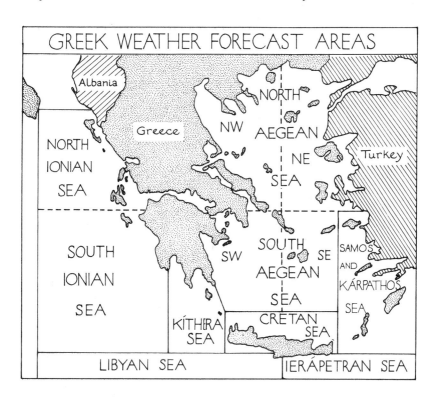

GREEK WEATHER FORECAST AREAS

E. Wind

Winds. The early Greeks associated the eight winds with certain seasonal conditions, and this phenomenon may best be summarized by the symbols carved on the octagonal marble Tower of the Winds standing intact below the Acropolis in Athens. It once had a water clock and a sundial. Its eight sides still face the important points of the compass, each being portrayed by a carved figure symbolic of the eight winds:

N.

Boreas
now called
Tramontána
or *Voriás*

the violent piercing north wind: a bearded old man well wrapped and booted, holding high the hood of his cloak.

N.E.

Kaika
now called
Grégo or
Vório
Anatolikós

the north-east wind, so cold on the Attic coast. The olives falling from the old man's charger depict the unfriendly nature of this wind to the vital Athenian fruit crop.

E.

Apiliotis
now called
Levánte or
Anatolikós

the more kindly east wind is portrayed by a handsome youth carrying the various species of fruit favoured by this wind.

S.E.

Euros
now called
Sourókoz or
Nótio Anatolikós

the frequently stormy south-east wind represented by an old man.

S.

Notos
now called
Óstra or
Nótios

the south wind – an unhappy clouded head, implying heat and damp. The fact that the figure is emptying a water-jug implies that the wind brings heavy showers and sultry weather.

S.W.

Libs
now called
Garbís or
Nótio Thitikós

the south-west wind so unfavourable to vessels leaving Athens. A strong severe-looking man is pushing before him the prow of a ship.

W.

Zephyros
now called
Pounénte or
Thitikós

the soft and kindly west wind, represented by a lightly clad youth carrying flowers and blossom, and gliding along contentedly.

N.W.

Schiron
now called
Maístro or
Vório Thitikós

the dry north-west wind: a robust bearded little man, wrapped and booted, pouring water from a vase to denote the occasional rain from that quarter.

During the last few centuries evidence from ships' narratives reveals that the Greek pilots had almost no logical understanding of changes in weather. Their predictions were invariably dictated by certain changes in shrubs, plants and other omens, e.g., certain pilots believed that the first appearance of the egg-plant was followed by a north-easter of some continuance. If at sea when confronted with foul winds they would always seek shelter, having too great a deference for the elements to think of contending against them.

Not only do seafaring Greeks use the Italian names for most of their winds, nowadays they also box the compass in Italian; this is a legacy from the Venetians.

The Prevailing Summer Wind, so often referred to in this book, is the Meltemi ('Etesian' wind in British *Sailing Directions*). According to Herodotus it begins with the 'Rising of the Dog Star' and continues until the end of the summer. It may be expected to begin, therefore, in early July and to continue sometimes until the middle of September. Caused by the low-pressure area over Cyprus and the Middle East, this wind has a mean direction between N.W. and north, except in the Turkish Gulfs, Kithera Channels and towards Rhodes where it blows almost west. It may be expected to start each day towards noon, reaching a velocity of force 5 to 6 and sometimes 7 by afternoon, and falling off towards evening. Quite often, without warning, it blows all night without diminishing in strength. When these conditions obtain, the wind on the Anatolian coast suddenly veers to N.N.E. during the hours of darkness. The Meltemi blows with the greatest strength from the middle of the Aegean towards the south. In the extreme north this wind is light, and in some northern areas a light sea-breeze is drawn in from the south.

The tall islands, which might be expected to form a lee for a sailing yacht working to windward, do not help, for the wind is always more violent under the mountainous coast than it is a few miles off. Certain islands, Andros and Amorgos for example, develop a heavy cloud formation over the mountains, an indication of strong north winds.

Summer Anchorages, July to early September, are therefore on the southern or south-eastern side of the islands, and though often open to the south, there is small risk during these months of the wind suddenly shifting in that direction. Vessels with power, wishing to work northwards, often start at night or early morning when the sea has gone down, and continue their passage until the Meltemi begins to impede their progress the following afternoon.

Other Seasons. In May and June there are usually light variable winds, also after the Meltemi season in the latter part of September and early October, when there are often pleasant sailing breezes. After the autumn months, gales blow from N.E., from S. and S.E. in December, January and February. Though nowadays many of the caïques take their chance of putting to sea during this period they formerly laid up, and in Venetian times vessels were actually fined for attempting to return home during the winter season.

Tides and Seiches. Admiralty predictions indicate a maximum rise of a few inches at some places to $2\frac{1}{2}$ ft at others. The level of the water is far more influenced by wind and seasonal conditions than by tide and, therefore, for practical purposes tide need not be considered.

It is necessary to watch the sea-level during a strong wind of long duration, and to bear in mind that in certain gulfs in the northern Aegean the sea-level during winter months may drop at least $2\frac{1}{2}$ ft and remain at this level for many weeks.

In places where violent squalls sweep down from the mountains miniature 'tidal waves' or Seiches may be formed; the surge from this is apt to sweep round the quay and call for some attention to a yacht's stern warps.

Currents. There is a general trend of current from north to south; in light settled weather it is slight, but with strong sustained northerly winds it can start running with a maximum velocity of up to 4 or 5 knots in certain channels – especially those between Evvia, Andros, Tinos and Kea.

Only in the rare event of a strong southerly wind in the autumn is this current likely to be reversed. A wind-induced current in open water or parallel to the coast may run at a speed of 1.5–2 per cent of the wind speed.

There is a gentle northgoing stream setting up the southern part of the Turkish Anatolian coast. This meets the general southgoing stream in the area north of Kos and the junction of the two currents is believed to have deposited the sand which has gradually raised the fringes of the Turkish coast and silted Kos harbour. Again, further south along the Turkish coast fishermen maintain that S. of Cape Krio a south-going current runs.

Taxes on Foreign Yachts. Law 438 of 1976 prohibits foreign yachts from engaging in the charter business in Greek waters without a permit. It also states that private foreign yachts not engaged in the charter business are to pay U.S.$15 per foot of length overall from the completion of one year's stay in Greek waters. Periods spent subsequent to that date are to be aggregated; each time the total reaches twelve months the tax becomes due. It was reported in late 1982 that the period has been reduced to six months.

Laying-up Ports and Repairs. Yachts normally stay afloat during the winter months and may be moored by arrangement with the local authority.

Near Piraeus are two large marinas: Zea, 350 yachts; Alimos & Vouliagmeni, 9 miles southward, 110 yachts. Repair and slipping facilities are close at hand at Perama; but most foreigners being unable to speak Greek sometimes have to employ the services of an agent. Also at the former Olympic yard at Gaideromandri a yacht yard with a travel lift is again in operation. Arrangements may also be made for receiving yacht stores from England without paying duty. It is often referred to as the Lavrian yard.

Rhodes has good facilities for laying-up ashore and afloat, but limited skilled labour for fitting out. (See under Rhodes.) There are possibilities of wintering afloat at other places: Spetsai, Porto Heli, Skiathos, near Volos etc. but help for repairs or fitting out is very limited.

Yachts are usually slipped on a skid-cradle, a treatment sometimes rather rough on the more delicate hull of the modern craft.

The sketch shows a yacht having been hauled out, now supported on keel blocks and shores while the dismantled skid-cradle lies beneath. (See overleaf.)

Running Repairs. During a cruise it may be necessary to make good some misfortune which is beyond the scope of ship's resources. It is then a matter of

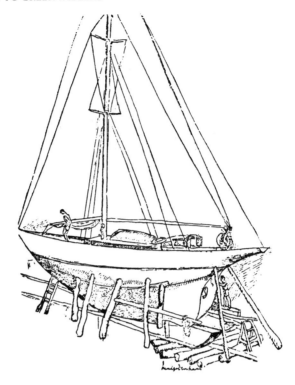

chance whether or not outside help can be obtained. At many islands and small ports there is a boatbuilder, or a joiner's shop, or a mechanic in the village willing to help.

Ship's Mails. It is usually quite safe for a yacht's mail to be directed care of the Harbour Master at any major port of call.

Yachts in Greek Waters are frequently referred to as being 'large, medium or small'. Times have changed and all categories tend to be smaller.

    large yacht   : over 35 ft
    medium yacht   : 26–35 ft
    small yacht   : below 26 ft

similarly draught has become less:

    deep implies   : over 6 ft
    medium implies : 4–6 ft
    shallow implies : less than 4 ft

Berthing. Normally yachts berth with an anchor laid out to seaward and stern to quay with a gangplank, but a dinghy slung in stern davits can be a hindrance. Small yachts often berth bows to the quay; anchor laid out astern.

This method of securing has certain advantages: the yacht's side does not get rubbed by the quay; one has some privacy from the gaze of onlookers; but perhaps more important still, one is less likely to be invaded by cockroaches or other vermin which sometimes frequent the quayside. In this unfortunate eventuality, the only successful way to eliminate the pest is to purchase 'Fumite' tablets made by Waeco Ltd, of Salisbury, Wilts. (Seal all apertures, ignite the tablets as directed and leave the yacht for 24 hours.)

Cockpit awnings and side-curtains are essential, not only to protect the crew from the burning rays of the sun, but also to shield them from the gaze of the idlers on the quayside.

Greek Nautical Terms, almost all of Italian origin:

Karína	Keel	*Lásca*	Pay out
Plóri	Bow	*Víra*	Haul in
Prími	Stern	*Flókos*	Jib
Kouvérta	Deck	*Mezzána*	Mizzen
Taboúkio	Coach roof	*Paní*	Mainsail
Albouro	Mast	*Mandári*	Halyard
Bastóuni	Bowsprit	*Aristerá*	Port
Mátsa	Boom	*Dexiá*	Starboard
Timóni	Helm		

Turkish nautical terms are given on p. 91.

Chartering. There are a number of fleets of small yachts available for charter, some for 'cruise in company' in parties of six to a dozen boats under supervision, others for independent sailing; they are advertised in the British yachting press. There are also larger yachts available, usually with professional crews; the National Tourist Organisation of Greece (195 Regent Street, London W1) can offer advice and it also publishes a pamphlet, 'Greece for the Yachtsman'.

Cost of Living. The cost of repairs, laying up, food, etc., comes no longer within the term modest, for Greece like other west European countries has been caught by inflation. Recently prices of many commodities have more than doubled within a few months.

I

Western Approaches to the Aegean

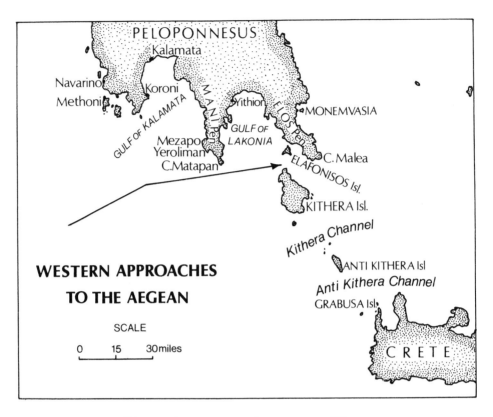

WESTERN APPROACHES

TO THE AEGEAN

SCALE

0   15   30 miles

Cape Matapan (Tenaron)
   Yerolimin
   Mezapo
Island of Elafonisos
   Poriki Lagoon
   Sarakiniko Bay
   Elafonisos Village anchorage
   (Vrakhonisos Petri)
Neapolis

ISLANDS IN WESTERN
APPROACHES
Island of Kithera (Kithira)
   Ayios Nikolaos
   Kapsali Bay
   Makri Cove
   Panaghia
Island of Anti-Kithera (Andikithira)
   Port Potamo

I
Western Approaches to the Aegean

Coming from the west one often makes a landfall at Cape Matapan (Tenaron), the low-lying point where the tall Taygetos range of the Mani peninsula falls insignificantly into the sea. The cape is so low that one can often see the lighthouse before the point of land.

Taygetos Range

In the event of strong E. or N.E. winds a west-going current of 1–2 knots may set in and one might find it prudent to seek shelter under the lee of the steep rocky coast at one of the small ports a few miles northward – Yerolimin or Mezapo.

Yerolimin, with a comparatively modern westernized village, has a good sheltered anchorage in northerly weather.

A short pier with a quay enables the mail steamer to berth in settled weather, but the place is very exposed to the westerly quarter; the Piraeus steamer on occasions has had to berth on the E. side of Cape Matapan at Vathi.

This little port has grown up since the middle of the last century and is a distributing centre for manufactured articles to the hill villages. Previously it had been a great haunt for pirates.

Mezapo, a small bay a few miles N. of the prominent C. Gnosso, is protected from S.W. by the southern headland, the great rock of Tigani ('frying pan'). Sprawling on its peak are the ruins of the fortress of Maina, one of three great defensive works set up by Geoffroi de Villehardouin in the late 12th century to protect his S.E. domain of the Peloponnesus.

A partially deserted hamlet with a few shattered towers (the result of earthquake damage) is all that remains of the substantial village.

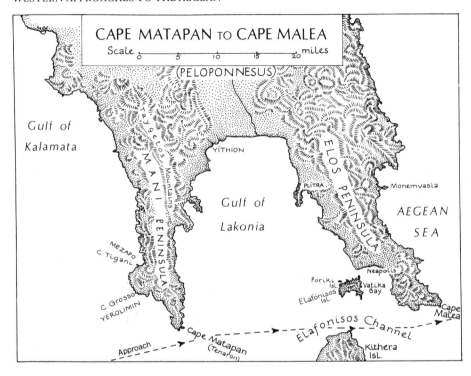

Rounding the uninspiring C. Matapan (Tenaron) one crosses the Gulf of Lakonia and heads for the bold, mountainous C. Malea.

To the British the name Matapan recalls the victorious battle in the Second World War at a time when Britain's strength was seriously threatened. Admiral Lord Cunningham's fleet brought the Italians to battle in a night action about 100 miles S.W. of Cape Matapan, successfully disabling one modern battleship and sinking three armoured cruisers and two destroyers for the loss of one aircraft.

Crossing the wide Gulf of Lakonia are a number of inlets with degrees of shelter (described in *The Ionian Islands to the Anatolian Coast*) but there is only the one port of Yithion near the head of the Gulf. One then enters the Elafonisos Channel – $4\frac{1}{2}$ miles wide, separating Elafonisos Island from Kithera.

Island of Elafonisos

With its undulating hills and somewhat barren country, Elafonisos is separated from the mainland by a 7-ft 'Boat Channel'. The island forms the western shore of Vatika Bay. Off its hamlet on the N.E. corner under the lee of Petri Islet is a reasonably sheltered anchorage. Off the west coast, Poriki Island's isolated

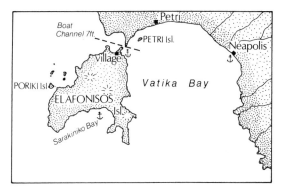

lagoon provides anchorage in fine weather, and the bay of Sarakiniko on the S. coast offers good shelter against northerly gales.

Elafonisos Village anchorage, Vrakonisos Petri, provides shelter and good holding for a yacht close to the Boat Channel, off the village.

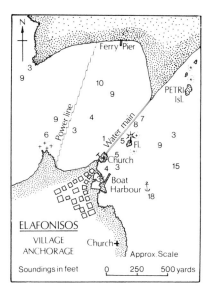

Anchorage. With winds in the western quadrant anchor E. of the village in 3 fathoms, but in the event of S.E. winds a small yacht should pass through the Boat Channel and anchor N.W. of the village. In N. and N.E. winds shelter in Sarakiniko Bay.

Facilities. The village provides one general store, a taverna and three cafés. There are bathing beaches on the north shore.

5

Earlier History. In prehistoric times there was a commercial port on this site which handled the trade between the Aegean and Ionian Seas. On the sea-bed between the mainland and the islet of Petri are Bronze Age remains of an extensive village with some chamber tombs and Cycladic pottery. At that time Elafonisos was joined to the mainland by a low isthmus. So it continued certainly until the 2nd century A.D. (Pausanius). By 1677 Elafonisos had become an island but the newly formed channel was still fordable. [Now it is 7–8 ft deep.]

Neapolis, a large village in the N.E. corner of Vatika Bay, has a pier 120 yds long affording only limited protection.

Approach and Berth. Chart 712. The pier has recently been extended with 2-fathom depths at its extremity and a Lt.F.(R). There are landing steps towards the root on either side with depths of 7 ft. A few yachts call and berth alongside as convenient.

Facilities. Water near the steps, transit fuel by lorry, good fresh provisions in the village, two small hotels, a small crane on the quay. Buses run three times daily to Sparta and Athens – steamers call twice a week from Piraeus, Kithera and Crete. Hydrofoil to Piraeus.

Officials. Harbour Master, Customs.

The rugged coast of the Elos peninsula continues southward, and then after bending eastwards it reaches the magnificent headland of Cape Malea (p. 13).

CHANNELS AND ISLANDS IN WESTERN APPROACHES TO AEGEAN SEA

South of Elafonisos Island is the 4½-mile wide Elafonisos Channel separating it from Kithera Island. This channel provides the main route for vessels entering the Aegean from the west.

> *Forsaken isle! around thy barren shore*
> *Wild tempests howl and wintry surges roar.*
> WRIGHT (*Horae Ionicae*, 1807)

Island of Kithera (Kithira)

This island is mountainous and steep-to with a barren-looking coast. There are two sheltered bays: Ayios Nikolaos (Avlemona) on the south-eastern corner of the island, and Kapsali Bay with the Chora (capital or main village) on the south coast. Plans are given on Chart 712.

There are also two places of shelter on the north-east coast, suitable only under

favourable conditions: Panaghia with its 100-yd breakwater and the sandy lagoon of Makri sheltered by an islet. (Details – see *The Ionian Islands to the Anatolian Coast.*)

Ayios Nikolaos is often known to local Greeks as **Avlemona**. This is the safest harbour in the island, sheltered in all weather, though open to southerly swell.

> **Berth.** A small quay with depths of 3 fathoms is sometimes occupied by caïques, otherwise it is the most suitable place for securing a yacht's sternfast, with her anchor laid out to the southward. The basins are small, there is swinging room if desiring to anchor in the outer basin in depths of 3 or 4 fathoms.

Though the configuration of the port is attractive, the barrenness of the surrounding country and the rebuilt hamlet make no appeal for a visiting yacht.

History. There was an occasion, however, in Nelson's day when the approach to this little harbour was causing much concern:

On 17 September 1802 the small brig *Mentor* conveying 17 cases of the famous Parthenon frieze was on passage to Malta; seeking shelter from a westerly gale she put in at St Nikolo Bay. Her two anchors began to drag, and in trying to make sail she cut her cables but drifted on the rocks and was holed; she sank in 60 ft close off shore, the crew managing to reach the rocky coast, all being saved. It was two years before divers from Kalimnos and Symi (whose sailors continue this vocation today) were able to complete their task, and retrieve all these cases from the wreck. Finally on 16 February 1805 the transport *Lady Shaw Stewart*, under orders of Lord Nelson, called at St Nikolo, loaded the cases and conveyed them to England.

Kapsali Bay. Shown in a plan on Chart 712, it lies in a mountainous setting with an anchorage open to the south; it is dominated by a massive Venetian castle. The Port Authority emphasises that the port is unsafe in strong winds between S.E. and S.W.

Approach and Berth. A yacht can anchor in the bay or berth behind a short breakwater extending from a rocky spur where the lighthouse stands, and where shelter is better. The new quay has a depth of only 8 ft but is useful for securing a sternfast when the yacht has laid out an anchor to the westward. (If laying out to the N.W. caution is needed to be sure of avoiding a reef lying off the beach.) The sea bottom in the anchorage is sand, but near the quay among patches of sand are loose rock and stones, giving uncertain holding. The bay is susceptible to swell and untenable in Sirocco winds. In the summer months westerly winds predominate, with an occasional spell of north-easterly weather. Ferries and freighters also use the quay; the former especially can much endanger a yacht when berthing.

Port Facilities. Fresh water, which is good, is sometimes available from a tap and also from a hydrant at the quay. Here also is a pump for diesel fuel which can be bought at one day's notice; limited provisions can also be bought, but for greater demands one must go to the main village. A hydrofoil operates from Piraeus in summer as well as a bi-weekly steamer.

The Chora, a full half hour's walk up a steep hill, lies in a commanding position beyond the Venetian castle. Its winding, fascinating streets with well-stocked shops are remarkably clean and neat. Good fish, including crawfish, are often obtainable there and in the port; there is a modest hotel and restaurant. People are friendly everywhere and tourists are few. There are one or two motor-drives to the other villages in the centre of the island.

The island continues to export palatable retsina for which it was once famous. The meteorological station may offer a useful forecast.

Earlier History. After the Napoleonic Wars, Kithera, together with the Ionian Islands, was ceded to Britain. Kithera was garrisoned by a small detachment under a subaltern's command, being regarded as a watch-post for the gateway into the Aegean. The garrison was relieved every six months, as it was considered 'a very lonely station'. Some English cannon, a bridge and a few graves are the only remains of this British occupation.

Though caïques and small mail boats sometimes land passengers at Makri Cove and at Panaghia (Pelayia) on the east coast, neither is recommended, the former having but little interest and the latter lacking shelter.

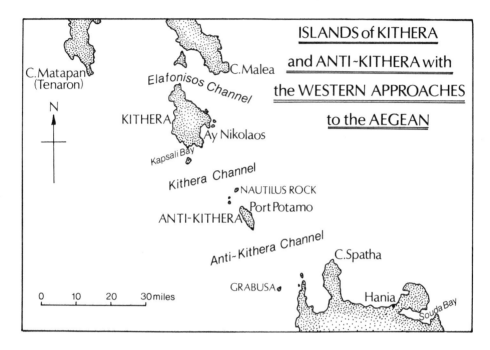

Island of Anti-Kithera (Andikithira)

This lies between Kithera and Crete. The 10-mile wide navigable channels on either side of it are used by vessels proceeding in the direction of Crete.

Port Potamo with its small hamlet is shown on Chart 712, but few vessels call, partly because of the heavy swell created by fresh northerly and westerly winds, and on account of poor holding on the rocky bottom.

This small island, of no significance today, was much in the news about Easter 1900 when a sponge-boat returning to Symi discovered the wreck of a Roman vessel close S.S.E. of Potamo. This resulted in the National Museum of Athens acquiring some of its finest 4th-century B.C. bronze statues, marble figures, pottery and glass.

History. The sponge-boat had been driven off course and was sheltering under the lee of Anti-Kithera. The divers decided to examine the bottom in case there might be sponges. Instead of sponges they were astonished to find statuary, and had the good sense to get in touch with archaeologists in Athens. After some months' work, diving in depths of more than 30 fathoms, several statues and other relics were recovered. The site was then abandoned and was not re-examined until 1952 when Cousteau and his divers arrived; they have been here since. Meanwhile, the salved objects, now in Athens, were awaiting analysis by modern methods, which revealed interesting facts; though some of the statues were of the 4th century B.C., others proved to be copies. One of the more remarkable finds was parts of an astronomical clock which, by careful deciphering of the inscriptions, was partially reconstructed.

The vessel herself was judged to have been about 300 tons burden; her underwater planking was of elm, which by carbon analysis of the small piece recovered, dates the tree from which it was formed to be between 260 and 180 B.C.; she was copper fastened and lead sheathed. None of her lead anchor stocks, although recovered by divers, ever reached Athens.★

Five miles N.W. of Anti-Kithera are some rocky islets. One, named Nautilus Rock, is so called in memory of H.M.S. *Nautilus* wrecked during the dark hours on the morning of 3 January 1807.

This frigate was carrying important despatches from the C-in-C to the Admiralty and, running before a strong N. wind, had in the darkness mistaken the silhouette of the islets for part of Anti-Kithera Island. She altered course to the west and so ran hard up upon the rocks. The ship soon began to break up and of her crew of 122 only 64 survived. The story of their great privations on the islet makes harrowing reading, and inspired Byron to write:

> . . . and you might have seen
> The longings of the cannibal arise
> (although they spoke not) in their wolfish eyes.

The Anti-Kithera Channel separating Anti-Kithera from the N.W. cape of Crete (C. Agria Grabusa) is nearly 5 miles wide, and without obstruction. (For Crete see Chap. 8.)

★ See *Shipwrecks and Archaeology* by Peter Throckmorton, Boston, 1970.

2

Cape Malea to Sounion

ATHENS
Piraeus
Corinth Canal
Salamis
Vouliagmeni
Sofikon
Aiyina
Nauplion
Methana
Sounion
Khaidhari
Poros
Tolos
Kremidhi
Astros
Dhokos
Heli
Idra
Spetsai
SARONIC Gulf
(Chart 1657)
Leonidhion
Gulf of ARGOLIS (Chart 1518)
Kyparissi
Yeraka
Monemvasia
Ay. Phokas
C. MALEA
Kithera
Scale
0   10   20
miles

CAPE MALEA TO THE GULF
OF ARGOLIS
Cape Malea
Port Paolo
Ayios Phokas
Monemvasia
Palea Monemvasia
Krenidhi
Yeraka (Ieraka)
Kyparissi
Fokianos

Gulf of Argolis
Leonidhion
Astros
Nauplion
Tolos
Khaidhari
Koiladhi (Kranidhi)
Porto Heli (Port Kheli or Cheli)
Kosta
Island of Spetsai
  Boat harbour
  Balza (Baltiza)
Island of Spetsopoula

IDRA (IDHRA) AND SARONIC GULF
Island of Dhokos
Ermioni
Island of Idra (Idhra, Hydra)
  The Port
Island of Poros
  The Quay
Methana Peninsula anchorage
Island of Aiyina (Aegina)
  The Port
  Ayia Marina
Palaia Epidavros
Sofikon (Korfos)

Corinth Canal

Island of Salamis
  Cape Konkhi anchorage

PORTS OF PIRAEUS
  Zea or Passalimani
  Mikrolimano
  Piraeus – commercial port
    Ayios Georgios
  Glifadha and local marinas
  Vouliagmeni
  Sounion

2

Cape Malea to Sounion

CAPE MALEA TO THE GULF OF ARGOLIS

Slowly sinks more lovely ere his race be run
Along Morea's hills, the setting sun;
Not, as in Northern climes, obscurely bright,
But one unclouded blaze of living light.

BYRON

CAPE MALEA

This bold mountainous headland rising to nearly 2,000 ft forms the turning point into the Aegean. Completely isolated and standing on the hillside close westward a few hundred feet above the sea stands a low, white monastery now inhabited by half a dozen nuns.

With westerly winds the cape should be rounded at least a mile off, especially when turning northwards towards the Gulf of Argolis.

This noble headland makes a profound impression, and to the ancient Greek sailors on a long voyage to some distant colony it was perhaps the last they were to see of their own country for many months to come. 'Round Malea and forget your native country' was the saying attributed to these early sailors. Many centuries later, shortly after the heyday of Venice, small vessels of the British Levant Company,★ after a voyage of 6 or 7 weeks from England, used, in their turn, to round this Cape into the Aegean. Shipping cargoes mainly at Constantinople and Smyrna, they also visited the Port of Lions (Piraeus) and Monemvasia; but the Aegean islands, except perhaps Chios, were of no interest for trading purposes. Having entered the 'Arches' (a corruption of archipelago) they called at Milos for a pilot, and sometimes an armed naval escort, for the Aegean was then a hunting-ground for pirates.

Today the shipping activity off Cape Malea is nothing compared with that off such headlands as St Vincent and Europa Point.

From Cape Malea northwards a 2,000-ft mountainous spur stands steeply

---

★ The French, more successful in the Levant, had as many as 700 vessels in this trade shortly before the Napoleonic Wars.

above the coast; the foothills are partially cultivated. There are some small villages concealed in the valleys. Only indifferent shelter can be found before reaching Monemvasia and Yeraka.

Port Paolo lies 1½ miles W.S.W. from Cape Kamili. It is a very small fishing cove with 12-ft depths protected by a 50-yd mole extending in a southerly direction from the northern shore; a very small white church at the root of the mole makes an excellent sea mark. The cove should be used only in settled weather, and it is susceptible to an easterly swell. There is no habitation apart from a small farm and the hamlet 2 or 3 miles distant. Except for some cultivated valleys and noble mountains there is nothing of particular interest.

Ayios Phokas, 5 miles south of Monemvasia, consists of a very small inlet behind an islet. It can be recognized from seaward by the few houses of the hamlet, and the islet by its small church. The approach is in a north-westerly direction, leaving the islet with its protruding underwater rocks to starboard. The channel is narrow with 2-fathom depths, and on no account should a vessel attempt to enter in the event of an easterly swell, which can be seen breaking on the rocks. Within the inlet there is just room to swing in 2 fathoms.

Monemvasia. A small Gibraltar-like headland is joined to the mainland by a causeway. This acts as a breakwater and affords temporary anchorage either north or south according to the weather.

   Anchorage. Chart 712. The new concrete mole shown in the plan is suitable for a yacht berth. It has about 20-ft depths alongside for the outer half of its length, shoaling rapidly towards its root. There are bollards and rings on the west or inner side, and the outer side is also deep and

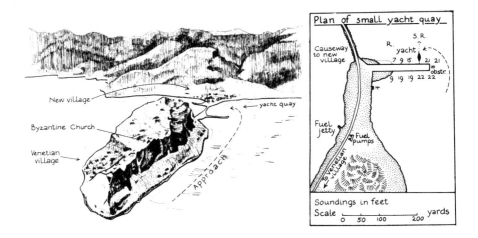

free from ballasting. The small basin shown in the picture at the S.W. end of the bridge to Monemvasia is used by local boats and the hydrofoil occupies the W. end of yacht mole.

Facilities. Water and fuel uncertain. At the new village with over a thousand people are restaurants, shops with fresh provisions, wine, post office and ice. In the Venetian village on the rock the old houses are once more inhabited mainly by tourists; there is a restaurant for tourists and a taverna.

The peninsula with its walled Venetian town is worth visiting, and the Byzantine church of St Sophia on the summit even more so. From here the outer walls of the fortifications are impressive and lend support to the stories of the many sieges this stronghold has withstood, during Venetian rule, ending in 1540.
Monemvasia was also a centre of commerce famous in medieval days for its Malmsey★ wines, which were of wide repute. Here the jars of wine were assembled from places on the Morea coast and from some of the islands to await onward shipment to Western Europe, including England.

Palea Monemvasia. A small bay sheltered from N. and W. with depths of 3 to 5 fathoms over an irregular smooth rock and sandy bottom. This is a better place for a yacht than Monemvasia in unsettled weather.

Anchorage. Chart 712. It is safe to anchore anywhere convenient on a sandy bottom.

Facilities. There are half a dozen fishermen's cottages and a small taverna where basic provisions may be obtained. A road leads to Monemvasia – an hour's walk.

Krenidhi, a bay 2 miles N.N.E. of Monemvasia, affords good holding on a broad sand-shelf on its west side. The afternoon day breeze causes squalls in the western bay, but shelter is good; open only S. to S.E.

Yeraka (Ieraka). This is the best sheltered and most pleasant port between Cape Malea and Spetsai.

Anchorage. Chart 712. This is well protected by the configuration of the steep coast; the only inconvenience is the occasional down-currents of wind under certain conditions. One should anchor in 5 fathoms rather than get into lesser depths, when the bottom becomes too hard for a plough anchor to be sure of holding. Strong N.E. winds set up a dangerous swell in the circular basin making it untenable.

A few cottages line the waterfront at the foot of the steep sides of the anchorage. The village lies on the hillside. The steamer from Piraeus calls twice a week, also the hydrofoil for which the quay has been extended.

★ Corruption of Monemvasia.

Kyparissi is an anchorage in a spacious bay at the foot of steep, wooded mountains off a small hamlet. Though subject to strong down-draughts during westerly winds, there is protection from the swell in the S.E. corner behind the sharp rocky point marked by a light beacon. Also anchorage in 8 fathoms; with stern warp to a quay by a small chapel, but beware of underwater wreck W.N.W. of chapel.

This is an attractive setting and is frequented by only a few local fishing craft.

Fokianos. This is a large, deep inlet in the mountainous coast with a few deserted houses at its head. It is an unsuitable anchorage.

THE GULF OF ARGOLIS

Entering the Gulf between Cape Sambateki and Spetsai, some of the small ports and anchorages only a few miles apart are of interest to a yacht.

Local Winds. Under fine weather conditions the day breeze blows from the S.E. up the gulf, starting before midday. There is a light breeze beginning before dawn and lasting until about 10 o'clock, blowing down the gulf from the N.W. With fresh westerly winds the mountainous shores of the gulf are subject to down-blasts, and the coast should be passed with an offing of about 3 miles. In some of the ports at the top of the Gulf the more violent squalls may set up a series of miniature tidal waves. With a rise and fall of 1 to 2 ft they may occur at few-minute intervals and can be embarrassing to yachts secured with stern warps to a quay.

West Side of Gulf

Leonidhion. The small port (Scala), chart 1518, lies $2\frac{1}{2}$ miles S.E. of Leonidhion village and is conspicuous for its white church and small cluster of white houses. It is open to S.W. and W. and in strong northerlies gusts come down from the mountains. In settled weather this place is well worth a visit. It is still unspoilt and has attractive shaded market gardens.

Approach. The mole, now extended to 120 yds with a Lt.Fl. (g) at extremity, has depth of 6–7 fathoms (3 fathoms against quay), bottom is gravel. A heavy mooring chain runs from the shore to W. of caïque jetty on the N. quay.

Facilities. Excellent fish meals at any of the four tavernas on shore. Buses and taxis to Leonidhion village (4 miles) where provisions of all kinds may be obtained. Hydrofoil to Piraeus four times weekly.

The monastery of Elonis lies 12 km up in the mountains along a newly surfaced road.

Astros. A pleasant small fishing port protected by two breakwaters. A good

summer anchorage with the new breakwater providing much better shelter in
S.E. weather.

Berth. Nearly 2-fathom depths extend along the mole. A yacht can berth stern to the quay,
anchor towards the village.

Facilities. Excellent water from a tap at the root of the mole. Good provisions, hotels, tavernas,
cafés. Bus to Leonidhion and Nauplion. Hydrofoil to Piraeus four times a week.

Tourism has considerably revived the village, also the building of a new
cotton material factory. Fortunately the old houses have now been protected and
the new ones have to be built either behind the village or on top of the peninsula.
A number of fishing boats still work out from here.

A delightful half hour's drive takes one to the Byzantine monastery of Moni
Loukas on the mountainside, whence the water is piped down to the harbour.

Nauplion lies at the head of the gulf and is one of the rare towns in Greece where
old buildings have been preserved by law and the new ones confined to an area of
their own behind the trees on the E. shore. The town is therefore clean and quiet
and has great character with its old churches, Venetian houses and converted
mosques. The port is well sheltered in summer and is a good place from which to
visit the Mycenaean Argolid.

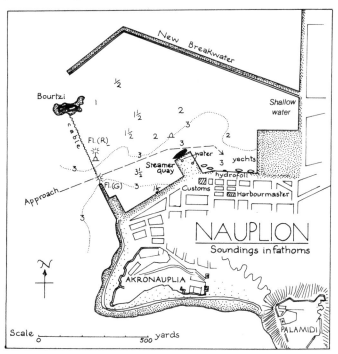

Approach and Berth. Chart 1518. The harbour is spacious and easy of access. A breakwater over 1,000 yds long has been built out in a W.N.W. direction from the E. shore with a 300-yd arm pointing S.W. A new jetty has also been built 350 yds E. of the former E. jetty. Yachts are expected to berth alongside between the two in 3-fathom depths, though it is not very salubrious because the town sewers discharge here. The hydrofoil also berths here, its bollards being painted yellow. The E. basin is eventually to be dredged to a uniform 3 fathoms. Water and fuel are laid on and the quay asphalted. N.W. squalls sometimes come down from the Arcadian mountains and cause a surge abreast the quays.

Officials. A Port of Entry. Customs on the quay, Harbour Master in the town.

Facilities. Water by hydrant at the extremity and on the E. side of the central jetty. Fuel by lorry. Good shops, hotels, tavernas; excellent wine. (The old Venetian fort, Bourtzi, is no longer a hotel-restaurant.) An archaeological museum. Buses to Athens, Tiryns, Mycenae, Epidavros theatre, Astros', Leonidhion. Hydrofoil three times a week to Piraeus.

The Venetian citadel on the summit of Palamidi approached by 857 steps is well worth the ascent, especially on a clear day when the views across the Argos plain are magnificent.

History. When Greece first obtained her independence in 1832 Nauplion became for a short while the first capital of the country, Athens at this time being a village of little significance. At St Spyridon church, Capodistria, the first governor of modern Greece, was assassinated; bullet holes can still be seen by the door.

East Side of Gulf

Karathona Bay (Chart 1518), 3 miles S.E. of Nauplion, provides good anchorage for those who prefer independence and bathing. Shelter in the southern part of the bay has been improved by the construction of a mole extending from the chapel almost half-way to the islet.

Tolos (or **Tolon**). A partially sheltered anchorage protected by an island off the seaside village of Tolos (Tolon).

Anchorage. A small harbour has been built at the S. end of the village with a 90-yd quay and a mole projecting from it 45 yds in an easterly direction and then 45 yds northwards. There are depths of 16 ft inside and yachts berth stern to mole. Many fishing boats moor off, but with northerly winds the anchorage is susceptible to strong gusts off the hills. There are convenient depths of about 3 fathoms with good holding about 100 yds offshore.

The village, only 12 km from Nauplion, has become a minor resort with some small hotels, modest restaurants and shops.

East of the village are some ruins on the promontory. This is ancient Asine whose harbour is now silted and filled with sand; from here Agamemnon's expedition set off for Troy.

Khaidhari. A sheltered inlet near the ruins of Mezes, on the W. side of entrance. The sea-bed rises sharply at the head of the bay to 2 fathoms – rather bleak and steep hills either side of the inlet, catching strong gusts with N.W. winds. The few houses of the fishing community are lost among the hotels, tavernas and cafés which form the new ribbon development along the road to Irio.

> **Anchorage** is off the beach west of the houses, in 3 fathoms, heavy clay bottom.

> **Facilities.** A fish meal may be obtained at one of the tavernas.

Koiladhi, the port for the large village of Kranidhi, lies in a sheltered bay whose entrance is difficult to discern. Once a small primitive village, mostly inhabited by fishermen who, after their night's fishing off the coast, land their catch at Porto Heli for conveyance to Athens, their small houses are now, however, almost totally obliterated by the ugly buildings of the new resort; these include an enormous and very conspicuous church. The island at the entrance has been bought by a Greek shipowner, planted with trees and grass, and a small private harbour built on the S. side.

> **Approach.** Kranidhi village with its white houses stands out in the distance. The small light structure, painted white and standing on the S. shore and a small white church are conspicuous.

> **Anchorage** is at the extremity of the new quay built out over the piers shown on chart 1518; 10-ft depth but shallowing towards the root. The trawlers lie on the E. side of the quay or nearer the head of the bay. In strong westerlies there is excellent shelter behind the island at the entrance. With northerly winds a slight swell enters the port, but in this shallow anchorage holding is good and the sea breeze steady.

> **Facilities.** Shops, tavernas, cafés, hotels. Bus to Kranidhi.

Porto Heli (or **Port Kheli**) is a large but shallow enclosed bay with perfect shelter. During recent years much building has taken place, new hotels and villas having spread themselves along the shores of this former unspoilt natural harbour.

> **Anchorage.** A broad, dusty quay has been completed. It runs parallel to the old waterside road and is well provided with bollards. See plan. There is 10-ft depth at the quay and 2 fathoms in the middle. Fresh water is available from a tap at this quay and at the 'Fish Quay', but it is inclined to be brackish at both places. This is a safe place to lay-up in winter, but is usually occupied by local craft.

> **Facilities.** Water by the quay. Provisions are sometimes in short supply but can be obtained from Spetsai by the ferry. Hotels and restaurants have recently grown up. A bus service operates between here and Nauplion, connecting with Epidavros. An airstrip for Athens flights. Hydrofoil operates to Piraeus and berths at corner of yacht quay (yellow bollards).

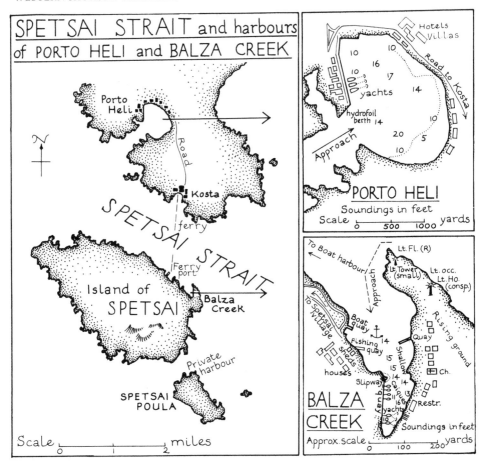

Kosta is a small ferry terminal for the Island of Spetsai. A partially sheltered cove with a few houses and a pier – of no interest.

Island of Spetsai

Well known to Athenians as a summer resort, this island is hilly and wooded on the north. There are two harbours: the Boat Harbour is off the village centre where the Piraeus ferry calls, and Balza (a creek at the N.E. end of the island) which is suitable for yachts, berthing, servicing and laying-up.

Balza (Baltiza)

Approach and Anchorage. Chart 1518. The lighthouse stands out and the port may be approached by day or night.

Yachts usually anchor to the S.W. of the lighthouse off a small stone pier in depths of $2\frac{1}{2}$ fathoms. This is open to N.W. and a swell sometimes rolls in, but the holding is good. Land at stone pier in dinghy – 8 min walk to village.

Berth. There is a quay (with shallow depths close in) usually very crowded. Towards the head of the creek there is usually more room, though it is necessary to berth well away from the quay. Here are a few suitable berths for yachts up to 20 tons to lay up for the winter, where shelter is better than at many Aegean ports; but one should bear in mind a drop in sea-level of $2\frac{1}{2}$ ft in the winter months.

Facilities. Provisions may be bought nearby from a caïque that brings them across from the mainland. The large Hotel Poseidonion and several smaller ones, also restaurants, are all 10 min walk from Balza and close by the Boat Harbour. Water can be obtained from the quay; also diesel fuel, petrol and paraffin. Hydrofoil to Piraeus, Porto Heli, Nauplion, etc. Two Piraeus services daily, also steamers.

There are two small shipyards where local caïques are built and small yacht repairs can be undertaken, including the slipping of a yacht up to 7-ft draught. The technical resources on the island are limited.

A large finishing school for boys lies to the westward of the hotel, both buildings being conspicuous when approaching from the west. Many new villas have grown up on the Balza area but they are mostly empty in the winter months, and only the small local population remains.

Island of Spetsopoula, lying close S.E. of Spetsai with a yacht harbour, is privately owned by Mr Stavros Niarchos, the Greek ship-owner.

IDRA (IDHRA) AND THE SARONIC GULF

Both the mainland and the island ports are within 50 miles of Pireaus and can be reached by ferry steamers within 3 or 4 hrs, or in summer by hydrofoil far more quickly. Chart 1518 shows Idra and the mainland coast (with the island of Poros) beyond the Methana Peninsula.

Before entering the Idra Strait there is the unattractive and largely barren island of **Dhokos** with two partially sheltered coves on the northern side, suitable as a temporary yacht anchorage, the westernmost has a large mooring buoy. There is also on the mainland the shallow little port of **Ermioni** with its adjoining hamlet connected to the main road system. Though pleasant for a night anchorage, none of these places is recommended for a special visit; Ermioni is frequented by 'flotilla' yachts.

Island of Idra (Idhra, Hydra)

This long barren island with a central spur rising to 2,000 ft has a picturesque

small port, where almost the whole of the island's 3,000 population live. The attractively built houses of early Idriot families rising one above the other form an amphitheatre round the three sides of the harbour. (Chart 1657.)

Approach and Berth. The entry is straightforward day or night, and a yacht should berth off the main quay near the church, or if this is congested with caïques (as it sometimes is in summer) berth stern to the breakwater. Though appearing to be a well-sheltered port it can, in fact, be very disturbed in N.W. winds, and Idra is certainly not such a safe harbour as Spetsai. This small harbour is very crowded in summer.

Facilities. Except during the height of the tourist season it is easy to step ashore on the clean broad quay where all the shops are, and to find a wide choice of fresh provisions (brought across from the mainland). Fresh water expensive. There are a number of restaurants on the quay, many modest hotels and a bathing place on the rocks outside the harbour. Small repairs can be done by a yard that builds local motor-boats. A school of navigation stands above the steamer quay where the Piraeus steamer calls 3 or 4 times daily in summer – a 3-hr passage; also a hydrofoil. Local ferry connections with Spetsai and Epidavros.

Apart from the little church of Ayios Ioannis (with original frescoes) close above the town, the only excursion is an hour's climb to the monastery of Prophitis Ilias. It stands high on the mountain, and a mule can be hired.

Though the monastery is uninhabited and without interest except for its bell-tower, the neighbouring convent is attractive and well maintained by a few nuns. It affords a magnificent view.

Though crowded with tourists in summer during the day, Idra is a colourful little port much animated by the gaily painted caïques unloading their produce, and by the arrival of the fast ferry-boats from Piraeus embarking and disembarking passengers many times a day. By night the place quietens down, for the tourists have left, and only those with summer villas and the local people remain.

Earlier History. From the harbour looking up at the houses it is at once apparent that many of them were built for people of wealth and, except for Spetsai, have nothing in common with the humble dwellings on other islands. Relatively large and constructed of a grey stone now weathered, they are usually approached by a small garden with shrubs through which can be seen a panelled door with a richly moulded knocker. On the seaward side is a loggia standing on the steep parapet with a commanding view over the port.

They were built in the 18th century by Albanian-speaking families, who migrated here at the time of Turkish suppression, and by the latter part of that century had developed a maritime trade with many parts of the Mediterranean. A large number of sailing craft were built here; schooners and brigs were soon earning big profits.

When the War of Independence broke out in the early twenties of the next century, these families together with those from the islands of Spetsai and Psara put their ships at the disposal of the newly formed Greek Navy. At that time there were 4,000 seamen on the island, and about 150 ships of which no fewer than 80 were of 300 tons burden or more; most of them well manned and armed.

History has handed down accounts of spirited actions against Turkish warships. On one occasion they captured a Turkish corvette and decided to name her after the island: she thus became the first *Idra* of the Greek Navy.

Some Idriot leaders have been highly praised for their part in the War, especially Admiral Miaoulis whose statue now stands outside the church, and other Greek patriots such as Thombazi and Condouriotis, whose descendants still own their original family houses.

Commerce recovered after the War and thrived well into the latter part of the last century. The presence of bollards and moorings facilities in the more sheltered coves of Idra and Spetsai reveal where these schooners and brigs were laid up in the winter months.

Island of Poros

This has an attractive, landlocked bay sometimes used as a Fleet anchorage. It is a pleasant place to visit in a yacht, with its green shores and one or two coves; the small town is pleasant.

The Quay

Approach. Chart 1657. The northern entrance can take unlimited draught; tortuous eastern channel, which is used by the Piraeus ferry-steamers, is now buoyed. Here the northern shore must be followed within 100 ft in certain places – see sketch.

Anchorage. It will be noted that the 10-fathom sea-bed rises sharply at the sides to 3 fathoms or less. Yachts are now required to berth with stern to the new West Quay – midway between the ferry landing and the naval hospital. One should avoid mooring close off the yacht station for here the water is shallow and it is exposed to the north.

The Inner Harbour is used exclusively by naval boats. It is, however, possible to anchor in the small coves on the north side of Poros Bay, which, though somewhat far from the town, are claimed to be fairly sheltered and afford pleasant anchorage.

Port Facilities. Fuel and water at Yacht Station, but berth well clear of the quay.

View from the eastern entrance to Poros looking towards N.W.

Summer hotels and some reasonably attractive restaurants are close to the steamer landing place. A tourist hotel with bathing place has been built outside the town, being approached by the one and only road, a couple of miles distant from the main quay.

A steamer service during the summer months connects with Piraeus via Aegina, taking about 3 hrs. There is also a less frequent service to Idra and Spetsai.

Two miles N. of the naval establishment is Neorion Bay, where the Nauticlub Hellenic Marine fit out their charter yachts. They are always most helpful in an emergency.

The monastery and the ruins of the temple of Poseidon are worth a visit. The monastery can be reached by bus or taxi in 15 minutes and also by motorboat, and the ruins of the temple are an hour's walk above the monastery – mostly through pinewoods.

An interesting visit can be made to Troezen where in 1827 the first meeting of the Greek National Assembly was held, and Capodistria was elected president. Troezen can be reached either by bus from Galata, or by 40 minutes' easy going on foot from Vidhi, a poor anchorage at the western end of Poros Bay. Though the ruins of the temple of Hippolytus and the Byzantine church are fragmentary, the mountain views across the fertile plain are magnificent.

Proceeding from Poros to the island of Aegina one passes the tall, massive Methana Peninsula. There is anchorage at the head of the isthmus on either side and also at the small port of Methana on the east side where all the Piraeus ferries call. Few yachts make use of these places, preferring the more convenient ports and anchorages of nearby Poros and Aegina. The peninsula, however, with its steep, green slopes rising abruptly from the sea is most impressive from the deck of a yacht.

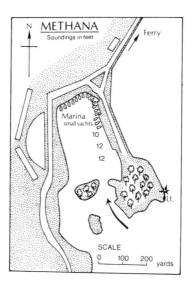

Methana has a small, well-sheltered yacht basin by the sulphur springs, the water from which is said to be good for cleaning the underside of a yacht. Small yachts sometimes lay up here. Entrance is difficult to see when coming from the north.

Island of Aiyina (Aegina)

(Spelt 'Aiyina' on Admiralty charts and 'Egina' on Greek maps.)

This is a hilly island, cultivated in places, with a well-sheltered though shallow little port – a seaside resort for Athenians.

The Port

Approach and Berth. Chart 1657, plan. The approaches to the port have recently been dredged and the shoals removed. Now the one obstruction remaining is marked by a buoy. The shoals were caused originally by concrete and stone blocks believed to have been set in the sea-bed by the early Greeks to form a protective zeriba round the mouth of their original harbour. Inside the port has also been dredged, and yachts now berth off the yacht station, stern to the quay, at the southern breakwater in 2-fathom depths. It is usually crowded.

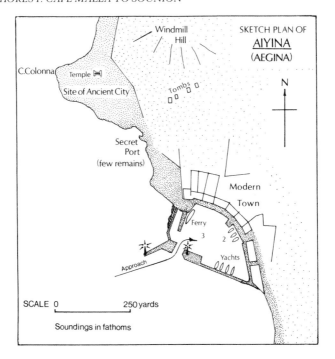

Port Facilities. There are provision shops and a fish market close by. Petrol and fuel may be obtained from a pump, and ice is available. Water is not easily come by; but it can be obtained by water-cart rather expensively. Taxis are available. There are several modest hotels; a palatable white wine may be bought locally. Frequent ferry communication with Piraeus and also with Poris, Idra, Spetsai and Leonidhion.

The small town of Aiyina is of no special interest; the island, though green in early summer, and partly wooded, dries up in the hot weather.

Brown's Hotel standing on the seafront was the former town house of the Brown family nearly a century ago when the original John Brown was manager of a sponge fishing company based on Aiyina. Their country house was by the site of the ancient city bordering some Mycenaean sarcophagus tombs. In one of these was discovered a most valuable treasure which was eventually identified as Cretan jewellery of the most skilful period of the goldsmith's craft. How it was acquired by the British Museum in 1891 for the sum of £4,000 makes a fascinating story told by R. Higgins in *The Aegina Treasure*, a booklet sold by the British Museum.

It should be borne in mind that divers came from a number of Aegean islands and that the waters south of Crete were a popular area to work – other Mycenaean treasures have also been recovered from the sea depths by divers during recent years.

Though the local museum is hardly worth a visit, the drive to the Doric temple of Aphaia is picturesque and the temple very fine.

History. In classical times Aegina had become a rival to Athens. After a four-year siege by the Athenian fleet the island was captured and its population deported. Many centuries later, Aegina suffered a worse catastrophe when the pirate Barbarossa overran the Aegean islands, and in Aegina he butchered the men and carried off 6,000 women and children. When the French fleet put in there soon afterwards they could find no people living on the island.

Ayia Marina Bay, though rather exposed, lies almost beneath the temple and affords suitable temporary anchorage in its N.W. corner off a sandy beach. Off the rocky foreshore further E. the holding is poor – sand on rock.

The small hamlet has grown into a popular resort with many hotels and villas.

On the north side of the island at Planaco is a boatyard which has been recommended for hauling out and repairing small yachts.

In later years, sponge fishermen, encouraged by the growing trade, were examining the sea-bed off this bay when they found considerable Minoan treasure, now in the British Museum.

Palaia Epidavros is a charming anchorage at the foot of the Peloponnese mountains with an interesting approach.

Approach and Berth. Chart 1657. The leading marks through the narrow approach channel are still described in *Sailing Directions*, the passage through the Narrows now being facilitated by prominent port and starboard beacons with lights Qk. Fl. (R) and (G).

Either anchor in 2–3 fathoms in the middle of the bay or berth off the quay. The yacht station is at another shorter jetty below the church: it has only 4–5 ft depths alongside.

Facilities. The village is growing and now has several hotels and restaurants, butcher, baker, grocer, etc. Water tap at the root of the jetty.

One should hire a taxi and drive to the ancient theatre at Epidavros – the finest in all Greece, less than an hour along a good road.

Continuing in a N.N.W. direction, close under the tall mountainous coast is a well-sheltered bay with a hamlet, Korfos, on the waterfront:

Sofikon, an attractive, spacious anchorage in mountainous surroundings.

Approach and Anchorage. Chart 1657. After avoiding obstructions both outside and at the entrance, anchor in the N.E. corner of the bay, off the eastern end of the village, in 3 or 4 fathoms. Shelter is all-round.

The hamlet has shops and tavernas, and modern villas are now extending round the bay. A new road leads to Poros.

Towards the N.W. corner of the Saronic Gulf lies the undiscernible entrance to the Corinth Canal at Kalamaki. Before reaching this, however, is the small cove of Kenchraie, the ancient Aegean port of Roman Corinth. Recent excavations have enabled some interesting mosaics and glass panels to be recovered. As the Gulf narrows, a mountain with medieval fortifications stands out prominently in the distance. This is Acro-Corinth and, though it lies on the west side of the Corinth Canal, it is the best distant mark for the Canal approach; the Canal entrance cannot be discerned until one is almost there.

Corinth Canal

This 3-mile cut much used by local steamers and caïques saves a distance of 140 miles on the sea route round the Peloponnesus. The canal is 80 ft wide and 25 ft deep in the middle. Chart 1600. (See Plate 5.)

The canal office is at the Aegean end of the canal. A yacht wishing to pass through should go alongside a quay at the entrance, when an official will come aboard to calculate the dues. When the canal is clear, the red flag is hauled down and a blue one hoisted; the yacht then proceeds without a pilot, passing between vertical limestone cliffs 250 ft high.

In 1981 a yacht up to 20 tons net might expect to be charged a sum of nearly £30. Fees are based on a vessel's net tonnage, and the denomination of the currency has varied over the years.

Though originally it was feared that there might be an inconvenient current, there is, in fact, seldom any flow of consequence, and only on rare occasions does it reach 2 knots due to strong winds. The sides of the canal are continually breaking away and the work of repairing has, for some years, been done on Tuesdays. This involves closing the canal to traffic, vessels being warned by 'loud hailer' as they approach the entrance.

Early History. This waterway was not cut until the 1880s. The project was, however, seriously considered by both Caligula and Nero; the latter ordered a survey, and appeared in person to inaugurate the digging, lifting the first clod of earth with a golden shovel. Pausanias states that work started in A.D. 67 with a labour force of 6,000 Jews, but owing to the troublesome times which followed the undertaking had to be abandoned, and thus the custom of hauling the galleys across the isthmus 'on rollers' continued throughout the centuries. The serious need for a canal did not again arise until the Austro-Lloyd Steamship Company secured the monopoly of the Levant trade during the last century. They found it necessary, though inconvenient, to build a good carriage road across the isthmus to convey the passengers arriving by sea at Loutraki to the steamer awaiting them at the other side.

During the 16th century British sailing vessels came to the roadstead W. of Corinth, to load the small dried grapes known to the French as 'Raisins de Corinth'. The British adopted the word currant – a corruption of their port of origin, Corinth.

Eighteen centuries had passed since the Romans abandoned their work, but when the French engineer, Gerster, came to construct the canal in 188‧ he found two sections of Nero's excavations at the western side of the isthmus – one of 2,200 yds and another 1,700 yds in length, and each about 50 yds wide. The French took about twelve years to complete the task, and the canal was opened in 1893.

> *. . . Salamis – where fame*
> *In noontide splendour shone,*
> *and blazed on Greece the deathless name*
> *That dawn'd at Marathon.*
>
> CARLYLE

Island of Salamis

A hilly island with clusters of trees and partial cultivation and small villages, overrun by modern villas. Leading into the much polluted Elevsis Bay are winding channels at either end of the island (Chart 1513). See p. xviii.

At the eastern end of the island lies the strait where in 480 B.C. the decisive battle against the invading Persian fleet was fought. Today this area is mostly taken up by the Greek Navy and repair yards. The ledge where Xerxes is said to have sat watching the destruction of his 2,100 galleys by the 480 vessels of Themistocles is marked on the chart. An open yacht anchorage on W. side.

Cape Konkhi on the southern tip of the island provides for a small yacht an unusual summer anchorage among some rocky islets.

PORTS OF PIRAEUS

Close eastward of Salamis is the great commercial port of Piraeus which since earliest days has served the city of Athens. Beyond it is the small but ancient port of Zea, which, during recent years, has been enlarged and dredged to become a modern yacht marina within less than an hour by road from Athens. Other marinas are Vouliagmeni, one-third the size of Zea and 9 miles south of it, and Alimos. Many visiting yachts crowd into these marinas during the summer months and many lay-up here in winter; but there are other possibilities for laying-up in safety at more remote places such as Spetsai, Porto Heli, Skiathos, Rhodes and near Volos, all of which are described under the port headings. Nearer to Piraeus is **Lavrion**, where since 1978 the yard at Gaidaromandri has been in operation.

Zea was planned as a yacht harbour about 1960. Breakwaters were constructed to form a deep outer basin known as Freatitha, and the ancient inner port, Passalimani, was dredged. Quays have been built in the outer port (4-fathom depths) to enable the larger yachts to berth stern-to, and in the inner port ($1\frac{1}{2}$ to $2\frac{1}{2}$ fathoms) stone piers have been completed to moor the smaller yachts in a similar manner. Altogether about 320 yachts can be accommodated; facilities are being arranged to provide convenient service in summer and when laying-up for the winter. The resources of the town of Piraeus are close at hand.

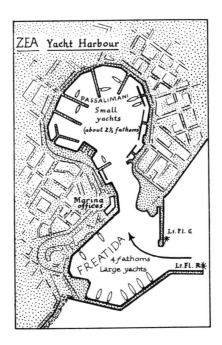

Approach and Berth. The entrance is well lit and there is no difficulty day or night. As all berths are normally taken for the season it is wise to arrange for one beforehand. Roger Stafford & Co Ltd, 11 Casanova Street, Piraeus, can often do this. Visiting yachts on arrival are expected to seek a berth immediately on the port hand when entering.

Officials. A Port of Entry: harbour office is on W. side of the Narrows, together with Tourist Office.

Facilities. Water, fuel and electricity are to be laid on at the berths. Provision shops and restaurants are close by. The Piraeus bus passes close to yacht berths with connections to Athens (see under Athens, p. 32). Yacht chandlers on the seafront and in the main harbour (Piraeus). Sailmaker: Manolis Pantelis, 55 King Paul Avenue, Piraeus 17, is the agent of Bruce Banks Sails Ltd, and can effect all normal repairs. One should realize that British paints, cordage, fittings etc, are 80 per cent more expensive here than at home; but all are obtainable out of bond though only in large quantities. Stores, however, can be sent by land or sea from England, consigned direct to the yacht via a Customs agent in Piraeus.

Harbour Dues. A tariff of charges for yachts berthing at Zea and Vouliagmeni is based on the vessel's gross tonnage, and the charge is made for a minimum period of 3 days' stay. At Vouliagmeni the charges are about 20 per cent more. One should examine the brochure on tariff charges, printed in English, and handed to the yacht on arrival; there are certain clauses which might be of benefit to a yacht when deciding upon her length of stay in the port. A deposit is required to be paid on arrival.

With southerly gales a reflected swell enters the outer port. In winter, gales occasionally cause seas to surmount the breakwater and cascade on to the quay, endangering the yachts within. The inner harbour is inclined to be dirty and smelly but, were the sewage pipes to be diverted, there would be an improvement. Its great advantage is that it is safe in all weathers.

Hauling-out and slipping cannot be done locally; a yacht must go to Perama – about 3 miles in the direction of Salamis – and arrange with one of the many yards whose resources are very limited. While waiting to slip, a convenient anchorage with all-round shelter can be found at Paloukia, Salamis. Individual arrangements must be made if desiring the services of a painter, plumber, engineer, metal-worker etc. Most of these artisans are to be found in Perama or Piraeus. For those who speak no Greek there are a few agencies who can arrange these services, but very few yacht-owners report favourably on this indirect way of approach. When laying-up afloat it is essential to leave a caretaker on board, or alternatively and less satisfactorily, make arrangements with an agent. An English agent who can be helpful is Mr Roger Stafford of 11 Casanova Street, Piraeus, Attica. See also p. 30.

Mikrolimano, the small harbour for Greek yachts and Class boats only, is always crowded. Foreign yachts may not enter without permission from the Yacht Club of Greece whose palatial white building stands on a promontory overlooking Passalimani. The Club secretary is willing to give helpful advice to a visiting yacht.

The sides of the port are lined with expensive restaurants and one or two yacht agencies. On summer nights the scene is animated by crowds of Athenians dining at the waterside in the cool of the evening.

Southerly gales during winter make the place uncomfortable. Except for the modern quays this little port has survived practically unchanged since the days of Themistocles. Formerly called Tourkolimano.

The Commercial Port of Piraeus (Chart 1520) has been greatly extended during the recent centuries, and today presents a scene of much activity, for not only does it accommodate the large liners and freighters, but all the local ferry services to Aegean ports. It is dirty and quite impossible for a yacht to berth here, all wharves being occupied by steamers, loading and unloading usually in the proportion of one to three respectively.

Ayios Georgios, the huge commercial harbour sheltered by the E. tip of Salamis, has recently been rebuilt to handle larger ships; but this port is forbidden to yachts. Caïques, trawlers and small coasters from the islands still land their cargoes here. One used to see many wine schooners from Rhodes, Kos and Khios; corn came from Macedonia; marble from Tinos, Naxos and Paros, olives from Mitilini and Itea, goats and cattle from many islands. For the return voyage caïques loaded largely with imported goods, machinery, tinned food – even Yarmouth bloaters.

The whole area between Perama and the eastern shores of Salamis is crowded with antiquated merchant ships awaiting their turn at the shipbreakers' yards nearby. Recently here and in Elevsis Bay 160 laid-up vessels were counted – nearly all tankers. Considerable development including the construction of breakwaters and wharves continues to progress, but the water being filthy, yachts are advised to avoid the area. Details of pollution here and in the adjoining Elevsis Bay are given on page xviii.

> **Brief history of the harbours.** With the exception of Ay. Georgios, the harbours were originally laid out in 493 B.C. when, in consequence of the Persian danger, Themistocles persuaded the Athenians to build stone breakwaters. These were largely of 10-ft square stone blocks on rubble foundations fastened with iron cramps run in with molten lead. The harbour approaches were then fortified and the two long walls leading to Athens were provided with adequate protection against enemy attack. Throughout the Venetian era the commercial harbour of Piraeus was known as Porto Leone, and although the marble lion was removed to Venice by Morosini in 1687, the port continued to be known by this name for at least another century. The lion now resides outside the Arsenal at Venice. The remains of the walls can be seen at Zea.

Athens can be reached from the marinas by taking a bus to Piraeus Station whence the electric trains (every 6 min) reach Omonia Square in 20 min. Green buses (every 15 min) reach Syntagma (Constitution Square) in 35 min. Alternatively, blue buses pass the Stadium (Athens) and go on to Kifissia. Both may be boarded in Korai Square by the Demotic Theatre, Piraeus. A taxi takes 20 min.

The guide-book gives details of all that is of interest in Athens. No one should miss seeing at least the Acropolis and the National Archaeological Museum. (All museums are free on Sundays and closed on Mondays.)

There is air and train communication with England: by aircraft in 3 hrs, and by rail in $2\frac{1}{2}$ days. Local Greek airlines fly to some twenty Aegean islands mainland ports – see p. xx. Terminal on W. side of airport.

On the Attic coast just south of the airport is the residential coastal area of Glifadha. Here a marina has been built, but it is somewhat exposed to southerly gales and is very noisy because of its proximity to the airport.

Alimos Marina (37° 54′ 50″ N, 25° 42′ 30″ E; not yet charted). Completed in 1981, Alimos is becoming more important than Zea. It lies immediately N. of Kalamaki at the foot of the Phaleron Second World War British Cemetery, and is scheduled to accommodate 1500 yachts.

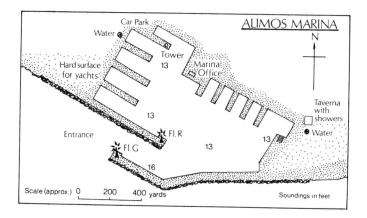

Approach. The entrance facing N. is through a protected gap approximately in the middle of the long sea-wall, not easily distinguished from seaward.

Caution: Submerged rocks, level with the airport and shown on Chart 1657 approximately 37° 53′ 40″ N, 23° 42′ 30″ E, extend further to seaward than shown. Vessels approaching from S. should keep well to seaward until the marina can be approached on a bearing of about 90°.

Berth. Where space permits. About 4 m depth generally.

Facilities. Water available at all berths except for those by the sea-wall. Fuel is supplied by bowsers; electricity is being installed and already available at some berths and in the laying-up area. Average depth alongside is 4 m.

The marina offers good laying-up facilities with a number of travel-hoists and mobile cranes with a capacity of 60 tons and possibly more, and a large area for parking yachts ashore. Repair facilities arranged through the marina office. Good provisions and chandlery, shopping facilities within a few minutes' walk of the marina. Good bus connections to Athens East and West air terminals, to Piraeus and to Athens city centre.

This marina is cleaner and more pleasant than Zea, but it has the disadvantage of being so near the airport.

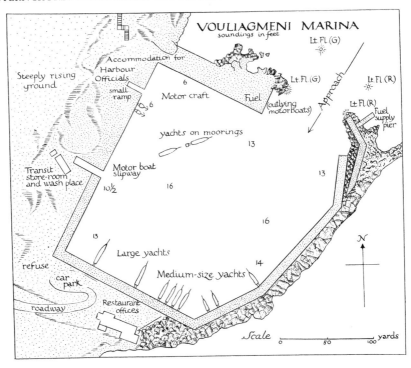

Vouliagmeni, the first yacht marina to be constructed in Greece, lies on the Attic coast 9 miles from Piraeus, and provides accommodation for 100 yachts; here are also many facilities both in summer and when laying-up in winter. The limited space available is usually fully booked; in the sailing season a visitor may be allowed to use the berth of a resident away cruising, but for lay-up it is prudent to make arrangements in advance.

Approach and Berth. The plan illustrates that entry is easy by day or night, but in the summer months when crowded a visiting yacht may have to look elsewhere as anchorage in the bay outside is prohibited.

On arrival one must be ready to pick up a buoy tailed to a chain bow mooring – the club boat assists. The yacht's stern is then hauled into the quay. Anchoring inside the port is forbidden. A copy of Port Regulations, printed in English, is handed to the yacht on arrival.

Shelter is normally good; only during winter strong southerly gales send in a reflected swell which necessitates yachts easing out stern warps and working fenders.

Officials. A Port of Entry, Harbour Master and Customs.

Facilities. Fresh water, telephone and electricity are laid on at each berth as well as at the pier. Fuel is available at the pier with permission. Laundry on the quay. Bread, vegetables, fruit and

1 The tower of Methoni, Peloponnesus

2 Night fishing-boats with their gas-lamps at Spetsai

3 Local craft: Bratsera with Trehandiri hull; nowadays only with a steadying-sail and motor power

4 The old Venetian fort, Bourtzi, at Nauplion

ice vans at the Club house. Vouliagmeni village is a mile distant with good restaurants and shops: from here there is a half-hourly bus service to Athens (40 min) – there are also occasional buses from the Marina to Athens. One or two smart hotels are near the Marina. The airport is 20 min by taxi. Only small motor-yachts and dinghies can be hauled out for refitting. Vouliagmeni's facilities however are expensive, and to lay up here is more costly than at Zea. One reason for high charges is that the services of technicians, artisans etc. can be obtained only from Athens; cost of transport by taxi is no small matter. For laying-up and repairs, see also p. xxvii.

It is possible to bathe from the rocks on the far side of the offices and restaurant, which is one of the attractions in hot weather, compared with Zea.

Sailing south-eastwards along the Attic coast towards Cape Sounion a yacht may pass between Gaidhari Island and the shore. During Meltemi conditions violent gusts sweep down from the hills, and sailing yachts are advised to follow the custom of local craft by shortening sail when passing through this passage.

> *Here in the dead of night by Lonna★ steep*
> *The seaman's cry was heard along the deep*

> FALCONER – after his shipwreck in *Britannia* on
> this Cape in 1762. He was one of the three saved.

Sounion. One can see Cape Sounion in the distance and, against the blue sky, the temple of Poseidon whose columns of Attic marble now appear quite white, and are in fact crystallized and glazed with the salt spray of twenty-four centuries. To the early Greek seamen this headland with its historic temple was the last they saw of the mother country as they sailed out to the Ionian colonies and the distant domains that were once the glory of the Greek Empire. (Plate 7.)

'Place me on Sounion's marbled steep,' wrote Byron; and here the poet, in common with many others, has chiselled his name at the base of one of the columns.

The view from the cape is magnificent. In the north are the peaks of Hymettus, once 'the happy hunting ground of bees', and sweeping towards the west lie the islands of Aiyina, Poros and Idra; farther to the south and the east can be seen the dark silhouettes of the mountainous Cyclades with Kithnos and Kea, and the nearby Makronisi. Much of this has been spoilt by enormous hotels on the beach and a motel close by the temple.

The Anchorage is frequently used by yachts throughout the summer and by caïques and small

---

★ Lonna, a corruption of Colonna, the Venetian name for Sounion.

coasters during N. to N.E. gales when the anchorage may be crowded. The bottom is largely sand, but there are stones and rocks causing the holding to be very uncertain. Open only to south, shelter from other directions is good. A short stone pier facilitates the landing by dinghy. *Note*. The nearby anchorage at Legraina is claimed to be better holding than Sounion.

By day there is a constant stream of motor coaches bringing tourists from Athens to see the temple, but by the evening the place is relatively quiet.

'A range of columns long by time defaced'

3

Cape Sounion to Salonika

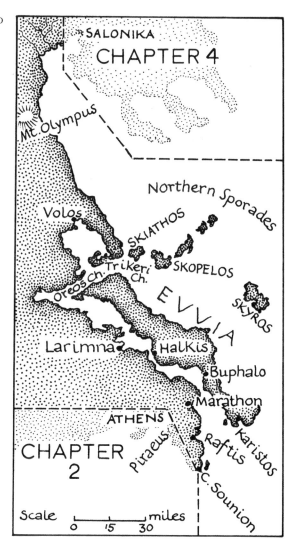

GULF OF PAGASITIKOS (VOLOS)
Trikeri
Palaio Trikeri
Vathudi
Port Pteleos
Mitzellas
Loutraki Amalioupolis
Port Volos
Trikeri Channel
    Andriami
    Platania
    Pondiko Islet

NORTHERN SPORADES
Island of Skiathos
    The Harbour
    Koukounaries

Island of Skopelos
    Port Skopelos
    Glossa (Klima)
    Panormos Bay
    Agnonda
    Staphilis

Island of Alonissos
    Murtia Bay

Patitiri
Stenivalla
Ormos Yerakas

Island of Peristera
    Vasiliko

Island of Pelagos
    Ayios Petros
    Planitis (Port Planedhi or Planoudhi)

Island of Skantzura
    Parausa
    Ormos Skantzura

Island of Skyros
    The Port of Linaria
    Linaria Cove
    Port Trebuki, with Akladi Cove
    Renes Bay
    Glifadha Cove

COAST FROM NORTHERN SPORADES
    TO GULF OF SALONIKA
Salonika
    The Marina
(*Mount Olympus*)

3
Cape Sounion to Salonika

CAPE SOUNION NORTHWARD

There are two routes:

(a) Leave Evvia to the westward and, sailing in more open water, a yacht passes through Doro Channel (Stenon Kafirevs) northwards. A similar choice was made by Odysseus when returning from Troy: 'In this dilemma we prayed for a sign, and heaven made it clear that we should cut straight across the open sea to Evvia.'

(b) Pass through the narrow inner passage between the long island of Evvia and the Attic–Boeotian shore.

Island of Evvia

With tall rugged mountains, fertile plains, forests and mines, Evvia is, after Crete, the largest island in the Aegean with a population of 160,000. The more interesting places and anchorages lie on the S.W. shores, and are described when considering the Inner Passage between Evvia and the mainland.

Evvia has its principal port of Halkis in the narrow Evripo Strait (described later). Karistos, lying in a bay the southern end of the islands, is a small town standing beneath Mount Ohi with a small port. Kimi lies on the east coast; protected by two breakwaters, Kimi is the supply port for the island of Skyros, and much used by caïques and steamers.

The Open-Water Route

Until after the First World War when caïques still had no motors, they always chose the open-water route to make their northing. When bound for Salonika they took advantage of the fact that the N.W. wind blowing from the Attic shores in the summer changes its direction as one moves farther eastward. Thus sailing vessels, having stood across, were often favoured with an easterly slant enabling them to fetch right up the Salonika Gulf.

The open-water route takes a sailing vessel to the north-eastward, passing S. of Evvia and through the Kea and Doro Channels, where anchorages on Andros Island are described in Chapter 9. A yacht can also put in at:

Karistos, a pleasant growing village by a small port lying in an attractive mountainous setting.

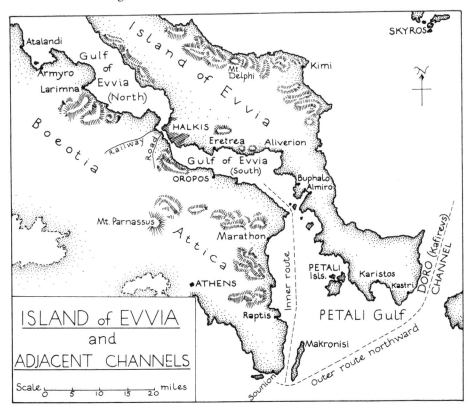

Approach and Berth. Proceed to inner basin, berthing stern to the quay by the village square and Harbour Office. Deep water until close to the quay (10 ft). Harbour lights. Shelter is good in all weather, except for very strong Meltemi gusts from the mountains.

Facilities. Excellent fruit, vegetables and fish; tavernas close by. New hotels with bathing beach E. of village. Communication by bus with Halkis and other villages. Daily steamer service Rafina–Andros calls here. Water-tap outside corner of town square; water is excellent. Ice from the cold store at W. end of village.

The modern village lies at the foot of a Venetian fort built on the site of an ancient Greek acropolis; west of the village is a cultivated plain; the whole district is partially wooded with plenty of vegetation. A number of mineral springs well up from the sand at the E. corner of the bay.

In Roman days the port was used for the export of green marble which is still quarried in the hinterland.

Pilotage notes for this route. Both the Kea Channel and the Doro Channel (Stenon Kafirevs) are notorious for the strong winds which funnel through them, and for the short steep seas and the strong currents which a strong Meltemi causes, particularly in the Doro Channel where it can reach 5 or 6 knots. If desiring to await better conditions, there is good anchorage in Gavrion Bay on Andros Island (p. 236), Ay. Nikolaos Bay on Kea Island (p. 242), and in two small sheltered coves on the opposite shore of Evvia.

    (a) Kastri Bay, with good holding on firm sand in 3 fathoms.

    (b) A bay unnamed 1 mile N. of Kastri.

Both bays (with fresh-water springs) afford good shelter from the Meltemi; but after the cessation of a strong Meltemi, the steep short sea in this channel can be very dangerous to small vessels.

Kimi, a small caïque port protected by breakwaters; the only useful port on route northwards before reaching the Northern Sporades, it has convenient depths, but has nothing to recommend for yachts. It owes its importance to being the ferry terminal for Skyros with good bus communication via Halkis to Athens. Water and fuel are available.

The Inner Passage via the Gulf of Evvia

This makes a very pleasant cruising ground for a small yacht with the choice of so many attractive anchorages close at hand. During the summer months the Meltemi may cause short choppy seas, but shelter is always near.

    Passing by the Petali Gulf to Halkis and thence the Gulf of Evvia, altogether 76 miles, the passage first leads between the uninteresting narrow island of Makronisi (formerly a military area) and the Attic shore. Here are some sheltered bays suitable for temporary anchorage, but of no particular interest to a yacht:

Gaidaromandri is a shallow but well-sheltered cove with a few cottages. It has recently become popular among yachts and there are permanent moorings and yachtyard facilities at the head of the cove.

Approach. On entering the cove make towards N.W., carefully avoiding the submerged wreck of a Turkish steamer which in 1981 lay between 1 and 8 ft below the surface. It was reported to extend several hundred feet N.W. of an unlit green wreck-buoy.

Berth at the head of the cove by the T-head of a main pier extending from the modernised shipyard 'Olympic Yachts S.A.' with a Travel Lift, where yachts can be laid up.

Facilities. Water and fuel. Winter laying-up arrangements. Provisions at Lavrion.

Lavrion, an open roadstead with an ore port and a large village, ore-tips and quays around the bay. A Port of Entry.

The mines which were renowned for their silver in the 5th century B.C. were out of production by the time of Pausanias. Re-opened in 1860, the mines now produce zinc and manganese, and from the rubble rejected by the ancients modern methods now enable small quantities of lead and silver to be extracted.

Port Raftis, 15 miles from Sounion, is a useful anchorage. It is also a popular summer resort and the coast is now built up with houses and blocks of flats.

> **Approach.** Chart 1630. On the small but steep islet which forms the protection for the bay stands a marble statue of the headless tailor from which the place takes its name. This is a splendid seamark and enables one to identify the port.

> **Anchorage.** On the S. coast of the N.W. arm of the bay are convenient depths on a sandy bottom off Ay. Spiridon – a small hamlet. A slight swell may come in but easterly winds do not blow home. Alternatively one can anchor off the beach W. of the light in 3 fathoms on a sandy bottom.

> **Facilities.** There are hotels and tavernas, fresh provision shops, and general stores. In the summer months, buses run frequently to Athens in about an hour. Fuel and water can be obtained near the landing place.

This little port, which now has a loading quay for caïques in the S.W. corner, appears to be increasing in importance.

> **Early History.** The origin of the headless statue is obscure. It could belong to the 6th century B.C.; but it is also said to be of Roman origin. It is believed that during the period of the Confederacy the annual ceremony of transporting the Theoria to Holy Delos took place here. In later centuries when sailing vessels from the west used these waters, the shelter of Raftis was well known: John Sellers states in *Sailing Directions* of 24 July 1677 'Port Raftis is one of the best and most commodious havens of all that are found in the archipelago to sail into in stress of weather.'

Rafina, with its sandy bathing beach patronised by Athenians, has now become a ferry port for Karistos, Andros and Erimoupolis. The ferries berth at the E. side of the inner mole leaving very little room for yachts.

Some $2\frac{1}{4}$ miles northward a chapel can be recognised standing above the shore – close southward is a short curved breakwater, affording protection to two small bays reported as being suitable as yacht anchorages.

Petali Islands

These lie close to the Evvia coast and provide a sheltered anchorage in all conditions. The best is close off a fine villa on S.W. corner of Xero Island.

The channel running south from this anchorage has a depth of 2–3 fathoms

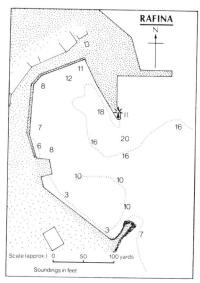

except for a narrow ledge of rock at the narrowest part of the channel where the depth is 8–9 ft (lead sounding).

On the S. side of Megalo Island is the deserted sandy bay of Vasiliko. This is sheltered on all sides except south and is a pleasant place to bring up. Anchor off the beach in 3 fathoms on a sandy bottom. Downdraughts can, however, be strong when the wind is northerly, and the holding is not reliable.

> *That man is little to be envied whose patriotism*
> *would not gain force upon the Plain of Marathon.*
>
> DR JOHNSON

Marathon is a large bay mainly of interest for its historical associations. There is anchorage in convenient depths off some small houses in the pinewood at the northern corner of the bay, where the peninsula projecting southwards affords some protection except in southerly winds; but it has little attraction. The modern summer village on the N.W. side of the bay has a pier and a few boats moored off, but this place is too exposed to the afternoon breeze and has been prohibited.

Early History. Behind the 'Dog's Tail' (Cynosura) was the anchorage of the Persian fleet, and where the pinewoods now grow is the site of the evacuation of the Persian army. It was here in 490 B.C. that the Athenians drove them back to their galleys drawn up on this beach. The famous tumulus where 192 Athenians lie buried has been tidied up, and there are now trees and gardens as well as a small pavilion for tourists.

Proceeding northwards one reaches the partially sheltered bay of Ay. Marina. Opposite is a group of uninhabited islands, where landing is prohibited. Here the Greek Navy has extensive recreational facilities and a pier in the northern part of the bay. Anchorage here is prohibited. On the east side of **Stira** is a rocky islet which provides partial shelter for temporary anchorage on a sandy bottom in depths of 3 fathoms with room to swing; but better places to anchor for the night are on the Evvia coast; only 10 miles from Marathon at

Almiros Pótamos, a long attractive fjord.

> **Anchorage.** At the entrance to a cove on the western shore (opp. '15' on chart 1597) in 5-fathom depths, with room to swing, open only to E. Also anchorage with better shelter in a cove in the N.W. corner of the fjord in 4 fathoms off the hamlet of Ayios Demetrios.

The village, with a bus service, lies in the bay E.S.E. of the islet.

Buphalo (Voufalo Cove). This is a charming sheltered little cove at the head of a small creek with only half a dozen cottages and some small fishing craft. The country around is grazing land and cornfields. A number of beehives can be seen on the hillside.

> **Approach and Anchorage.** Chart 1554. There is deep water everywhere except near the projecting sand spit from the eastern shore. Anchor in the middle of the small basin in 3½ fathoms on firm sand. Here there is nearly all-round shelter and sufficient room for several medium-sized yachts to swing.

Aliverion. A mole provides good shelter off a village, recognized by a Hellenic tower and Venetian castle. A yacht should round the mole-head (Chart 1597) and berth stern to a quay by the village close to a water-tap, and a restaurant nearby. This little place has been dwarfed by the nearby Pyrgos where a huge power plant has been built close by the waterfront; it is not worth a special visit.

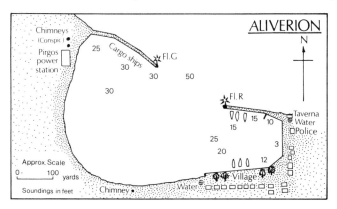

Eretria is Evvia's busy ferry port terminal; it can also be useful for a yacht wishing to gain shelter for the night and visit the ancient acropolis.

Approach. Chart 1554. A safe course into the middle of the port is about 020°, taking care to avoid the shoals indicated on chart.

Anchorage. On account of the depths and ferry traffic, one is limited to the small area in the S.W. near the root of the sunken mole. Depths here are about 4 fathoms, sand and mud bottom open only to S. The ferries are continually crossing to Oropos on the opposite shore conveying lorries and cars but also a regular bus service which reaches Athens in just over 2 hrs. Land in the dinghy at the quay.

Eretria, now a village of about 2,000 people, was once a city state. Remains of the ancient acropolis can be seen on the hill above the village and also a Greek theatre. In modern times during the Greek War of Liberation refugees from Psara, when sacked by the Turks, fled to the hospitality of Eretria.

Oropos, an open bay on the green and hilly Attic shore, has anchorage off a stone pier near the S.W. corner. Ferries are continually coming and going, conveying lorries with produce from Evvia to Athens.

So they passed by Crouni and Chalkis a land of fair streams
ODYSSEY XV

Halkis (Khalkis or Chalkis) is a pleasant, modernized town with 25,000 inhabitants; a sliding bridge connects the island of Evvia with the mainland. The narrow winding channels through which a vessel approaches from the south are interesting from the pilotage point of view as well as the scenery; the fortress, defended towers, and campanile are all Venetian.

At the narrowest part of the Strait, crossed by a bridge, the tidal stream runs swiftly changing direction about every 6 hrs, but considerably influenced by wind and barometer. The stream can occasionally run as fast as 6 knots and it begins almost immediately after the turn of the tide. Yachts are only allowed to pass at slack tide when the bridge is opened for a very short period and signals (see under) are hoisted to indicate which side will be accepted first. Yachts must be ready to seize this opportunity and must recognize the appropriate signal. (Inquire and pay fee at Port Office west of the Bridge.)

About 15 min. before opening the bridge signals will be hoisted:

(a) Cone (point up) above 'hour-glass' shape means that traffic from N. to S. will have priority.

(b) Ball–Cone–Ball signifies that the traffic to move first is from S. to N.

Note: Sometimes the bridge controller declines to open the bridge unless there is a quorum of at least three yachts waiting but never on Sundays.
Sailing Directions may be consulted for slack water predictions.

Approach. Chart 2802. There is no difficulty in beating up the channels even against a strong Meltemi and then berthing temporarily to await the opening of the bridge and for day and night signals.

South of the bridge: The commercial quay on the eastern shore provides the best berth. (The current can be dealt with by adjusting warps). The area behind this quay, although out of the current, has the disadvantage of difficulty in landing and the inability of observing the bridge and its opening signals. (Water is obtainable by the police-boat mooring pontoon on the east side of this quay.) One may also anchor off the railway station, but here tugs and ferries are frequently obstructing.

North of the bridge: The area south of the pilot cutter berth is now infested with local small craft. The best berth is on the east side of the channel immediately above the bridge alongside a new small quay. The current can easily be coped with by adjusting springs.

Facilities. Water on the quay. The Mobil garage in the street behind; it also supplies diesel fuel, but not duty free. Fuel and fresh water are available at the yacht station.

There is an excellent market. Modern hotels, some good restaurants and shops have given Halkis a new and thriving look. A train service connects with Athens in 1½ hrs. There is also a half-hourly bus service which is slightly quicker than the train.

After leaving Halkis and entering the northern part of the **Gulf of Evvia** the scenery now becomes more grand and the Evvia mountains reach their greatest height – nearly 6,000 ft of limestone cliff – standing almost sheer above the green coastline. A sailing yacht should keep towards the mainland shore, as the mountain squalls can be hard; moreover the anchorages are all on the Boeotian coast of the mainland.

Larimna (Larymna), the present name of the ancient port of Larmes, lies 16 miles N.W. of Halkis, at the mouth of the River Kifissos. Off the small village are convenient depths for anchoring, but the interesting approach is somewhat marred by the buildings of an ore company, the smoke belching from their furnaces often covers the surroundings with an oily dust. Ferronickel is one of Greece's most valuable exports. (Chart 2802.)

An alternative anchorage can be found by a small yacht in an attractive small bay about 2 miles S.W. of Cape Larmes. It is open only to the east and holding is excellent. It could be affected by the smoke from the ore furnaces but only if the wind were S.E.

The ancient river still flows and provides cooling water for a bathe at the anchorage. Formerly running underground, it was used to drive the mills of the early Greeks, and shafts were sunk to enable men to descend and prevent blocking. Some of these shafts may still be seen.

Continuing N.W. one reaches:

Atalandi Island. Off its western shore an islet forms two small coves with a quiet anchorage in each.

Port Armyro, although a small mining port, seldom used, is a mediocre settled-weather anchorage rather near the noisy motor highway.

> **Approach.** The dangerous sunken rock at the entrance is sometimes marked by a buoy, but recently it has been reported as unmarked and the port unused.

> **Anchorage.** A yacht should anchor, before reaching a line of stakes, in a depth of about 3 fathoms. Alternatively she can anchor more peacefully in the cove immediately north of the loading jetty, but here the holding has been reported as poor. The lines of stakes at the head of the bay should be treated with respect as some are largely submerged.

Atalandi Jetty. In settled weather it is pleasant to anchor off a small jetty where a road leads to Atalandi village standing on a hill about 3 miles distant. Unfortunately this anchorage is also near the motor road from Athens to Salonika which follows close along the shore passing two ferry landing points:

Arkitsa. Close under the cape is the car-ferry terminal linking the Athens bus route with Edipsos and the north of Evvia Island. Although this little bight in the coast is of no interest to a yacht the communication route can be useful – see under Orei.

Ayios Constantinos, comprising a wide bay with modern summer village at the foot of a green crescent-shaped mountain range, is the ferry point linking the Athens bus route with the steamer to Skiathos and Skopelos.

> **Anchorage.** In fine weather only, on the E. side of the bay near an old river mouth; good holding in 3–4 fathoms on mud, but very exposed. Alternatively berth off the steamer quay (which lies N. and S.); anchor in 7 fathoms, stern to the quay.

> **Facilities.** As for a summer resort, hotels, restaurants etc. Bus from Athens $2\frac{1}{2}$ hrs, steamer to Skiathos 3–4 hrs.

The Evvia Shore. In fine weather when there is not a fresh N. wind it is interesting to cross to the Evvia coast and follow it westwards from the point where the steep-to mountains recede from the shore. Here the green slopes become more gentle with forestry, olive groves, vineyards and cultivation generally. At the foot of each torrent bed is a hamlet with small houses lining the waterfront and usually an olive oil factory. Limni, the largest village, has nearly 3,000 people, but most places are only a cluster of houses. Before sighting the large hotels of Edipsos one passes a bay beneath the monastery of the Prophet Elias, standing boldly on a spur close under the 3,000-ft Mt Balanti.

Unfortunately none of the places along this charming Evvia coast has a suitable anchorage, and a yacht should always bring up for the night at one of the anchorages described on the mainland coast.

At the end of the Evvia Gulf and 42 miles above the bridge of Halkis are the **Islands of Likades** with passages leading into the Oreos Gulf to the N.E., and the Maliakos Gulf to the west. The narrow N.E. Passage (350 yds wide) between Evvia and the small island (see plan, Chart 1196) is quite practical by day. Here the tidal stream can run at 3 knots but its direction cannot be accurately predicted as it is much dependent upon the wind; a yacht can always anchor under the red cliffs to await a favourable tide. In the main channel the tide runs at about half this velocity. (See also sketch-plan on p. 50.)

One should not be discouraged from making this inshore passage; it is necessary to pass within 200 yds of the point to avoid underwater rocks on the western side of the fairway and to keep a cable from the Evvia coast until the N. shore of the northern islet bears west. Then keep half a mile offshore.

It is not proposed to describe the western or Maliakos Gulf which leads to the ore and bauxite loading quays at Stilis with the pass of Thermopylae beyond. This gulf has no appeal. Turning eastwards, however, is the **Oreos Channel** which

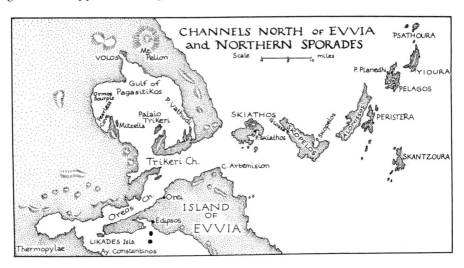

separates Evvia from the Thessaly coast and leads past the Gulf of Pagasitikos (or Volos) towards the attractive islands of the Northern Sporades. Every afternoon in summer the N.E. breeze blows freshly down the channel and whips up a short, steep sea.

There is only one good harbour in the gulf; this is on the N. coast of Evvia:

Orei, a pleasant modernized fishing village with a small harbour protected by a mole against the prevailing winds, but exposed to east.

Berth. Chart 1521. Should there be room berth stern to the mole near its extremity in depths of 3 fathoms or berth alongside between the light and the steps. Alternatively anchor off the pile pier and haul in the stern. The harbour is clean, the bottom sand, shelving towards the quayside. The little port is apt to be crowded with fishing boats and charter yachts. In event of swell from strong W. to S.W. winds shelter in Pirgo – southern shore. An extension of the quay at Orei was projected (1981).

Facilities. Water at a tap on the mole (own hose required). Ice and limited fresh provisions can be bought close at hand. Post office and telephone nearby. Two tavernas with tables under the tamarisks on the waterfront. A daily caïque ferry runs to Paleo Trikeri Island and Volos. Bus service to Edipsos, thence car ferry and bus to Athens (4 hrs altogether).

By the village square stands a marble bull of early Greek times recently recovered from the sea by fishermen. Beyond it are the ruins of a Venetian fort built on the foundations of an early Greek boundary wall, and S.W. of it is a canning factory. The village was built near the site of ancient Histiaia after which the present village on the hill is now called. The foundations of a marble temple are still to be seen.

Brief History. One cannot leave Evvia without touching on its history during Venetian times; then known as Negropont, this island, 120 miles long, had been for more than two centuries the Venetians' main fortress of the Aegean, the centre of commerce for trade with Constantinople and a base for the fleet to operate against piracy. Castles grew up all over the island, the ruins of some remain. Like all great empires Venice began to crumble, and in 1470 came the attack on the fortress of Halkis by a determined Turkish fleet, which after a long dramatic siege captured the port, and the whole of Evvia fell.

On the mainland is the small village of Glifa. A car ferry now operates from here to the opposite coast of Evvia. The two coves in this bay, E. of the ferry point, though appearing suitable anchorages for a small yacht are, in fact, too deep for convenience.

Ormos Vathikelon, lying $1\frac{1}{2}$ miles west of Glifa, is a deep but well-sheltered cove. Anchor in 7 fathoms and run out a warp to a tree. The place is attractive, being well wooded and devoid of habitation.

GULF OF PAGASITIKOS (VOLOS)

On entering this large gulf one sees to the N.E. a substantial village perched on the mountainside. At its foot lies the Skala:

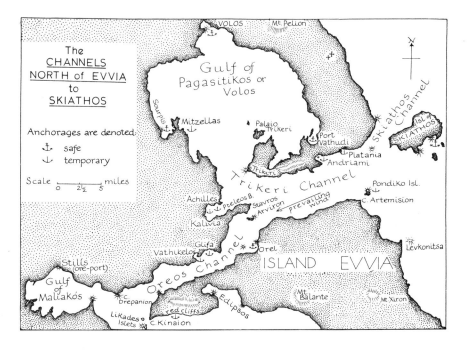

Trikeri, an open bay with a primitive hamlet, Skala Trikeri, guarding the approach to the Gulf of Volos.

Approach and Berth. There is no difficulty by day for the water is very deep and the village is conspicuous on the hill. On account of the sea-bed rising too steeply to permit anchoring off, a vessel must proceed to the N.E. corner of the bay, letting go in 10 fathoms and hauling in the stern to a small pier. (A couple of mooring buoys lie close off, whose ground cables should be avoided.) The mail steamer calls daily.

Historical. A spirited action took place in this little bay during the Greek War of Independence. On 23 April 1827, Captain Abney Hastings, then fighting for Greece, was commanding one of the earliest aux-steam gunboats, named *Karteria*. This 4-masted vessel was built of iron, with a tall thin funnel, fore and aft rig with square topsails, and also driven by paddles. She had already harassed the ships of the Turkish Navy then blockading the Greek coast off Volos, and on this occasion her opponent was a large Turkish brig moored close to the shore and protected by a battery on the hill above.

She was sighted by *Karteria* who, approaching from seaward, immediately prepared for action. Driven by her 40-horse-power engines she rapidly closed the enemy. Meanwhile, in the

5 The Corinth Canal

6 Patmos: the harbour

7 The Temple of Poseidon at Cape Sounion

boilers – each 23 ft long – cannon shot was being heated and when within range Hastings opened fire. The red-hot shot soon had the brig alight and in an hour she was a completely burnt out. Hastings has not been forgotten by the Greeks, for his statue stands in a prominent position in the Garden of heroes at Missolonghi.

Island of Palaio Trikeri is the larger of two wooded islands inside the E. arm at the entrance to the Gulf. Its most prominent feature is a monastery which has recently become an hotel. Although most of the inlets have been examined with a view to finding convenient anchorages, none has been found. The best place to secure temporarily in a small yacht is at the Skala – a charming cove with three or four small houses on the S. coast. Let go the anchor in 7 fathoms and haul in the yacht's stern to a wood pier where the Volos caïque-ferry berths.

A small well-sheltered bay will also be found east of the Skala.

In the S.E. corner of the Gulf is

Vathudi. Chart 1556. This is an attractive wooded bay affording shelter and convenient anchorage at the mouth of any of the small coves in depths of about 3 fathoms. During the Meltemi the best shelter is S.E. of the shipyard beyond the caïque moorings.

Facilities. Limited provisions, including fish and ice, can be obtained at the café-store belonging to the shipyard. This has been building large caïques for some years and has recently accepted yachts for slipping and laying-up. (Caïques have moorings S.E. of the yard.)

This large enclosed bay is quite unspoilt and inhabited only by a few peasants. It is well worth a visit, being cooled in summer by an unfailing day breeze.

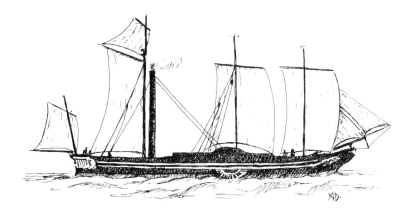

Petraki, lying a mile north of Vathudi, is a charming cove with olives and shrubs.

Approach and Anchorage. North of Alatas Islet can be seen a quarry, and then the cove opens to the N.W. Anchor in 2–3 fathoms, complete shelter. Temporary anchorage can be found in a cove west of Vathudi entrance, and also under a small headland S.E. of Cape Maratea.

Inside the western arm of the gulf is

Pteleos Bay, a long mountainous inlet with two villages believed to be where Achilles set off for Troy.

Approach and Anchorage. Charts 1521 and 1556. The best place for a yacht to make for is **Pigadia** (or **Paralia Pteleou**) village. Anchor off the ramp in 3 fathoms – sand. Alternatively anchor 200 yds westward in 6 fathoms where shelter from the day breeze is better. The whole gulf is exposed to the prevailing N.E. breeze coming in from the Trikeri Channel and there is always a swell after the wind has fallen off in the evening.

Off the larger village of Achilleion at the head of the Gulf, where the fishermen land their catch for Volos, the anchorage is very exposed; and under the shelter of the Achilles Tower peninsula the depths are too great. Off Pigadia village is the best choice.

Facilities. Pigadia is only a poor little hamlet with a road to Volos. The taverna sells basic provisions including fish.

The Achilles Tower is part of an early medieval stronghold with foundations of defending walls and much piled-up rubble. The view from the top of the hill is rewarding, for apart from the magnificent country surrounding the gulf, one can see the Achilleion peninsula with its ancient port, now silted, beside it.

Further N. Westward is

Mitzellas (Chart 1196, plan), or Amalioupolis, a small village with a stone pier off which a yacht can anchor and haul in the stern. A taverna and a water pump are close by. At night with N. winds, one should proceed to an anchorage in the large cove off a sandy beach in the N.W. corner of the bay where there is shelter from the swell caused by the day breeze.

Loutraki‾Amalioupolis, leading off Ormos Sourpis, is a delightful place among pines and olive groves; a perfect anchorage with excellent shelter and almost deserted. Marked on some charts as Fearless Cove.

Anchorage. Chart 1196. Let go off the beach, about 5 fathoms, sand and mud. A couple of caïques have permanent moorings here and in winter one or two yachts lay-up afloat. Shelter is claimed to be all-round. Land in the dinghy at a stone pier.

Facilities. The village of Amalioupolis is 15 min walk over the saddle. Fish and simple supplies can be bought. A bus service on a new road plies to Volos.

Volos, a town of 51,300 inhabitants, lies at the head of this large gulf. Though the port is clean and sheltered, it is seldom that a yacht makes this long detour for a special visit.

The Port

Approach and Berth. Chart 1196. The entrance is straightforward by day or night. Yachts and coasters berth stern to the quay off the yacht station, near the centre of the town; the bottom here is soft mud. In the summer months the afternoon breeze is usually from the southward.

Port Facilities. Good water is available from a hydrant at the root of the mole, and a hose is provided. Diesel fuel and petrol can be bought and ordinary repairs undertaken. Ice can be bought. Some yachts lay-up here in winter, the shelter being adequate, and the assistance of mechanic, carpenter and sailmaker being available. At the eastern end of the town is a small but unique collection of painted stellas.

At Volos modern hotels have been built and there are some good restaurants on the waterfront. There are frequent buses to Larissa, Athens and Salonika, and sea communication with Skiathos and islands of the Northern Sporades. Air connection with Athens.

Officials as for Port of Entry.

Volos has developed considerably since the Second World War and is now the fourth largest town in Greece. It suffered early in 1955 from a severe earthquake when a number of the older buildings were destroyed, but prompt action by the authorities soon restored the town to working order.

The country round Volos, both on Mt Pelion itself and on the coast beneath it, is attractive. To avoid the heat of Volos in the summer evenings, a drive to Portaria (half-way up Pelion) or Macronitsa is recommended; each is picturesque with hotels, good restaurant and a terrace with plane trees. Along the coast are little villages among olive groves where one may also dine simply but well. Returning to the Trikeri Channel and then proceeding north-eastwards along the Magnesian promontory one comes to two coves suitable for temporary anchorage:

Andriami, well sheltered in attractive scenery affording anchorage in 3 fathoms in the N.E. corner of the bay. Chart 1556.

Platania, with its small hamlet in wooded surroundings, and an anchorage in 3 fathoms on a sandy bottom. There is a small hotel, provision shops and bus connections to Volos. Of the two coves, Andriami provides the better shelter from the day breeze.

Following the *southern* shore of the Trikeri Channel and heading north-eastwards one reaches Cape Artemision where in 480 B.C. a hundred Athenian warships had their first brush with the invading Persian fleet. There is no anchorage here, but on the south side of the offlying islet of **Pondiko** is a small attractive cove affording convenient anchorage for a small yacht.

> **Historical.** Only a few years ago, with the discovery of a white marble slab at Troezen, details came to light of the naval strategy employed by Themistocles to save Athens from the coming Persian invasion. The writing on the slab explains the employment of delaying tactics to be adopted by the Athenian warships off Cape Artemision: it directs that the trireme's crew should consist of a captain, 20 marines and 4 archers; and it gives the disposition of the other 100 triremes which were to lie off Salamis and the Attic coast to 'keep guard over the land'. Before these details were found, it was never realized how carefully Themistocles had planned the Battle of Salamis. Herodotus adds that a force of Greek galleys had been stationed at Skiathos in order to give warning of the enemy's approach by fire-signal.

Northern Sporades

Including Skyros there are nine islands, some of which are of great interest and beauty. Chart 2072.

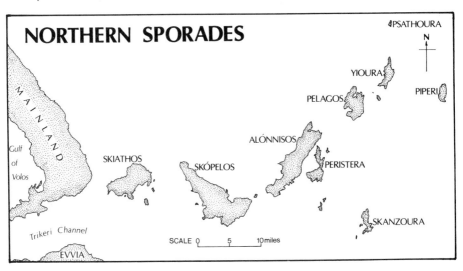

Island of Skiathos

The pleasant village standing on the hill-slopes behind its sheltered port makes Skiathos an attractive place to visit in a yacht. It has become popular for residents as well as tourists.

The Port

Approach. Chart 1196, and plan below. Since the construction of new quays in 1977 there are now convenient berths for yachts inside the sheltered bay. Proceed in a northerly direction passing between the small promontory of Bourtzi (with conspicuous red roof) and Dhaskalo Rock. Then converge towards the new quay.

Berths. Yachts berth stern to quay, leaving N. end clear for mainland ferry. Alternatively anchor at head of bay, land and then walk 15 min to town. Small yachts often prefer the old quay among local boats. Very crowded.

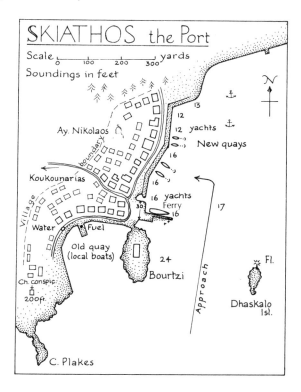

Facilities. Water at new quay, but fuel at the old town quay by the yacht service station. Petrol in drums should be ordered in advance. (Fuelling being a slow process a queue of yachts may be expected and it is sometimes more convenient to order a tanker from a service station; slightly more expensive.) Two ship chandlers supply limited hardware. Competent mechanics available by the waterfront. A chemist with variety of medical supplies. Well-equipped clinic with English-speaking doctors; also a dentist. The shipyard at the head of the bay still builds caïques. It has a slipway with skid–cradle capable of hauling out vessels up to 45 ft in length, but there are no repair facilities.

Abundant provisions and fresh vegetables; usually ice. Restaurants, tavernas and self-service stores; modern hotels, pensions and private rooms; apartments and villas can be rented. Airport: two daily flights, $\frac{1}{2}$ hour to Athens. Hot showers at Meltemi (N. of quay).

The village was built in the early part of the last century on the suppression of piracy. Skiathos is proud of its writer Papadiamandis whose statue stands on Bourtzi islet. The inhabitants of the little white houses take great pride in their attractive gardens, always displaying an abundance of colourful flowers. The old capital, Kastro, up on the hills, has been deserted for some years and is now a mass of ruins.

The island's population is about 4,000 but in the summer tourist season it is doubled. Between the two wars the anchorage was popular with the Royal Navy and early in the last century was much used by pirates.

Koukounaries until a few years ago was renowned as the best bathing beach in the Aegean. Tourism has stepped in with hotels and villas, and now a small marina has been built.

A 4-ft high sea-wall at the E. end of the beach was completed in 1976 and now forms part of a small yacht harbour which can accommodate about twenty small yachts. Depths range from 4 to 10 ft with about 16 ft in the middle. This is claimed to be well sheltered and safe, even in winter, when ten medium and ten small size yachts are reported to have laid up.

Island of Skopelos

The island is green and rocky with sharply defined mountain ridges. Some of the wooded valleys lead steeply upwards to attractive monasteries still inhabited mostly by nuns who have recently established a weaving industry, selling blouses and skirts to the tourists. Skopelos, the capital, with about half the island's 4,500 population, is unfortunate in having an artificial port so exposed to N.E. gales that sometimes it becomes almost untenable. It lies in a lovely setting, with the houses of the town, rising like the sides of an amphitheatre almost overshadowing the port. Above are olive groves; here and there clusters of cypresses, and vineyards beyond.

Port Skopelos

Approach. Chart 2072. The breakwaters have been rebuilt, the harbour dredged and shelter improved by extending the outer mole. A yacht should not attempt to enter the port in a strong Meltemi, but seek shelter instead at an anchorage on the S.W. coast.

Berth. Proceed to W. side of the harbour and secure stern to the quay off the yacht station. Should the Meltemi blow strongly it is best to shift berth to the centre of the harbour and ride to the anchor, or ease off the warps if moored to the quay. Depths at the entrance are 3 fathoms shelving to 2 at the quay; the bottom is mostly firm mud.

Facilities. Water, fuel, fish and ice at the quay. Baths at Tourist Pavilion and the new hotel. A

mechanic is available at a workshop on the waterfront. Restaurant, tavernas and bank. Bus service to Glossa for Skiathos. Steamer services almost daily to the mainland connecting with Athens and Volos.

Two monasteries can be seen in a commanding position on the slopes high above the port; a 9th-century church with frescoes lies north of the town, and to the S.E. is a pottery works. Charming scenery forms the object of some delightful mountain walks.

On the S.W. coast of the island are the following anchorages:

Glossa (Klima). Chart 2072. With its small harbour of Loutraki 4 km distant this is a charming place to visit. The breakwater helps to provide shelter for caïques and also for the mail steamer during strong north winds.

Approach. The long breakwater has been further extended.

Berth inside the breakwater at a quay which until half-way along affords sufficient depths. A new mooring-quay has been built and mole extended to 220 yds; the harbour dredged to 16 ft.

Facilities. Water is laid on at the quay. Two tavernas are at the port and ice can be ordered (24 hrs). The village, above, can be reached by an occasional bus, which connects with Port Skopelos.

57

The walk up the hilly slopes is rewarding, for not only are there fine views from the top, but one passes through luxuriant vegetation with masses of fruit trees including plums, an island speciality.

Panormos Bay is a charming small cove, at the S. end of the island, affording complete shelter for a number of yachts.

> **Berth.** Entering the cove one sees several villas lining the shore. Anchor in 5 fathoms, bows N. and run out a warp to a pine tree on the beach. Winds N. or S., no swell, complete shelter; N.W. winds bring strong gusts. Entrance lights (1981).

> **Facilities.** The main road from Glossa to Skopelos passes by. Occasional buses, but no amenities nearby. There are two houses, both occupied during the summer months.

Agnonda, a charming steep-to-bay with pebbly beach at its head and a quay with 2 fathoms depth the S. side.

> **Approach** from an E. direction between two light towers.

> **Berth** at quay (bollards and rings) or anchor off beach on sandy bottom in 3 fathoms. During Meltemi leave room for ferry which berths here instead of at Skopelos.

> **Facilities.** Two tavernas, which also provide water. Road to Port Skopelos.

Staphilis, a more open bay, affords the nearest safe anchorage to Port Skopelos in the event of a strong Meltemi. A few houses and a camping site.

> **Anchor** off the sandy beach in 3 to 5 fathoms, on sandy bottom.

Staphilis was named after the son of Theseus and Ariadne. In recent years his alleged tomb on the rocky peninsula has been excavated and certain gold treasures recovered which are now in the museum at Volos.

Island of Alonissos

With a population approaching 1,500 this island has a rocky forbidding N.W. coast without inlets; this contrasts with the S.E. shores which have some attractive anchorages suitable for a small yacht. On the summit of the S.W. peak, nearly 1,000 ft up, is the attractive village of Alonissos, evacuated after the last earthquake and now mostly inhabited by foreigners.

Murtia Bay, on the S.W. of the island, provides anchorage in either E. or W. coves in 4 fathoms. In W. cove beware of submerged telephone cable close to the shore; E. cove has a submerged rock close S. of above-water rock. The sea-bed is

mostly sand with rock and weed patches. A mule track ascends to the village –
half an hour's climb.

Patitiri, a charming small cove, partially protected by a mole, with a large
modern village.

> **Approach and anchorage.** Steer for centre of the village, leaving molehead to starb. Anchor
> where convenient or moor at a quay (rings and bollards). Open S.E. quarter, sometimes S.
> swell. Harbour sometimes overcrowded; then advisable to proceed to Votsi, $\frac{1}{2}$ mile S; anchor in
> the N.E. corner of bay.

> **Facilities.** Plenty of provisions, small hotels and tavernas. Ferry and caïque service to Skopelos.

Stenivalla, lying midway along S.E. coast of Alonissos, is a small but pleasant
cove with sufficient room to berth a dozen small yachts.

> **Approach and Berth.** Entering on a westerly course a small, but shallow quay may be seen on
> the N. side. Where the quay bends to W. there are 6 ft depths. Beware of heavy chain cable on
> the seabed about 150 ft S. of the quay; it runs roughly E. to W.

> **Facilities.** Small hotel and restaurant, well-stocked shop, but no baker. Water being laid on
> (1982).

Ormos Yerakas, lying on N. tip of island, is a small cove useful for anchorage
only in S. winds. Anchor at head of cove or in small incision E. shore.

Island of Peristera (Xero)

Lying close east of Alonissos this island is barren with a population of only
twenty-five. It has some small inlets at its southern end.

Vasiliko, the principal bay, is almost landlocked with only a couple of ruined
cottages and one small dwelling by a slipway.

> **Anchorage.** The inlet lies in the centre of the island. Anchor in the middle of the bay in 3–4
> fathoms. Avoid anchoring on a dump of old wire ropes close opposite two cottages.

Island of Pelagos (Kyra Panagia)

Tall and wooded with a population of fourteen, almost all shepherds. There are
two delightful anchorages, mountainous and green with all-round shelter.

Ayios Petros is a remote cove on the S. side of the island.

> **Approach and Anchorage.** Make for the furthest E. cove and anchor in 3 to 4 fathoms on sand

and stone bottom in very clear water. Almost entirely sheltered. Room for three or four yachts to swing. No sign of habitation, only large herds of goats.

There is evidence of the place being populated throughout the early centuries, neolithic remains having been found.

Planitis (Port Planedhi or **Planoudhi)** is a charming anchorage in N.E. of the island with complete shelter and no habitation.

Approach. Chart 2072. Coming from the west, the first channel to open is the shallow cut between Pelagos Island and Sphika Islet. An easterly course should be continued until the main channel opens east of Sphika Íslet. Though only a minimum of 90 yds wide there is no difficulty in tacking through to the two basins at the head of the islet.

Anchorage. A convenient berth is in the W. corner of a beach where one can run a warp to a boulder ashore; also one can use the E. arm. Bottom is firm mud and shelter is complete.

Despite the fact that the anchorage is entirely enclosed by high mountains, it is refreshingly cool and there is a potent scent of herbs. The only summer visitors are the fishing boats and caïques that call here for charcoal which is prepared close to the shore and then shipped to Salonika. Recently a herd of wild horses belonging to the monastery were roaming over the countryside.

The Monastery Landing lies on the east coast beneath a conspicuous group of white buildings which form the deserted monastery.

Anchorage. On a calm day a yacht may find temporary anchorage in this open cove, and run out a warp to a large rock on the E. side of the shore.

One may land here to scramble up to the 11th-century church and to enjoy the splendid view across the sea and islands. The sea here provides good fishing and the soil is fertile; of great benefit to the two or three shepherd families who form one of the more primitive communities in Greece.

The remaining three islands of the group lie to the N.E.:

Yioura, Piperi and **Psathura** are uninhabited, without suitable landing places and of no interest to a yacht. With northerly winds one should be mindful of the south-going current.

Island of Skantzura

On the route to Skyros. This low-lying island may be of use to a yacht on passage seeking a night anchorage. There is a choice of two places.

Anchorages

(a) **Parausa.** In the bay are 3-fathom depths on a sandy bottom with weed; partial shelter.

(b) **A bay on the west coast** of the island has better shelter with more room to swing, but barely depths of 2 fathoms, weed on sand. Shelter from east winds.

The island is uninhabited.

Island of Skyros (Skiros)

This is the largest island of the Sporades, but its population (2,350) is considerably smaller than both Skiathos and Skopelos. Skyros could be considered as almost two islands joined by a low-lying isthmus in the middle. The northern half is wooded and cultivated, the southern half with its barren hills is largely stony with occasional olives, maple and holm-oaks. The main port is in the north, Linaria, with its small harbour and nearby sheltered anchorage; in the south is the large deserted bay of Trebuki, more suitable for steamers.

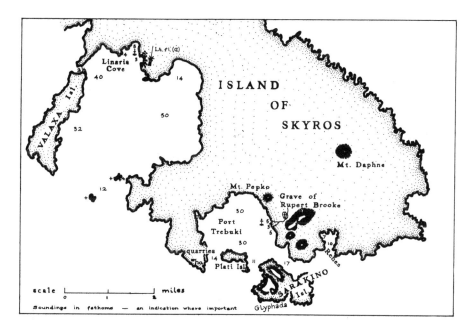

Port of Linaria

Approach and Berth. Chart 2048. The passage north of Valaxa Island has slightly less depths than charted; one cannot depend upon more than $2\frac{1}{2}$ fathoms and the passage should not be attempted at night. By the small harbour entrance the white house and the green flashing light are easily distinguished; beneath them a 50-yd mole trends northwards and has been recently extended. The short quay, also on the S. side of the port, has depths of only 4 to 6 ft, but this too is being built out to afford depths alongside of 6 to 12 ft. When berthing in a yacht one should lay out the anchor northwards and haul in the stern towards the quay. (Every morning and evening the quay is taken up by the Kimi ferry-steamer.) The bottom is clay or mud and it rises steeply; when letting go care must be taken to avoid heavy mooring cables of the caïques which can usually be seen through the clear water on the sea-bed.

Facilities. A water tap is on the quay by the nearer taverna. Petrol and diesel fuel may be bought. Basic provisions are obtainable. Ice arrives daily by the ferry-steamer and is sent to the Chora (Skyros village). Two tavernas and two modest hotels. A bus runs to the Chora twice daily. The Piraeus steamer calls and so does the Kimi ferry.

Linaria Cove. In the event of the harbour being too congested, there is good anchorage in 5 fathoms in Linaria Cove – weed on clay and mud. This is the best place for newly arrived vessels and a useful anchorage in unsettled weather.

The Island of Skyros, with a population of about 3,000, has its main village, or Chora, on a rising slope on the east side of the island. It can be reached in 20 min by bus and is well worth a visit. There are some interesting houses, the Byzantine church of St George and local crafts, also a well-arranged small museum. A small hotel is on the beach at the foot of the village.

In ancient times the acropolis stood just above the present village, and the walls connecting it with its port beneath can still be traced; the mole is shown on Admiralty chart. Until the end of the last century Skyros exported wheat, wine, honey, oranges and lemons; nowadays goats are grazed and sent by caïque to Athens.

The original herd of wild ponies sometimes to be seen in the country is now largely diminished, and the remaining ponies are cared for by a British organization.

The statue to Rupert Brooke stands in an imposing position north of Skyros village looking across the brilliantly coloured sand and over water of many shades of blue towards the distant islands beyond. Brooke died on St George's Day 1915 on board the French hospital ship *Duguay Trouin* at Port Trebuki when on the point of sailing for Gallipoli.

Port Trebuki (Tres Boukes), a large enclosed bay surrounded by barren hills, is unsuitable for yachts. There is only one anchorage with good holding suitable for a yacht, but with northerly winds strong gusts sweep down from the mountains and spoil the tranquillity. The only interest here is the grave of Rupert Brooke.

Directions. Anchor off the mouth of a small stream (see plan), in depths of 3 to 5 fathoms; bottom is weed and sand, good holding. Position: from river-mouth Mt Daphne bears 045°,

N.W. point of Sarakino Island 195°. The mouth of the dried-up stream can be identified by a loose stone cairn.

About 400 yds. S. of the mouth of the dried-up stream a small stone jetty has recently been built. It is now convenient to land here from the dinghy, and follow a well-defined and easy path from the jetty to the grave, about 20 min. walk.

For those visiting the poet's grave, a brief description of the burial written immediately after the ceremony by Edward Marsh may help to recreate the scene on 23 April 1915:

'We buried him the same evening in an olive grove ... the ground covered with flowering sage, bluish grey, and smelling more delicious than any flower I know. The path up to it from the sea is narrow and difficult, and very stony; it runs by the bed of a dried-up torrent. We had to post men with lamps every 20 yards to guide the bearers. The funeral service was very simply said by the chaplain, and after the Last Post the little lamp-lit procession went once again down the narrow path to the sea.'

Winston Churchill, writing to *The Times* on 26 April 1915, said, 'A voice had become audible, a note had been struck, more true, more thrilling, more able to do justice to the nobility of our youth in arms engaged in the present war than any other. . . . The voice has been swiftly stilled.'

> *If I should die, think only this of me:*
> *That there's some corner of a foreign field*
> *That is for ever England.*

Akladi Cove is reputed to have prehistoric dwellings, visible on the bottom in clear weather; but an examination of this cove has failed to locate anything of interest. The holding here, weed and fine sand, is unreliable.

Renes Bay, deserted and rocky, has a small cove in the N.W. corner. Although well-sheltered, one must anchor in not less than 7 fathoms to ensure room to swing. The bottom is weed on fine sand, the holding poor.

The south coast of Skyros is almost forbidding; only a few goats are to be seen, and the rubble mounds of early quarries on the hills. The bays on the west coast are used by small fishing craft, but are not recommended for yachts.

Glifadha Cove, on the bottom side of Sarakino Island, affords anchorage in 3 fathoms on a sandy bottom, open only to south.

It was on Skyros that Thetis decided to protect the young Achilles by disguising him as a maiden among the daughters of Lycomedes. 'What songs the Syrens sang, or what name Achilles assumed when he hid himself among the women' wrote the witty 17th-century writer Sir Thomas Browne 'though puzzling questions, are not beyond all conjecture'.

The bones of Theseus were also found on the island, and according to Thucydides were then conveyed to Athens to be enshrined in the Theseon.

Mainland Coast from Northern Sporades to Gulf of Salonika

The coast is straight and without shelter for 100 miles. The predominating feature is Mt Olympus, nearly 10,000 ft, and the high mountains in the vicinity. Chart 1085.

Thermaïkos Gulf leads into the Gulf of Salonika and, though there are some night anchorages close off the coast, they are completely open and practical only in flat calm weather. One passes the great delta formed by four rivers: Aliakmon, Loudhias, Axios and Gallikos, called after the major tributary – the Axios Delta. Much reclamation work has been done during recent years thus restricting the marshland area, and limiting the breeding ground of the large number of wild birds.

There are still to be seen, even in the summer, shellduck, plover, tern and many species of the smaller birds. In winter it was renowned for the duck shooting.

The Meltemi can blow in strength from the Axios River down the Gulf. This happens for periods of only 2 or 3 days, often followed by a S.W. sea-breeze blowing up the gulf every afternoon.

Unfortunately as one penetrates deeper towards the head of the Gulf and the port of Salonika, pollution gets very much worse. (See page XVIII.)

SALONIKA (THESSALONIKI)

The second city of Greece, with a large commercial port, has been the capital of Macedonia since earliest times. A Port of Entry.

The Marina

Approach and Berth. Chart 2070 and plan below. A yacht marina completed in April 1973 lies 12 km on the motor road S.E. of the city in Thermaïkos Bay. One hundred and fifty yachts (max. length 100 ft) can be accommodated in depths of 3 to 4 m. It has recently been enlarged.

Officials. Port authorities, a British Consul-General.

Facilities. Water, fuel, telephone, power; shops and restaurants nearby. Hauling-out arrangements. Berthing charges slightly less than at Zea. (Tel: 426.261)

Salonika is connected to Athens by air (25 min); train and bus (about 7 hrs). Express to London (2½ days) and Istanbul. There are archaeological, folklore and medieval museums.

With a present population of nearly 700,000, Thessaloniki takes its name from the sister of Alexander the Great, wife of Kassandra who founded it in 316 B.C.

The modern city presents a great contrast to the walled oriental town captured from the Turks in 1912. Three large war cemeteries with about 3,000 graves outside the town are evidence of its occupation by Allied troops during the First World War. Between the two wars some progress was made in rebuilding, but in 1940 with the German invasion the place sunk to a low ebb. However, all these misfortunes have now been forgotten and one sees the bold façade of a modern and prosperous-looking maritime and university city with esplanades, public squares, large hotels and skyscrapers though many of its buildings were damaged in the earthquake of 1978. Many of the inhabitants are workers at the industrial plants on the outskirts of the city. It is best known for its International Trade Fair held annually in September. Unfortunately the pollution caused by industry has had a contaminating effect on the fish normally caught in the Gulf.

History. In Roman days the port became more important when the Via Egnatia was completed. This great military highway from Dyrrachium (now Durres, Albania) linked Rome with her eastern empire. It passed through Thessaloniki, Amphipolis and Phillipi before reaching Byzantium.

The guide-book describes the town's associations since the days of St Paul, and the historic Byzantine churches, which together with the three museums and the White Tower should be visited.

In the nearby village of Langada the famous fire dances take place from 20 to 23 May. Originally a pagan rite imported from eastern Thrace since Christian times it has been held in

65

honour of St Constantine: men and women holding red handkerchiefs dance over hot coals to traditional music.

Mount Olympus is within close reach.

Climbing. Information on the ascent of Mount Olympus can be obtained from the office of the Greek Alpine Club either at Salonika, Athens or Litochoron, the village from which the climb begins. There are now three huts, one low down, one three-quarters of the way and one on top. Only the last few hundred feet involve a climb. Mules may be hired for the first two stages of the ascent; the second stage passes through wooded country and is much the more attractive. A guide is compulsory for the last stage. Three days are necessary for the expedition which can be made from late June to the end of August.

4

The Northern Coast

The Khalkidhiki Peninsula

KASSANDRA PENINSULA
  Nea Moudania
  Nea Potidea
  Siviri
  Nea Skioni
  Paliourion (Glarokambos)

SITHONIA PENINSULA
  Porto Koufo
  Toroni
  Port Carras
  Neos Marmaras
  Sikias Bay
  Dhimitri
  Ayios Nikolaos
    (Ormos Paganias)

AYION OROS PENINSULA
(MOUNT ATHOS, HOLY MOUNTAIN)
  Ammouliani Island
  Ouranoupolis
  Daphni
  Vatopedi Bay
  Nea Roda

Khalkidhiki Peninsula to the Turkish frontier with the Islands

MAINLAND
  Stavros anchorage
  Amphipolis
  Elevtero Bay (Neo Peramos)
  Kavala
  Keramotis

ISLAND OF THASOS
  Port Thasos (Limenas)
  Potamias anchorage
  Prino
  Limenarias

  Vistonikos Bay (Porto Lagos)
  Alexandroupolis

ISLAND OF SAMOTHRAKI
  Kamariotissa

ISLAND OF LIMNOS
  Port Moudros
  Kastro Merini

4
The Northern Coast

The western part of this coast, especially the Khalkidhiki (or Chalcydice) Peninsula and the island of Thasos, is of great beauty. Here, the summer winds blow with considerably less strength than in the southern Aegean.

The Khalkidhiki Peninsula (Chalkidhiki)

Looking at the chart, this unusual shape appears like a folded hand with three fingers sticking out into the Aegean. These are the peninsulas of Kassandra, Sithonia and Ayion Oros or Akti (the Holy Mountain). All are green and wooded, with hilly or mountainous country.

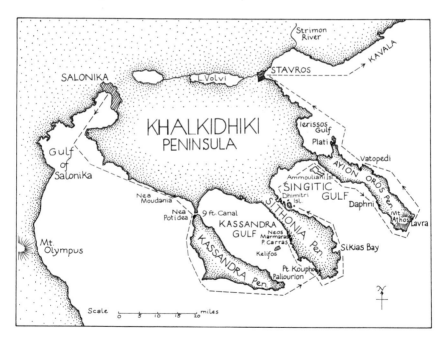

Nea Moudania, 40 miles S.E. of Salonika, offers good shelter in northerly weather. A breakwater with a high protecting wall runs 100 yds in a S.W. direction with depths alongside the quay of 3½ fathoms. (A further extension with a 110-yd hook running S.E. is projected.) A smaller jetty S.E. of the breakwater provides a working space for caïques.

Officials. Harbour Master and Customs in the town.

Facilities. Water and fuel at the foot of the mole. Shops of all kinds, restaurants, tavernas, cafés, hotels. Bus to Salonika, Alexandroupolis and the Kassandra and Sithonia peninsulas.

The Kassandra Peninsula is mainly pastoral and agricultural country and is separated from the mainland by a canal. From S. of Kalithea a continuous bus route runs both sides of it.

Nea Potidea lies on the S. bank of the canal which is spanned by a bridge with 56-ft clearance. On the S. bank of the western end there is a small boat harbour used by the 'grigria' fishermen. East of the bridge at the eastern entrance there is a small basin on the N. bank with depths of about 13 ft in the centre, shallowing towards the edges. It is possible for one or two yachts to lie here in northerly weather and run out a warp to the shore. All along the S. bank of the canal trawlers have moorings with small wooden jetties giving access to steps cut in the bank. The canal silts at the W. end, but as it is much used by fishermen, it is dredged periodically and is claimed never to have less than 10 ft (*S.D.* states 9 ft); there is said to be double this depth down the centre.

The village of 1,200 inhabitants was originally a 5th-century colony of Corinth and some of the ancient walls can still be seen along the S. bank and running out to sea. The modern town has the usual sprinkling of new houses and hotels; there are shops in the main square, and good fish restaurants and cafés near the W. end of the canal. Caïques are built opposite the E. harbour off which is good bathing.

Continuing down the W. coast of the peninsula there are two small anchorages at **Siviri** and **Nea Skioni**, both with jetties affording approximately 10-ft depth at the extremity and providing shelter from the Meltemi.

Paliourion is a small bay at the tip of the peninsula. Lying near the new coastal road the place has become a resort, with hotels, restaurants, etc. Known locally as Glarokambos it has a natural harbour, sheltered within in all weather. It was intended by the National Tourist Organisation of Greece to be developed as a marina, but the entrance, although dredged, has silted again to only 4 ft and is unapproachable in northerly winds because of the breaking seas.

Anchorage with good holding on sand and mud is very secluded and quiet with pine trees along the seaward side and sloping sandy beaches all round. The bay shoals west of the entrance, but to the eastward there are depths of 13 ft or more; yachts anchor towards the head of the bay out of sight of the camping area.

The Sithonia Peninsula, also pastoral and agricultural, is the most wooded and beautiful of the three prongs and still has one or two unspoilt sandy beaches. The road has now been completed right round the shore from Nikiti, although buses do not run on the section from Sarti to Ormos Panagias.

Porto Koupho lies 8 miles from Paliourion across the Kassandra Gulf in an attractive setting of pine woods, and is being steadily developed. Excellent shelter for several yachts.

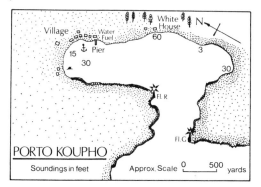

Approach and Anchorage. Chart 1679. Plan. The approach is easy day or night. Proceed to the head of Geras Bay and either anchor in 4 fathoms or haul in the yacht's stern to the pier (9-ft depth at extremity). Bottom is fine weed on sand, shelter is all-round. The port is much used in summer and winter as a base for fishing craft.

Facilities. Fuel and water at the quay. Excellent fish meals at three small tavernas. Provisions at small supermarket and at the grocer's shop. Bus service to Salonika and Sarti.

There are some interesting caves on the hillside, west of the hamlet.

The anchorages on the S.W. shore of Sithonia are all towards the southern end of the peninsula.

Toroni, an anchorage with convenient depths in a bay open to S.E., is much used by fishermen. This place had not been spoiled in 1978 and was beautiful with its trees and golden sand. Only a few shops, hotels and villas; a divergence from the new road runs along the shore making it accessible to trucks for the fishermen.

Continuing on up the coast there is the new marina:

Port Carras, a modern safe marina, surrounded by a holiday resort.

Approach. A large pyramid-shaped hotel complex marks the northern entry to a 30-ft wide channel, the sides of which have silted. There are harbour lights and leading lights.

Berth. The fishing port lies on a bight on the south side, but yachts berth stern to the N.E. quays as convenient.

Facilities. Water and electricity at each berth. Fuel is supplied by bowser. There are restaurants and bars, but no food shops, in the marina. Provisions can be bought in the village of Marmaras, 30 min on foot but scooters or bicycles can be hired in the marina; taxis also available. Alternatively, one could proceed by motor dinghy to Marmaras. At Port Carras is also a museum, open-air theatre, art gallery and local craft centre. Bus to Salonika three times a day.

The laying-up and berthing charges are based on the calculation of the yacht's overall length. The site was formerly owned by the monastery of St Gregory on Mount Athos.

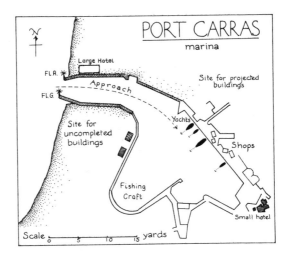

Three miles S.W. of Port Carras lies the little island of Kelifos, the only place apart from Kalimnos where coral is found in Greece. It is sometimes available in the tourist shops in Nea Moudania.

Neos Marmaras, close north of Port Carras, is an attractive, sheltered anchorage, but tourist development has already begun.

Anchorage is on sand in convenient depths.

Facilities. In the village N. of the headland are good shops, a bank, several good restaurants and tavernas. South of the headland is a caïque slip; a fire-fighting launch is permanently berthed off a little jetty. Ice can be bought.

Sikias Bay. Barely a dozen miles from Porto Koupho but on the E. side of the peninsula, it lies close to the mouth of the Singitic Gulf – a pleasant sandy bay with one or two new houses and a shop. It is sheltered on three sides, and worth a call.

> **Approach and Anchorage.** Chart 1679 – inset. There is no difficulty day or night. The best anchorage is in 3 fathoms where indicated in the southern corner of bay. It is firm sand, and a perfect bathing beach. If it blows from the N.E. this anchorage is no longer comfortable.
>
> An anchorage 3 miles southward (2 miles N. of Cape Pseudhokaves), behind a rocky spur in a sandy bay, is sometimes to be preferred in N.E. winds.

> **General.** The village of Sikia is 1½ miles inland, otherwise there is no connection with civilization.

Dhimitri. Lying deeper in this gulf is the lovely island of Dhimitri providing landlocked coves between it and the mainland, suitable for small yachts. The country is hilly and green with clusters of poplars and cypresses near the shore merging into olive groves close behind; a background of dark green pinewoods rises to the skyline beyond. There are only one or two small houses belonging to fishermen temporarily on the island; and on the mainland a number of farmhouses by a road connecting with Salonika. See plan.

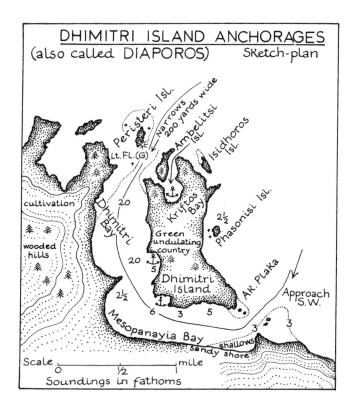

Approach. *Sailing Directions* explain it in great detail; the sketch-plan is intended to simplify.
There are two entrances, the southern one being recommended:
South Entrance. This should be approached in a S.W. direction: the rocks are above water and clearly visible, the rock with the white tower being left to port – minimum depth 9 ft.
North Entrance is between the two wooded islets of Peristeri and Ambelitsi (the outlying rocks are above water and clearly visible). The channel leads through a narrow passage (200 yds wide) which at night is covered by the sectors of a flashing green light, where there are a number of islets and rocks, not clearly shown on the chart.

Anchorages close under Dhimitri Island are shown in the plan. There is also the pleasant sheltered anchorage of Kriftos Bay, entered by passing eastward of Ambelitsi islet.

Ayios Nikolaos (Ormos Panagias) is an attractive, wooded bay open to N.N.E., but with a well-sheltered anchorage in the more easterly of its two coves. Bottom is soft mud and sand. Off the hamlet is a small jetty used in summer by the ferry boats which take tourists round Mt Athos and by the fishermen: 2-fathom depths off the extremity. Many summer villas ashore and more in the process of building. Three small cafés which also provide meals. Telephone. Provisions come daily by road from Nikiti, 8 km inland where there is also connection by bus with Salonika and Porto Koupho.

Forming the eastern side of the Singitic Gulf is the narrow isthmus of the Akti or Athos Peninsula where Xerxes in 481 B.C. dug a canal to enable his galley fleet to pass in safety and avoid the much-feared storms off the headland. Landing at Tripiti and walking inland, traces of some of the diggings can be discerned, and though the land here must still be about the same level above the sea as then, the sea-bed close by has sunk. In 12-fathom depths large stone blocks can be seen and also the outline of early wharves.

The Ayion Oros Peninsula, usually called Akti, Mt Athos or the Holy Mountain, is known generally for the monasteries.

Island of Ammouliani. Lying a mile off the isthmus this island has a small fishing population of 600 much increased in summer due to the number of new villas which have been built. Though indented and irregular in shape, it is unattractive and rather barren. Certain coves indicated on the chart afford useful anchorage to small vessels according to the weather.

The Port
It lies on the N.E. side of the island, well protected by a new mole from all winds except the N.W.; it is much used by fishing craft and the ferries. The new mole extends 125 yds in a N.N.W. direction with a projection near the root on the N. side for berthing the larger ferries: the smaller ones berth on the S. side and trawlers on both sides. Depths of 4 fathoms on the S. side, 3 on the N., decreasing gradually towards the ferry extension.

Facilities. Fuel on the mole. Fish tavernas, cafés, hotel, telephone. Frequent ferries to Tripiti, twice a week in summer to Ayios Nikolaos.

On the peninsula towards the frontier of the Holy Mountain is the prominent seamark of Prosforion, a Byzantine tower.* In contrast, the adjoining village of Ouranoupolis is relatively new, having been built to accommodate the Greek population deported from one of the Princes Islands, in the Sea of Marmara after the First World War.

This village has now become a tourist centre with several hotels (large and small), restaurants, tavernas and cafés all along the waterfront and a bus service to Salonika.

A jetty has been built in front of the tower, but it is in very shallow water and yachts should anchor off. In southerlies the anchorage is untenable and larger yachts should make for Ammouliani, smaller ones for the anchorage in Partheni Bay on the N. side of the most westerly of the Dhrenia islets.

Close offshore is a long reef, more than 2 fathoms underwater, on which the seas break heavily during storms. The sea-bed on the southern side of the reef falls away quickly and at one place the Cyclopean walls of some early construction, long since submerged, can still be clearly seen.

In fine weather it is convenient to anchor in $2\frac{1}{2}$ fathoms 200 yds N.W. of the Tower.

The Holy Mountain (Mt Athos or Akti Peninsula)

Less than a mile from the Tower is the frontier of the Holy Mountain with its recently increasing population of monks, still leading a monastic life. There are altogether twenty monasteries with their sketes and kellia, undoubtedly seen at their best from seaward and, therefore, a yacht should sometimes stand in close or, when desirable, go alongside a jetty. Some monasteries were built in the second half of the 10th century; others at later periods. Most of them stand dramatically on various mountain spurs, or are tucked into the mouth of some green valley, or have grown up on fertile land close to the sea. With the exception of one or two relatively modern ones, each monastery is usually a heterogeneous cluster of Byzantine buildings in colourful shades of red or blue and conspicuous for their domes and cupolas. Though varying considerably in size and shape, when seen as one unit they nearly all look attractive in their green mountainous setting.

The peninsula, which is nearly 25 miles long, is rugged and steep on its western side, whereas the eastern slopes are gentle and covered in a great variety of trees.

* See *A Fringe of Blue* by Joice NanKivell Loch (John Murray).

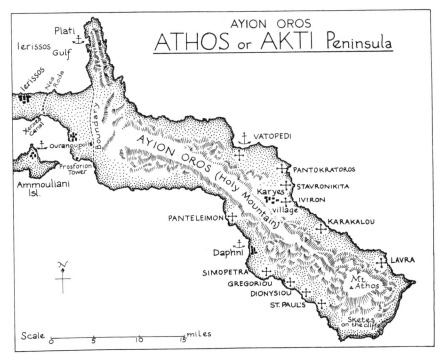

Close to the ridge itself on both sides there is afforestation – beech and chestnuts above, oaks and plane trees below – also a flowering undergrowth. The long ridge forming a backbone reaches a bare peak (Mt Athos) near the extremity of the peninsula where it rises to over 6,000 ft; here it is rather bare and stands abruptly out of the sea.

Daphni is the Control Port for the Holy Mountain – a temporary place of call if landing on the Athos Peninsula – and lies about half-way along the shores of the Singitic Gulf.

A Customs Officer and Police are stationed here to examine papers and possessions of visitors to the Holy Mountain. Women may not land.

Once there were 40,000 monks in the twenty ruling monasteries or sketes, but now there are only about 6,000. A civil governor now has to approve any decisions by the Holy Community. Civil police check the entry and exit of visitors landing from caïques at ports or jetties of monasteries. Russian monks, once in the majority, are now not permitted to exceed thirty in number; they keep to themselves and employ a Greek to entertain visitors. Male tourists having first been vouched for by their own consuls and then obtained Greek Foreign Office permission and the Holy Community's laissez-passer may land at Daphni and proceed by bus on a 5-mile journey to Karyes where after police inspection, they may spend 5 days touring the Holy Mountain. Mule and boat services are available.

Approach and Berth. About 100 yds S.E. of a light-tower is a small quay with a stone pier, having a depth of 6 ft at its extremity. The sea-bed rises sharply, and 70 yds off is a heavy mooring-buoy suitable for steamers; but near the pier-head is a patch of sand (which is not good holding) sufficient to hold off a yacht's bows when temporarily hauling her stern up to the end of the pier.

The prevailing wind does not blow home and though entirely open, one may expect sufficient shelter from the curvature of the coast during ordinary summer conditions.

Facilities. There are one or two rather modest little shops, and a fresh water tap close by. The mule track leads to Karyes, the principal village of Athos, where permits to land on the Holy Mountain are again examined.

Continuing along the shore one sees the striking monastery of Simon Peter built solidly into the cliff, reminiscent of those fortress-like structures in Tibet. Further towards the top of the peninsula, and standing on the steep mountainside, appear small houses. They are in fact the abodes of hermits and occasionally a monk may be seen under the shade of his black umbrella climbing up to one of these solitary habitations; some, even more primitive, appear as mountains caves, and are accessible only by ladder; others seem to have no visible mode of access at all and cling to the steep cliff like swallows' nests.

The sea off the extremity of the Cape can be very disturbed, and under certain conditions violent squalls sweep down from the mountain slopes. Mardonius experienced a phenomenal storm in 491 B.C. when from a clear sky a sudden Levanter blew up and wrecked the invading Persian fleet of 300 vessels.

Rounding the massive headland and approaching the north-eastern shores of the peninsula you come to one of the oldest and most attractive of the monasteries, Lavra – here, one may land to climb the mountain; the Lilliputian harbour cut into the cliff close under the monastery can accommodate caïques up to 35 ft in length. Other monasteries have short piers where landing can be made in calm weather. There is only one summer anchorage on the N.E. shore of the peninsula and this is beneath the large monastery of

Vatopedi. From seaward this well-known monastery appears as a huge manor, but certainly not as a monastery. Although the largest and second in importance only after Lavra, it fails to arouse admiration for its architectural merit. Perhaps the more interesting features are the clock-tower and the scattered little churches.

Approach and Anchorage. Steer for the monastery buildings and let go 100 yds off the small stone pier in 4 fathoms. Holding is good, but the bay is open to the northern quadrant.

General. A policeman is on duty at the quay to check the coming and going of visitors and local people who have no direct connection with the monasteries.

During part of the summer a few of the fishing fleet are based here. The monastery still has its ancient aqueduct, and there is plenty of water available in the buildings today.

In the **Gulf of Ierissos** are some useful anchorages:

Plati. This is a pleasant deserted anchorage convenient for making a day excursion to those monasteries with jetties when the sea is calm.

> **Approach.** Chart 1679. Pass to seaward of the islets off Cape Arapis as the inside passage has shoaled since the last survey.

> **Anchorage** is almost anywhere in Plati Cove in 4–5 fathoms, light weed on sand – open only across the bight to S.W. – a fetch of 5 miles; but normally only the night breeze is from here, although wind direction in the cove changes frequently. Room for half a dozen yachts to swing. The surrounding land is relatively low-lying and the anchorage peaceful.

Nea Roda. A well-sheltered little fishing port lying at the N. end of the former Xerxes Canal, now protected by a breakwater extending for 100 yds in a W. direction from the natural hook of land:

> **Anchorage** on a sandy bottom in $2\frac{1}{2}$–3 fathoms as far as the projection in line with the headland where the small boats lie.

> **Facilities.** A small hard for hauling up fishing boats at the head of the bay. The village lies a few hundred yards away and has basic provisions. Fish tavernas and cafés line the waterfront and there are hotels both large and small. Bus to Salonika and Ouranoupolis.

Summer villas are being built both near the port and by an open shallow anchorage.

Ierissos has a short mole for the fishermen. A great many summer villas have grown up and there are shops inland on the main road.

Stratonion. In the N.W. corner of the gulf is an open anchorage in a sandy bay with shops, houses and hotels. A metal factory and a disused tip are nearby.

KHALKIDHIKI PENINSULA (STAVROS) TO THE TURKISH FRONTIER WITH THE ISLANDS

Continuing northwards, you approach the mountainous wooded slopes at the head of the Gulf of Strimon. On the sandy shores lie the village of Stavros and behind it an extensive cultivated plain reaching to the foothills beyond.

Stavros Anchorage. Plan on Chart 1679.

The setting is appealing, though the anchorage off the pier by the village, being no longer sheltered by the mole shown on the chart, is exposed to the southerly swell. The village is now almost lost among the new hotels, villas, restaurants and shops. North of the village the waters of the Rendina River, flowing from Lake Volvi (Beşik), enter the sea. The green and wooded gorge is attractive and may be followed along the motor-road for 6 miles as far as the lake; it is also partly navigable by boat, though the stream can flow swiftly in places.

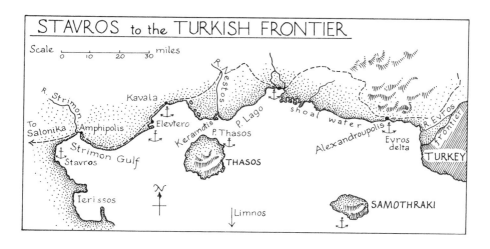

Ten miles N.E. the **River Strimon** empties its muddy waters into the Aegean. This is the first of the Macedonian rivers which flow from the Bulgarian mountains and empty into the north Aegean. There is also the Nestos (east of Thassos), the large lake at Porto Lagos fed by two rivers, and finally the Evros River forming the boundary between Greece and Turkey. The mouths and estuaries of these rivers are interesting to explore on account of the variety of wild birds; both the indigenous and the temporary visitors.

History. In Graeco-Roman days the Strimon formed an artery to the port of Eion close to the city of Amphipolis on the E. bank of the river sometimes visited by St Paul. The walls of the ancient city, some graves and part of its port are to be seen above the bridge, also the foundations of three basilicas of the 6th to 5th centuries. The famous lion commemorating the victory of the Spartans over the Athenians in 422 B.C. is by the road just below the bridge. The remains of the early wooden bridge, referred to by Thucydides, have only recently been excavated by archaeologists some 40 ft from the riverbank. The importance of the place in ancient times was due not only to its strategic position as a communication centre, but to its extensive forests and gold mines on Mount Pangaion.

The river no longer supports a fishing industry, for in recent years the rising levels of mercury, copper and lead are reported to have contaminated the fish. The river entrance is now almost blocked by a sand bar.

Elevtero Bay (Neo Peramos), 15 miles beyond the Strimon River, is a dull well-sheltered large bay with some loading wharves for steamers in the northern corner. The best anchorages for a yacht are near the medieval fortress (see Chart 1679, plan) or the north corner. A change of wind may quickly alter the sea level.

Kavala is a pleasant commercial port and interesting to visit in a yacht.

>   **Approach and Berth.** Chart 1679, plan. No difficulty when entering day or night, but the yacht station is exposed and has an inconveniently high wall for landing. Small yachts can sometimes shelter behind the S. mole, but the harbour is very crowded.

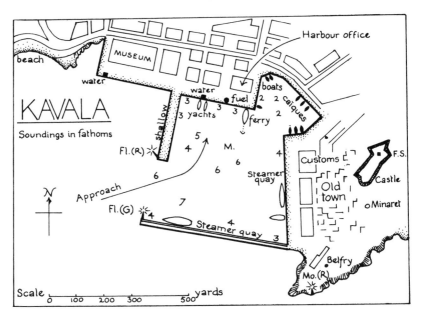

>   **Officials.** A Port of Entry. Harbour Office on the corner of the quay, British Consular official.

>   **Facilities.** Water and fuel, electricity are available at the yacht station. Ice at fishmarket in W. Harbour. Local speciality: fried mussels. A 25-ton crane and a 5-tone crane are available. Everything can be bought in the town, laundry, mechanical repairs, etc. available. Modern hotels, restaurants and tavernas, archaeological museum on the quay. Daily air services to Athens. Frequent ferry-service to Thasos, bus to Salonika and Alexandroupolis. Steamer to Piraeus, Rhodes, Samothraki, Limnos, Mitilini. Excursions to the little church of Ayios

Panteleimon and to the monastery of Ayios Silas in the pine forest. Also to Phillipi where St Paul converted Lydia, the purple seller and where Antony and Octavian won their famous victory over Brutus and Cassius.

The modern, well-built port is often busy with medium-sized steamers in the tobacco trade, and during the summer months it is active with ferry-boats plying to Thasos with tourists.

With a population of 40,200 the modern part of the town was built after the First World War to house refugees from Turkey. But it is the old town under the castle which is most worth a visit, especially the house of Muhammad Ali, founder of the Egyptian dynasty that ended with King Farouk. The unique and beautiful Imaret was built by him but it still belongs to Egypt and unfortunately has been allowed to fall into almost total disrepair, some of its courtyards being used as shops and stores. The old houses in this picturesque quarter are also gradually being pulled down.

History. Ancient Neapolis, which has been Greek only since 1913, previously had four centuries of Turkish occupation during which it declined from its earlier importance.

It was the first European town to receive St Paul and so came to be known as Christianopolis. It was about this period when the Roman aqueduct was built and part of it still remains. Later, under the Byzantines, the castle was built.

The future prosperity of Kavala seems encouraging, for although most of the tobacco-growers migrated to America, other industries have prospered. Grain is now exported from a loading quay $\frac{1}{2}$ mile W.S.W. of the port; a chemical fertiliser plant stands conspicuously 4 miles E. of the port and natural gas deposits have been reported in an area under the seabed.

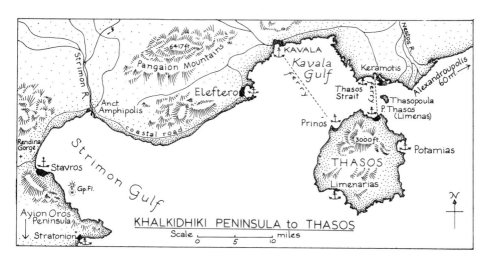

KHALKIDHIKI PENINSULA to THASOS
Scale 0 5 10 miles

Keramotis is a low-lying ferry port about 16 miles S.E. of Kavala. This small port is the nearest point to Thasos, but is of no particular interest to a yacht except for the fish hatchery and the local delicacy of dried mullet roe.

> **Berth.** Chart 1679, plan. Stern to the S. side of the quay (lit at night). Anchor in convenient depths – good shelter.

> **Facilities.** Water and fuel are available. Ice at the root of the quay. Some tavernas nearby.

The mouth of the River Nestos lying immediately east of Keramotis is much frequented by wildfowl. Between the channels is a delta where pelican and sheldrake are frequently seen, also egret and heron fly across from Thasos where they breed. Many smaller marsh birds are also to be seen.

Island of Thasos

Tall and wooded, is largely of marble, one of the most beautiful islands in the Aegean. Though the green mountains are visible many miles off, the low walls of the old Greek harbour cannot be seen until close to. (See plate 12.)

Port Thasos (Limenas)

> **Approach and Berth.** Chart 1679, plan. The harbour has been dredged to 10–12 ft off a quay extending E. from the small pier protruding from the middle of the S. shore. A yacht should berth off the pier, or the quay immediately E. of it, with anchor laid in a N. direction. Alternatively, if the quay is crowded, a yacht can berth off the N.E. wall and lay out an anchor southward; the depth is inadequate for going stern-to. Elsewhere is very shallow. Harbour lights are exhibited and shelter is all-round.
> Outside the harbour a few hundred yards westward is the ferry quay.

> **Facilities.** Water and fuel, but there is also a water tap near the stone pier in the harbour. In summer provision shops are good but since much of the produce comes by ferry-boat from the mainland in the afternoon, it is wise to shop late. This includes ice which must be ordered by telephone from Kavala. There are good modern hotels in the village and beyond, and tavernas by the harbour. Car ferries operate several trips daily both to Kavala and Keramotis.

The modern village of Thasos with its 2,000 inhabitants has expanded appreciably in recent years and is now much visited by tourists. The ancient town recently excavated by the French was surrounded by $2\frac{1}{2}$ miles of walls with a dozen towers and gates. It rises to the acropolis standing on the hill among pines and olives behind the port. One may climb leisurely to the sites of temples and a theatre enjoying at the same time splendid views of both the port and the green wooded mountain valleys behind. Some of the finds from the acropolis have been assembled in the small museum by the port.

8 Skiathos: the boat basin often used by small yachts

9 Athos: Simon Petra monastery

10 Athos: Dionysiou monastery

The countryside, often similar to the Tyrolese landscape, should be explored; there is a variety of trees and birds; running streams are everywhere. The bus service is helpful in getting one to mountain villages.

In early Greek days Thasos marble was sent to Samothraki and used in the construction of the temples and for statuary. Among distinguished early visitors were Thucydides, historian and admiral, and Hippocrates, the famous doctor of Kos. Today the island exports no more marble, but following the discovery of substantial high-grade oil deposits only 6 miles south of this lovely island, an oil-rig has now been established. The main exports remain olives and honey; these and tourism as well as remittances sent home by Thasiots abroad support the island's economy.

Prinos, lying 8 miles W. of Limenas, is a shallow and exposed harbour for the Kavala ferries. It has a small quay and jetty and a harbour master, but is of no interest to yachts.

Limenarias, on the S.W. coast, is a small fishing port sheltered in Meltemi weather and recently developed for tourism. The small fishing creek on the E. side of the bay is shallow and rocky; a quay has been built on its W. side.

> **Anchorage.** Let go in 2 fathoms on patches of sand at the entrance, or off the bay on a sandy bottom, where there is a landing jetty open to S. which can be dangerous in unsettled weather. On the bluff cliff N.E. of the creek is a large conspicuous house formerly owned by the now disused German factory company in the next bay.

The little port is pleasant and picturesque and has excellent tavernas and cafés as well as good provisions. Bus to Limenas via both east and westward routes.

Potamias, on the E. coast, is an attractive anchorage in suitable weather.

> **Anchorage.** The bottom is sand shoaling gently. No jetty.

> **Facilities.** Restaurants, hotels and summer houses ashore. Bus to the village of Panagia (tourist development) on the hill above and thence to Limenas.

Vistonikos Bay (Porto Lagos) consists of the small port of Lagos lying at the head of a low sandy bay, and a larger lake fed by a number of streams.

> **Approach.** Chart 1679, plan. After passing a light buoy 1 mile N.W. of Akri Fanari the harbour should be approached on a course 023°. The channel is marked by pairs of buoys and light-perches. After entering the lagoon turn to port.

> **Berth.** Concrete quays with bollards and fend-offs have been built on the N. and W. sides of the

bay. Yachts should berth on the N. side in depths of 3 fathoms. (In summer, steamers use the W. quay for loading wheat.)

Officials. Harbour Master on the N. quay.

Facilities. Fresh water from taps, fuel from garage, basic provisions, excellent fish restaurants and cafés also on the N. quay. Bathing on the far side of the pine trees on the S. shore where there are also fresh water showers and a café. Bus to Alexandroupolis and Salonika.

A rebuilt Byzantine monastery, a dependency of Vatopedi on Mt Athos, lies on the lake off the road to Komotini; there is always a monk in residence.

Between the lake and the sea a large number of birds can be seen most of the summer months. Many may be seen alighting on the saltpans and lagoons; waders and sand-pipers are common, while pelicans, herons and white-tailed eagles fly in from Thasos to feed on the lake.

From Thasos Strait the low uninteresting coast of Thrace stretches eastwards for 70 miles towards the last Greek port, Alexandroupolis, close to the Turkish frontier. About halfway lies the large landlocked lagoon. Shoalwater extends further seaward than charted, especially the shoals near Ak Makri, not marked on the chart. Vessels should keep at least one mile off.

Alexandroupolis. A Port of Entry, has been much improved with its two long breakwaters, but the depths both inside and offshore are barely 3 fathoms. The small town of about 22,000 inhabitants has important communications by air, road and rail between Salonika and Turkey, but its exports are limited to tobacco and agricultural produce. The presence of the army contributes to its prosperity.

Approach and Berth. Chart 1679, plan. The low-lying coastal plain extends for 2 miles inland until reaching a hilly range, making the port difficult to discern until reaching the 5-fathom line. Enter the harbour heading east to north basin and berth stern-to outer mole, S. of jetty; safe but dirty. Depths are nearly 3 fathoms but only 1 in the big basin in N.W. corner.

Officials. As for Port of Entry. Harbour office on quay opposite light tower.

Facilities. Water and fuel on yacht quay, good provision shops, mechanical repairs, 5-ton crane at pier and floating crane. A hospital. Daily air service to Athens, express trains to Salonika and Istanbul (12 hrs). Daily ferry to Samothraki and Limnos; twice weekly to Piraeus. Yacht Club on S. jetty. A library with rare editions at town hall. Wine festival July and August.

History. Alexandroupolis was recovered from the Turks in 1913 but lost again to the Bulgarians when it remained a wretched shallow little port still known by its Turkish name of Dedeagatch. It finally became Greek again in 1920.

Leaving Alexandroupolis and following the low, shallow, sandy shores for 10 miles one reaches the delta of the Evros River, the eastern side of which marks the Turkish frontier. This is the largest of the rivers on this coast and, rising in the Bulgarian mountains, it augments the outflow from the Dardanelles, causing a southgoing stream in the channels of the Aegean.

On the river estuary are fisheries and on the banks further upstream numerous mulberry groves with a flourishing silk industry. Much of the delta has been reclaimed, but there are still lagoons and marshes, the breeding grounds for a number of wild birds. One may see ibis, egret, stork, pelican and a variety of more common birds such as heron, bee-eater, and plover. In winter there are many wildfowl.

As the delta is an impractical place for a yacht to approach, those interested in bird-watching are advised to drive out on the coastal road from Alexandroupolis; but where the road bends northward towards Ferai, turn off along a track in an easterly direction leading to a riverbank.

Raised aloft like a woman's breast.   STRABO

Island of Samothraki (Samothrace)

A 'great lump of marble' rising from the sea; shaped like Fujiyama this 5,000-ft mountain is partially covered in woods and on its western side a low spit of cultivated land helps to form some natural shelter for the small harbour of

Kamariotissa. This is convenient for visiting the splendid archaeological sites.

> **Approach.** Chart 1086. One can enter harbour day or night. The curved breakwater, which has recently been extended by 100 yds, reaches from the western shore and trends for 250 yds in a S.W. direction. The quay has 2- to 3-fathom depths, and yachts should berth stern-to, anchor E.S.E., soft mud bottom, poor holding. Some yachts prefer to berth alongside if the ferry-steamer's berth (at the extremity of the mole) happens to be free. The Port can be crowded with fishing vessels. Shelter is good; only in S.W. winds can the harbour be uncomfortable. The Meltemi seldom blows here before the autumn months and causes little concern. (The quay on E. side, with 1–3 fathom depths, can sometimes be used by yachts, but is liable to be crowded with fishing craft).

> **Facilities.** Excellent water is available at taps on the quay. Basic provisions including fish are available at the hamlet close by. Ice comes daily by the ferry-steamer from Alexandroupolis. Bus and taxi (10 min) to archaeological sites at Paliopolis, where there is a hotel.

The Panhellenic Shrine, 'Sanctuary of the Great Gods', excavated by the Americans, is well worth a visit. The whole setting in a charming green valley lies beneath the great mountain peak. Its perimeter, now fenced off, assures an air of peace similar to Delphi before the tourist invasion. Near the theatre the famous 'Victory of the Samothrace' was discovered by the French Consul in 1863. In the well-arranged museum are some of the more precious finds.

The island with a population of only 4,000 is well worth visiting. Tourists come by the ferry-steamer from Alexandroupolis, but it was planned to extend other transport services.

Mount Fengari (5,500 ft) can be climbed, but local advice should be sought as to the best route.

Island of Limnos

This undulating low-lying island, 40 miles south of Thasos, is of great archaeological and historical interest and more beautiful than it appears from seaward being somewhat low-lying with a few hills. The large harbours of Moudros and Kondia, which were used as fleet bases during the Dardanelles Campaign in the First World War, are of little interest to a yacht today, and one should put in at Kastro Merini instead.

Port Moudros. Yachts should make their way towards the substantial modern village standing above the shore on the N.E. side of this large bay.

> **Approach.** Chart 1661. There is no difficulty but by day it is interesting to identify some of the hills marked on the British chart:
>
>   YAM Hill
>   YRROC Hill
>   EB Hill
>   DENMAD Hill
>
> By reading these names from right to left one learns what the British surveyors thought of their captain, whom they considered had worked them too hard and also had stopped their leave.
>
> **Berth.** The yacht and fuelling quays have now been established on the S.E. side of the harbour near the root of the mole. The other side of the port is occupied with fishing boats and small ferries. Some of the piers and quays were originally built in 1915 by the British during the Gallipoli Campaign when many casualties were landed for the field hospitals. The two war cemeteries commemorate the dead.

Kastro Merini (Limin Mirina) is the only harbour for small vessels and yachts though this is liable to be crowded with caïques. A Port of Entry, and a convenient place for obtaining clearance if intending to visit the Dardanelles. It lies beneath the ruined Venetian fortress.

> **Approach and Berth.** Chart 1661, plan. Depths are now greater than charted. A new breakwater, extending in a N.W. direction, projects from the S. headland. Note that the light is positioned inside the Genoese castle. A yacht should berth at the new pier stern-to in convenient depths. Good shelter.

Facilities. Water and fuel at the yacht station. Good shops for provisions and other stores. A hotel and some good tavernas. Mechanical repair facilities. Air flights to Athens once or twice daily, twice weekly to Salonika, steamer to Piraeus, Kavala, Alexandroupolis and Mytilini.

Limnos has a population of about 15,000 – the cultivation is limited and mainly cotton-plant on the eastern side of the island.

ARCHAEOLOGY. Limnos is remarkable for possessing the most advanced Neolithic civilization in the Aegean with unique stone baths still in existence. The earliest occupation was probably Thracian and Pelaegian and it was not Greek until the 6th century B.C. Its language still remains undecyphered, but its burial customs resemble those of the Etruscans. It is famous for its ancient cult of Hephaistos and the Kabiri, twin demons of the underworld of Anatolian origin. It was taken by the Persians in 513 B.C., subsequently became a member of the Delian league and was occupied in turn by the Venetians, Turks and Russians. It was ceded to Greece by Turkey only in 1920. The ancient remains are at Poliochini under Cape Voroskopos on the E. coast and show four superimposed settlements, two Neolithic (of which the earlier is older than Troy I), a Copper Age (earlier than Troy VI) and an early Bronze Age. Near the castle of Kokkino, above the Bay or Pournia on the N. coast is the famous 'Lemnian earth', a red bole containing silica much in use in antiquity and the Middle Ages as a tonic. Palaeopolis, the ancient classical capital of Hephaistos was wrecked by a landslide in 1395. On the opposite side of the bay is the site of the Pelaegian mysteries originally more important than those at Samothraki.

Island of Ayios Evstratios (Strati), about 17 miles southward of the S.W. corner of Limnos, appears from seaward as a barren lump of rock without interest. It does, however, grow some agricultural produce which is exported only with difficulty, for the island was without suitable shelter except for the small cove on the west coast, 4½ miles N. of Cape Tripiti.

Recently a breakwater has been built on the N. side of the cove and a quay constructed to enable small vessels of 9–10 ft draught to berth. Though open to S. and S.W. the harbours can be used except in a strong Meltemi, when the swell makes it untenable. The bottom is sand. There is a white-walled cemetery standing on a ridge easily distinguished close N. of the cove. The village is over the hill on the E. side and has a population of about 250.

Introduction to Turkish Coast

Before reaching Istanbul a visiting yacht sailing up the Dardanelles and Sea of Marmara will get an impression of rural Turkey which is dispelled on reaching the Golden Horn.

Istanbul, described briefly on page 107, is a westernized once-Byzantine city, something quite apart from the country towns and villages where three-quarters of the population live.

On the Anatolian coast the scenery is often very beautiful and there are expeditions to be made to ancient Greek sites,★ many of the greatest interest; but the amenities in the small ports are apt to be disappointing. The villages may well be without dependable drinking water, fuel supply or electricity, and lacking a doctor or technician. The Government are making efforts to better social and industrial conditions, and have greatly improved the roads, although local transport is often by donkey or camel, and cars are few. Bus services now link up towns and villages, but unfortunately drivers generally cannot be trained fast enough to keep up with the increased transport, and Turkey is said to have one of the highest accident rates in the world. Nevertheless fairly reliable taxi-drivers are usually to be found in the small towns for those wishing to make a country expedition.

Turkish officials are almost invariably polite and welcoming. Only recently have irritating formalities been abandoned and the port procedure simplified.

Formalities for Entry. The following instructions have been issued by the Turkish authorities (*Liman Reisliği*) or Port Captain (*Liman Reisi*):

Application to the Port Health Authority (*Sahil Sihhiye Memurluğu*) for a health clearance. Sometimes recognized by yellow flag with white crescent on red.

Presentation of passports, visas and a list of passengers to the Security Authorities (*Emniyet Amirliği*).

Passage through Customs control (*Gümrük*).

After a three-month stay a reasonable monthly tax is levied (1980).

★ It is recommended that every yacht should carry on board a copy of those excellent books *Aegean Turkey* and *Turkey beyond the Meander* by George E. Bean.

Ports of Entry are as follows: Çanakkale, Istanbul, Ayvalık, Dikili, Çandarlı, Izmir, Çeşme, Kusadası, Güllük, Bodrum, Datça, Marmaris, Fethiye and Kaş. The authorities whom it is necessary to visit if they do not come aboard are: *Sağlic* (Health); *Polis* (Police); *Gümrük* (Customs). In each case a yellow Bill of Health has to be obtained from the Health Officer, a passenger list (two copies) given to the Police. On leaving the country it is necessary to visit the *Liman Reisi* (Port Captain), Police and Customs. If leaving for another Turkish port only the Port Captain and Customs need be visited.

Military areas, sometimes signed *Yasak Bölgi,* are apt to vary from year to year, but for a long period the following were prohibited to yachts, although not marked on charts:

The Dardanelles, Sea of Marmara and Bosporus:
The two islands Imros and Bozcaada (Tenedos).
The area by Kumkale (south side of Dardanelles entrance), and by Cape Helles.
The Isthmus of Gallipoli – an area extending about 10 miles E.N.E. and W.S.W. of the old Bulair Lines. But restrictions have been eased recently.
At Büyük Çekmece which touches the coast at Ereğli for only about 2 miles.
The N. entrance to the Bosporus on both shores of the Black Sea and for 7 miles inside the Bosporus.
Avoid obvious military activity and warships; patrol craft must be respected.

The Aegean coast in the Gulf of Smyrna – Approaches to Izmir:
A small area extending southward from Eski Foça.
Uzun and Hekim Islands.
Two small frontages on the S. shore close to Izmir, both opposite fairly obvious military installations.

It is best to avoid zigzagging between Turkish and Greek waters as this may be misinterpreted.

The coasts are under rigorous surveillance and yachtsmen should strictly refrain from taking any antiquities from the coast or from coastal waters, as the penalty is the confiscation of the yacht.

Underwater diving with cylinders is at present prohibited in Turkish waters for security reasons.

Food is sometimes difficult to obtain when away from the towns, although with a few words of Turkish one can forage in the village and sometimes find eggs and tomatoes, an assortment of fruit and the local flat brown bread eaten by the peasants. Fish can usually be bought or caught (fishing by net is prohibited) and sometimes a farmer will sell an old fowl 'on the hoof'. In the towns food is abundant, good and cheap. Market-day is usually Friday, but it varies for different areas.

Some Food Terms

bread	ekmek	fruit	meyva
meat	et	orange	portokal
veal	dana	apple	elma
vegetables	sebse	cherry	vişne
water	su	apricot	kayısı
fruit drink	serbet	figs	incir
milk	süt	nuts	fındık
wine	şarap	ice	buz
beer	'bira	fruit juice	meyva suyu

non-alcoholic yoğurt drink *ayran*

steaks	cooked medium	iyi	
	rare	az	
coffee	with sugar	şekerli	} unobtainable
	without sugar	sekersik	} recently

Fish (Balik). On the Turkish seaboard fish is greatly to be preferred to meat. Some of the more popular fish are:

swordfish	kiliç	grouper or rock cod	orfo, or ofoz
gilthead bream	isipoura	whitebait	gümüs
red bream	mercan, fangri	sardines	sardelya
white bream, or dentex	saryos	anchovy	hamsi
sea bream	manda göz mercan		
small species of bream	sinagrda	prawns	karides
red mullet	barbunya		
grey mullet	kefal	crawfish	böcek, istakoz
mackerel	uskumru		

A great quantity of fish was to be found in Turkish waters especially in the Marmara, where many varieties exist. The mackerel, according to local opinion, are unsurpassed in quality anywhere, and this is believed to be due largely to an abundance of plankton on which the sardine and anchovy feed; they are eaten by the mackerel which in turn is devoured by the bonito. Tunny and occasionally the blue shark frequent these waters. Unfortunately pollution and dynamiting has had an ill effect on the spawning of fish especially on bonito and mackerel.

The tunny which pass into the Mediterranean early in spring were keenly fished off Sardinia, Sicily and other places before they reached the Aegean and Black Sea to spawn. They entered the Black Sea along the coast of Asia and returned along that of Europe, a peculiarity noted by Pliny who, following a theory of Aristotle, supposed that the fish see better through the right eye than the left!

Yachts should be cautious about fishing in Turkish waters, and to avoid suspicion one should be content with catching the odd two or three fish for the crew. Net fishing, aqualung or lamp fishing by night are prohibited.

Fuel is seldom available at the quay and must be fetched from pumps in the towns.

Fresh water though plentiful is not easily accessible and sometimes of doubtful purity. It has been found to be good at Ayvalık, and Fethiye, also at certain village wells.

Turkish nautical terms may be traced back through the centuries and it is interesting to note that so few words stem from the Ottoman tongue; the majority of terms and expressions have come in via the Greek and betray their Venetian origin. This is hardly surprising when one remembers that at about the time of the Norman Conquest of England the Turks only began to occupy Anatolia. Ionian Greeks were then building and manning all the trading craft which they continued to do until 1920, and for at least two centuries during this long period the Venetians controlled the Anatolian ports.

The following glossary of sea terms (most of which spring from Italian) may be of help on some occasions:

bow	*pruva, baş*	jib	*flokos*
stern	*kiç*	mizzen	*mezzana*
deck	*güverte*	halyard	*kandalisa*
mast	*direk*	'pay out'	*lasca*
boom	*bumba*	'haul in'	*vere, çek*
keel	*omurga*	port	*iskele*
mainsail	*pani, yelken*	starboard	*sancak*

Pilotage Notes. In this section certain names are spelt according to the common English practice, e.g. Dardanelles, Gulf of Smyrna, Mitilini, Rhodes, etc.; others are in Greek or Turkish according to the present sovereignty of the places. This diversity of nomenclature sometimes presents a difficulty when wishing to explain to the port authority of one country the yacht's destination which may be a port of the other; Tenedos (near the Dardanelles) known for centuries by this name, is Bozcaada to the Turks, Samos is called Sisam. Fortunately Turkish harbour officials are often supplied with British charts and misunderstandings can be overcome. British charts copied in Turkey may be bought at Istanbul.

In *Sailing Directions* the language difficulty sometimes arises, also, when referring to capes, bays, gulfs, islands, etc. To clarify a few of the more common words on the chart, the following brief glossary may be of help:

ENGLISH	TURKISH	GREEK	ENGLISH	TURKISH	GREEK
castle	*hisar*	*kastro*	new	*yeni*	*neos*
Customs	*gümrük*	*telonion*	old	*eski*	*palios*
great, large	*büyük*	*megalo*	river	*nehir, irmak*	*potamos*
gulf, bay	*körfez, koy*	*ormos*	sky blue	*gök*	*galaxios*
island	*ada*	*nisi*	small	*kücük*	*mikro*
harbour	*liman*	*limani*	strait	*bogaz*	*stenon, dhiavlon*
headland, cape	*burun, burnu*	*akri*	tower	*kale*	*pyrgos*
hill	*tepe*	*vouno*	valley, stream	*vadi, dere, su*	*koilada, vrýssis*
lighthouse	*fener*	*faros*	village (main place)	*kasaba, köy*	*khlora or chóra*

(a) All letters in a word are pronounced separately and do not influence others, thus sade (plain, or neat, as in drink) is 'sahdeh' – not 'sayd'.

(b) ç is ch

(c) ş is sh

(d) ḡ (soft g) is not pronounced.

(e) c is pronounced as j in English

(f) u is 'oo' ü is 'ew' (almost)

(g) 'o' is pronounced as in English hot, ö is like 'er' (in fact, ö and ü are as in German).

(h) ı (undotted) is (very roughly) 'er'

Winds. The Meltemi wind of the Greeks is always called the Imbat in Turkey and around the Aegean coast has unique effects quite different from that in the open sea.

5
The Dardanelles to the Bosporus
and Black Sea

GALLIPOLI AND THE DARDANELLES

Morto Bay (Anıt Limanı)
Çanakkale (*Port of Entry*)

SEA OF MARMARA
South Coast
  Karabiga
  Artaki Bay
  Erdek
  Marmara Islands
    P. Marmara
    Asmalıköy
    Saraylar
    Pasha Liman
  Imralı Island
  Mudanya

North Coast
  Ereğli
  Silivri
  Büyük Çekmece

ISTANBUL
  Dolma Bahçe (*Port of Entry*)
  Moda and Fenerbahçe

THE BOSPORUS
  Bebek Bay
  Tarabya
  Büyük Dere

Lapseki
Gelibolu

East Coast
  Gemlik
  Armutlu
  Yalova
  Aydınlı
  Pendik
  Tuzla Bay
  Princes' Islands ('The Islands')
    Büyükada
    Haybeli
    Burgaz
    Kinalı
    Yassı
    Sivri

THE BLACK SEA
Southern Shores

5

The Dardanelles to the Bosporus and Black Sea

GALLIPOLI AND THE DARDANELLES

The western coast of the Gallipoli Peninsula consists of cliffs and sandy beaches with minor indentations suitable for anchoring only in the summer months. The background rises gently to hills of less than a thousand feet covered largely in scrub. Chart 2429 enables one to make for the entrance to the Dardanelles (called by the Turks Çanakkale Boğazı).

It is impossible to sail past these shores without being moved by the sight of the Allied War Cemeteries. More than a dozen burial places of varying sizes were laid out, usually near where men fell in battle – a reminder of our heavy casualties in the campaign of the First World War where a million men fought for possession of the peninsula. Unlike the usual war cemetery elsewhere, the graves on Gallipoli are marked by plaques of marble lying horizontally on the ground, which is lavishly planted with cypresses and flowering shrubs. The southern end of the peninsula at Cape Helles is marked, not only by a Turkish lighthouse, but by the 70-ft British War Memorial, an obelisk cut in stone shipped from England. A French memorial can also be seen inside the entrance, and now the Turks have recently set up a large symbolic gateway on the high cape east of Morto Bay near the site of a famous battery called after Baron de Toth, the French engineer who modernized the defences early in the last century.

The Passage to Istanbul. From Cape Helles the distance to this former capital of Byzantium is about 150 miles, and much of the route passes through interesting scenery.

The Dardanelles continues for about 40 miles from the entrance until reaching Gelibolu where it begins to broaden out into the Sea of Marmara. The tall European banks broken by steep ravines are mostly covered in scrub with occasional clusters of trees. The land supports only rough grazing, and, apart from the village mentioned, is sparsely populated. A foul current estimated to average at least 1½ knots should be allowed for.

Although the approach may be made at night this is not recommended; for, added to the embarrassment of steamer traffic, is that of the searchlights at Seddülbahir, which sometimes like to focus their beams on each approaching vessel. Also, if compelled to anchor off the Cape (a small bay known by the British in the First War as V-Beach) or in Morto Bay, it is possible that the military would interfere. Hitherto the whole of the Gallipoli shores was a forbidden area, and consequently for a small yacht it became a problem how to arrange one's passage through the Dardanelles during daylight. In 1977 the eastern shore of Morto Bay (now Anıt Limanı) became a permissible anchorage with good holding (mud). The eddies however caused by the current prevent a yacht from lying head-to the wind. From this anchorage one may row for a mile in the dinghy to the pilot-boat basin at Seddülbahir, where a landing may be made to look at the War Memorial.

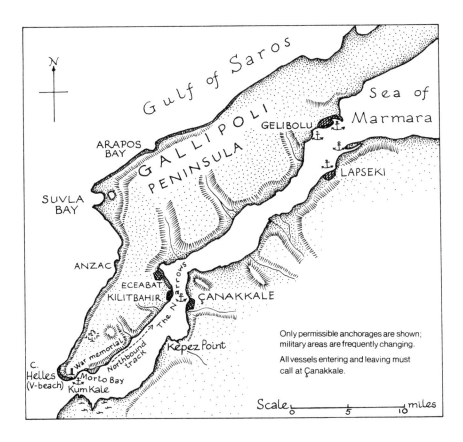

The Current. Sailing vessels seldom used to attempt to sail up the Dardanelles against the current without a fair wind, and often waited outside many days until conditions were favourable. On one occasion in 1807, Duckworth, anxious to press on with his squadron to Constantinople, had to remain at anchor off Tenedos for nine days awaiting a fair wind.

Since the days of Leander many attempts have been made by swimmers to cross from one shore to the other.

On 3 May 1810, Lord Byron in company with a young lieutenant swam from Sestos to the Asiatic shore in 1 hr 10 min. On board the frigate *Salsette*, which was at anchor nearby, it was calculated that the distance from the place where they had entered the water on the European shore to the finish of the swim below the Asiatic fort was upwards of 4 miles although the width across the Strait was only one. In the summer of 1923 some naval officers accomplished the swim without difficulty, but in later years the Turks raised official objections to prevent a repetition of the performance.

The chart of the Dardanelles is now marked with the positions of wrecks, some of them British and French battleships sunk by German mines and Turkish guns on 18 March 1915 when the Allies were attempting to fight their way through this vital passage to gain the greater prize of Constantinople. This date was a decisive one for both the Allies and the Turks; for the Allies because they had to abandon any further attempt to force the Dardanelles by warships alone, and were thus compelled to raise a military expeditionary force, while the Turks, profiting by this delay, gained the necessary respite to enable them to continue the war.

The positions where the battleships sank could not always be accurately plotted at the time especially in the case of *Ocean* and *Irresistible*, last seen abandoned but still afloat in the evening of 18 March. These two battleships and the French *Bouvet* (sunk at 2 p.m., author's watch) were recently located by Dr E. T. Hall with a proton magnetometer. *Bouvet* was found to be only a few hundred yards from her charted position, but *Ocean* had been swept down the Dardanelles some 3 miles beyond where she was presumed to have sunk. *Irresistible* was not far from her estimated position on the chart. *Goliath*, torpedoed by a Turkish T.B. at night in Morto Bay, had drifted down with the current, her position being assessed at the time with reasonable accuracy. The Turkish salvage party with the help of Dr Hall and led by Tosun Sezen have now recovered most of the propellers, torpedo tubes and engine-room fittings from the wrecks.

The wreck of the German cruiser *Breslau* sunk by British mines between the Dardanelles and Imroz during a sortie with *Goeben* cannot be located.

On a hillside by the Narrows, in large characters formed of white stones, may now be seen '18 March 1915'. But all the forts have vanished, and except for an old Genoese castle there are no visible signs of defensive works today.

Çanakkale, lying on the Asiatic shore of the Narrows, is the Turkish Control Port for all vessels entering or leaving the Dardanelles. Sometimes a Customs boat puts off to the newly arrived yacht with other port officials necessary for Clearance. Çanakkale can now boast of one or two modest hotels and a museum displaying some Hellenistic and Roman objects from Troy. It is also the residence of the Allied Graves Commissioner for the War Cemeteries on Gallipoli, which commemorate about 32,000 British and Commonwealth dead. One can visit Troy from here; a car may be hired, and in about an hour one arrives at the scene of Schliemann's excavations which can be best appreciated by a previous study of Professor Blegen's book *Troy and the Trojans* (Thames & Hudson).

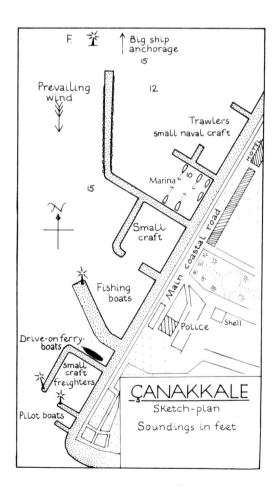

11 Prosforion Tower, Khalkidhiki

12 Thasos: the harbour from the acropolis

13 Moda, Istanbul

14 Tarabya Bay, Bosporus

The Port. Harbour works now enable a yacht to lie peacefully alongside while furnishing particulars to Turkish officials.

Approach. Proceeding northward, continue past three small basins until coming to a low rough breakwater (completed 1978) which lies close south of the big ship anchorage of Dardan Liman with its large mooring-buoy. Rounding the extremity of the breakwater one must turn south into the basin and berth in the marina as in plan. Harbour lights (R. & G.) are exhibited on the extremities of the breakwater where there are depths of 12 to 15 ft.

Berth. The marina is well sheltered from swell and steamer wash, depth 10 ft alongside. There is only the prevailing N. wind to contend with. One should choose whether it is preferable to lie alongside or possibly moor to the quay, head to wind. No limit on period of stay.

Officials. As for Port of Entry. Officials here have invariably been helpful to a yacht. British Graves Commissioner also resides here.

Facilities. Water on quay. Fuel from Shell station; good shopping, simple but good restaurants. Ferry to Gallipoli shore. Excursions to Troy.

The small town was rebuilt after the First World War when shells from the British battleships completely destroyed it.

A small War Graves cemetery lies about one mile east of the village.

The War Graves representative for the large cemeteries on Gallipoli can be found at Gası Bulvarı – Gul Sokak Dardeniz Apt, Kat 3 Daire 5. As these cemeteries are widely spread in the areas of C. Helles, Anzac and Suvla where the fighting actually took place, it is advisable to seek advice if wishing to visit Gallipoli. Altogether there are thirty-two cemeteries and five memorials commemorating British, Australian, and New Zealand dead.

Approaching Nagara above the Narrows, where the width is only a mile, the current usually runs at 2 knots, and rather unexpectedly flows faster at the sides than in the middle. It was here that Xerxes built his bridge for boats of the vast invading army he was leading into Europe in 480 B.C. The bridge crossed a little higher up than Abydos and touched the European shore between Sestos and Madytus. Herodotus wrote: 'And now as he looked and saw the whole Hellespont covered with the vessels of his fleet and all the shore and every plain about Abydos as full as possible of men, Xerxes congratulated himself upon his good fortune; but after a little while he wept.'

It was at Abydos that Alexander first set foot in Asia.

Today there is almost nothing to be seen at Sestos and only a few poor dwellings at Abydos, one of which, now a petrol dump, was the house where Byron stayed on his voyage from Smyrna to Constantinople:

> *The winds are high on Helle's wave*
> *As on the night of stormy water*
> *When love, who sent, forgot to save*
> *The young – the beautiful – the brave.*
> *The lonely hope of Sestos' daughter.*

In the Dardanelles a growing number of merchant ships may be passed, proceeding to or from Istanbul or the Black Sea ports most of which will be flying the flag of Iron Curtain countries. In recent years yachts have reported the passage of modern Soviet warships, but the captains of these naval vessels are very camera-shy and direct powerful spotlights on any yacht attempting to photograph them. Local caïques are also to be seen, ferrying either passengers or cattle from one shore to the other; but their graceful form has now changed. No longer do they resemble the Greek caïques with a low waist rising with a gentle sweep to a high pointed bow and stern. The modern design demands a high built-up waist where the weather screens used to be, and a raised poop on which is a wheelhouse. From head on, especially when lightly laden, they appear not unlike the original Roman freighter. There are no sails – only a stump mast and derrick.

Further northwards the undulating countryside on the banks becomes more attractive, and in early summer yellow-brown cornfields suggest England at its best.

Continuing up the Dardanelles it will be necessary for a sailing yacht to find an anchorage for the night, as the summer breeze normally drops immediately after sunset.

Night Anchorages in the Dardanelles

Lapseki, on the Asiatic shore, is a country town with a convenient roadstead protected by a stone pier.

> **Anchorage.** There are 3 fathoms depths in position 300–500 yds N.N.W. of the pierhead – well-sheltered except between N.W. and N.E. A fairway should be kept clear for the ferries.

> **Facilities.** Bread, fish, wine and fruit can be bought.

Lapseki, capital of the province, lies in an attractive position by the waterfront amidst vines and olives with a background of wooded hills. Mostly of modern construction, this small town was once the sacred city of the Priapus cult.

Should the wind be unfavourable for anchoring here, a yacht may cross to the European side and anchor at:

Gelibolu (Gallipoli). A small yacht can moor in the fishing harbour as directed. Otherwise there are suitable depths in line with the town jetty well-sheltered from the N. wind, alternatively the N.W. corner of the bay near a stone pier by a clump of trees near a hospital with an officers' mess. One can land by dinghy at the jetty where restaurants and shops are close by.

If wanting to press on to Istanbul it is recommended in summer to keep under the northern shore of the Sea of Marmara where the wind, especially at night, is better and there is shelter under the land. The coast however is of no interest, except for a couple of night anchorages which can be used by smaller yachts. The southern shores are interesting to follow.

SEA OF MARMARA

On its southern shores are a number of attractive anchorages. A yacht with a week to devote to cruising off this coast will find the ports and anchorages conveniently spaced and the coast green and partly cultivated. If one cruises along these shores on the outward voyage to Istanbul it is suggested that when returning to the Dardanelles a quick direct passage can be made by night under the lee of the northern shore. Here, in summer, the advantage of the night breeze could carry one on a fast broad reach to the northern approach of the Dardanelles by the next morning.

A yacht entering the Sea of Marmara for the first time and having, say, a week to spend on the south coast is recommended to call at the places in the Gulf of

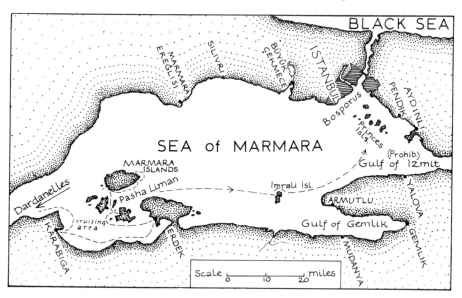

Erdek and in the Marmara Islands. The other places though of possible interest are rather far from the direct route to Istanbul.

Southern Shore (Charts 1004 and 1005)

Karabiga. Chart 844, plan. A primitive walled village at the head of a wide bay, with a new harbour.

> **Approach.** After rounding Kale Burnu make for the towers on the breakwater extremities (unlit) or consider anchoring N.E. of the above-water rock.
>
> **Berth.** Secure off the quay in 14 ft depths.
>
> **Facilities.** Limited provisions.

From the unattractive village it is a pleasant walk to the medieval walls standing on the cliffs some 2 miles distant.

Artaki Bay. There is a good anchorage in the open bay off a small summer bathing place.

> **Approach and Anchorage.** Chart 2242, plan on Chart 884. The channel between Tavsan Island and mainland has at least 3½-fathom depths. Anchorage is in the N.W. corner of the bay, the depths being convenient.
>
> **Facilities.** There are one or two small summer hotels. Bread can be bought.

Erdek. Chart 884, plan. An attractive small port protected by a breakwater from W. In summer the place becomes a bathing resort.

> **Approach.** Make for the buildings of the village, but do not enter the small harbour which on account of ferry traffic and shoal water by the quay is unsuitable.
>
> **Berth** alongside. Exposed in onshore winds, when the swell can be dangerous.
>
> **Facilities.** Water, provisions (fruit and vegetables), hotels, restaurants, banks, ferry connections with the islands and small resorts.

The village is pretty, being well laid out with trees and kept fresh with water-carts in summer. It is much given to tourism and has a small museum.

Marmara Islands (Charts 1004, 1005 and plan 844)

The massive mountains on the north side fall steeply into the sea, but the southern coast is wooded and attractive with settlements dotted along the shore where there is occasional cultivation.

The Port of Marmara lies E. of the town roughly in a direction N. and S.; it is long, narrow, and deep. Rather shut in and hot in summer.

Approach. The entrance is narrow and the breakwater extremities are lit.

Berth. Secure alongside western breakwater but beware of rubble about 50 yds from extremity; alternatively if not of deep draught, berth stern-to at N.E. side of the port off a wooden jetty with a small quay.

Facilities. Water, fuel (in cans by dinghy) provisions, ice from cold store.

The substantial village is becoming a tourist centre.

Asmalikoy on the S.E. coast, a pretty fishing village with a conspicuous minaret (not marked on chart), has a harbour formed by a breakwater extending westwards from Asmalı Burnu.

Berth. Secure to a quay about 50 yds inside the end of the breakwater (unlit) where fishing craft may also want to berth. Alternatively one may anchor off the breakwater, but here there may be a swell.

Facilities. A water-tap in the village but nothing much to be bought. One shop and a bar.

The walk through the village, with its crude carvings on the wooden houses, to the coastal road above is rewarding for the views over the wooded bay.

Saraylar (Palatia). An attractive village at the head of a bay on the N. coast, noted for its export of marble from the local quarries. The loading now takes place at a new small port $\frac{1}{2}$ mile W. of the village, which on account of noise and dust is not recommended for a yacht.

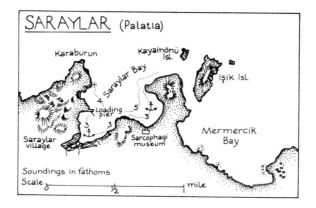

Anchorage
(a) Anchor off the village or berth close E. of it.
(b) A small bay ½ mile N.E. of the village provides a well-protected anchorage and is quite deserted.

Facilities. Groceries, bread, fish and fuel.

The quarries, which have been in use since classical Greek times, may be visited by jeep. One can see huge slabs of marble being cut and dressed still mostly by hand. On the drive from the village one passes a number of giant sarcophagi of early Byzantine period recently excavated. The village being difficult to reach by land has not yet been spoilt by tourism.

History. On 8 December 1915, during the Gallipoli Campaign, submarine *E.11* (Lt.-Com. Dunbar-Nasmith) chased an armed Turkish dispatch vessel during darkness into this little harbour. After a protracted action continuing until after dawn against the defending shore battery, the Turkish vessel was finally left ablaze.

Pasha Liman Island has an attractive landlocked bay on the N. coast with a simple village at its head.

Approach. Although leading marks are no longer in position, it is easy to enter by day. The shoals on either side of the entrance are clearly visible, the channel being about 600 yds wide at the narrowest point.

Anchorage. Let go off the village in 2–3 fathoms.

Facilities. Water from a spring; simple provisions.

Arabiar Island has no suitable anchorage.

Imralı (Kalolimno). Chart 844, plan. This island is a penal settlement and approach and landing are prohibited.
Alternatively, in settled weather, a yacht may find convenient anchorage in 2 fathoms (sand) along the Asiatic coast off **Kurşunlu** or between **Mara Burnu** and **Yeni Köy**. Both are open anchorages.

Mudanya is a commercial port with a substantial town, convenient for visiting Bursa (Brusa) and climbing the Uludag (one of the many mountains called Olympus). See plan on Chart 844.

Anchor behind the breakwater, but clear of the ferries, somewhat exposed to north N. winds.

Facilities. Provisions of all kinds, hotels. Ferry-boats from Istanbul land tourists here who continue to Bursa by road.

In the First World War when the port was sending war supplies to the Turkish army on Gallipoli, submarine *E.11* surfaced at 5 a.m. 28 August 1915 off the port. Although shelled by shore batteries, *E.11* succeeded in setting ablaze the railway station and installations before being driven off by Turkish gunfire.

Eastern Shore

The following are unimportant open anchorages:

Gemlik, a small summer bathing place at the head of the gulf.

Armutlu, chart 908, lies opposite Mudanya on the promontory – an open bay well-sheltered from N. A pier extends in a S. direction with 4 fathoms depth at its head.

> **Anchorage.** S.E. of Maykhane Burnu in 3 fathoms on a sandy bottom.

Yalova has become a popular little ferry-port for tourists from Istanbul when visiting Bursa. Their cars are embarked at Kartal (near Pendik) and landed here at a pier. Both Yalova and nearby Çinarçik are completely open anchorages.

Eastward of Yalova the Izmit Gulf leads towards the naval base, an area prohibited to yachts.

The large gulf of Izmir is largely allocated to the Navy, and yachts are advised to keep away.

Aydınlı has been developed and, though well-sheltered except during fresh W. and S.W. winds, it makes no appeal to a visiting yacht.

Pendik affords good anchorage except in strong W. winds when yachts must move closer under the lee of Pavli Island. Water, provisions, hotel and fuel available.

Tuzla Bay. Plan on chart 497. There is good anchorage in $2\frac{1}{2}$ fathoms (sand) either off the village or in the bay N. of Deserters Islands and E. of Porias Liman Burnu.

Princes' Islands ('The Islands')   Chart 2286

Before reaching the southern entrance of the Bosporus are the six Princes' Islands (Adalar), formerly used by the Greek colonists as summer resorts. They are now popular with Turkish tourists who pour out of the ferry-steamers from Istanbul to enjoy the fresh air, the flowers and the absence of motor traffic. These islands are largely green and wooded. Motor cars are prohibited and there is usually anchorage for a yacht.

Büyükada, a large and mostly wooded island, was known to the Greek colonists as Prinkipo. It is a fashionable summer resort with hotels, villas and cafés by the sea front.

> **Anchorage** off the sea front is too exposed, and the quietest place is in the southern bay of the island; open only to south.

Büyükada has a permanent population with a small village, and provision shops, but it lacks sufficient water.

Heybeli, attractive and wooded, has its village and ferry port on the N. coast. Its anchorage is off the S. shore in the bay of

Cam Limani. Unfortunately the present scenery is marred by buildings with two large government hospitals, tourist hotels and much boating activity.

> **Anchorage.** In convenient depths off the beach.

> **Facilities.** Only a buffet-bar by the shore. It is necessary to go to the main village for provisions, a walk of 2 miles or drive by horse-carriage.

The island was inhabited during Byzantine days; from this period some buildings survive and have been embodied into the naval college. The old church of Theotokos is worth a visit. There are pleasant walks in the pinewoods, and if passing by the N.E. corner of the island one can see the grave of Sir Edward Burton, one of England's Elizabethan ambassadors.

Burgaz, lying close to Heybeli, has similar terrain and an anchorage behind a sunken mole whose root lies 100 yds south of the ferry pier.

Kinalı, also inhabited, is without particular interest.

The four small islands are mostly uninhabited:

Yassı, sometimes used by the Navy, was once owned by Sir Henry Bulwer, who at the beginning of the last century built himself a mansion which has now become a ruin.

Sivri came into the news seventy years ago when the Turks rounded up all the dogs in Istanbul and put them on this island for extermination. **Sedef** and the small island of **Tavşan** (close S.E. of Büyükada) are without interest.

Northern Shore

There are some partially sheltered bays, none of which is worth visiting except for temporary anchorage:

Ereğli (Erekli). Chart 2230. A yacht may anchor N.W. of the jetty. During approach the lighthouse must be given a wide berth.

Silivri. Its new harbour is crowded with large fishing boats. Provisions can be bought; a small hotel; nothing of interest.

Büyük Çekmece

Berth in new harbour in N.W. corner.

ISTANBUL

Chart 1198. Yachts on arrival should anchor off Dolma Bahçe out of the tideway and haul their sterns into the quay. Here there are depths of 6 ft, but west of the palace by the mosque there are 2 fathoms 10 ft from the quay. The Turkish authorities do not board newly arrived yachts, but expect the owner to come to the office with Ship's Papers. While port formalities are being completed, one may watch the never-ending flow of traffic: large steamers, local craft and fast motor-boats all straining to enter the Bosporus and Golden Horn. At the same time one should not miss the opportunity of seeing the naval museum inside Dolma Bahçe.

Clearance may be obtained by visiting Yokulu Salonu on the 'old city' end of Galata Bridge. At the Police Office is an information centre with an interpreter who is there to lead one to all the officials concerned.

In 1977 it was reported that Turkish formalities had been relaxed and that the procedure for yachts was then unnecessary. Similar relaxation has occurred before, but on previous occasions formalities have again been tightened up.

After obtaining clearance, one alternative for a yacht is to berth in the bay of Moda at Fenerbahçe (on the south side) at the Istanbul Yacht Club. Though rather crowded it is more comfortable than being anchored on the northern side of Club Deniz. Moreover, the latter is more of a social club whereas the Istanbul Y.C. caters for the smaller yachts and is usually helpful with regard to provisions, repairs, etc.

Facilities. Water, fuel, provisions nearby. Bus to Kadiköy and then ferry to Istanbul; allow 70 min.

An alternative is to anchor off the European shore at **Yesilkoy**, south of the airport. Anchorage is off the village in $1\frac{1}{2}$ fathoms, from here the bus to Istanbul takes about an hour.

> Tall minarets, shining mosques, barbaric towers
> Fountains and palaces, and cypress bowers.
>
> HEMANS

The City. Guide-books describe the many interesting places to be seen in Istanbul, yet one is apt to forget that this city with its 3 million population has only recently acquired a western look. As late as the 1920s the alleys and bazaars were crowded with men nearly all wearing the red fez and clad in Asian costume. There were Arabs, Persians, Kurds, Armenians, Circassians and Greeks, all to be distinguished by their dress. The few women to be seen were veiled. In the narrow streets were Dervishes, lemonade-sellers with their huge brass apparatus, story-tellers, letter-writers and barrel-organ players. Threading their way through this gossiping crowd, laden donkeys would pass with their drivers, and porters bearing heavy loads.

On 1 November 1922, these outward signs of an eastern world began to change, for Kemal Ataturk had come to power. By deposing the Sultan many centuries of ancient Turkish tradition and customs were discarded. A new democratic state arose with the Gregorian calendar, the metric system, hand-writing in Latin characters and western clothes. Almost overnight the fez and the veil were swept away and the secular powers of holy men and priests abolished. More than half a century has now elapsed, yet apart from some of its architecture this ancient Byzantine city has shed all outward signs of its oriental past.

THE BOSPORUS

The Bosporus (known to the Turks as Istanbul Bogazi), 16 miles in length and in places only 1,700 yds wide, is remarkable not only for its beauty but for its many types of ships and local craft. On account of the 3-knot current and unpredictable whirlpools it is advisable to proceed under power. Though permission to enter the Bosporus is not required, no vessels may proceed into the Black Sea without notifying the Turkish authorities, and at the same time a study should be made of the prohibited areas.

When proceeding to one of the Bosporus anchorages it will be noticed that the Asiatic shore is more peaceful, the traffic being mainly off the European coast. The new bridge joining Europe to Asia crosses the Bosporus between Ortaköy and Beylerbeyi, passing 64 metres above the high water level.

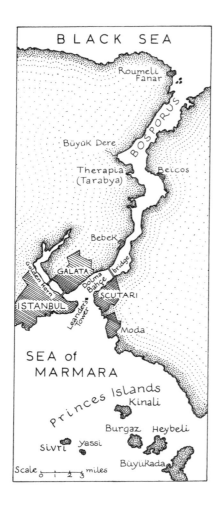

Anchorages in the Bosporus (Chart 1198)

Bebek Bay is probably the most convenient anchorage for getting into the city by road, but today the place is so crowded that it is difficult for a visiting yacht to find a berth.

Anchorage. The only possibility is to moor bows or stern to the waterfront in between other boats similarly moored. There is a great deal of oil pollution here.

Note. When approaching this place from the south the violent current off Arnavut Köy should be avoided by keeping in mid-stream or even nearer the Asiatic shore.

Facilities. Fuel and ice may be bought. There are provision shops and good restaurants;

laundry and dry cleaning. One can land in the dinghy close to a bus stop for the city – nearly an hour's journey following the sea.

Istinye. A deep creek between Bebek and Tarabya with a large government shipyard which in emergency can slip the largest yacht.

Tarabya (Therapia) is also convenient for a yacht to berth when visiting Istanbul, but is normally very crowded.

Berth stern to a quay on the S. side of the creek with anchor laid out to N.N.E. in somewhat deep water (about 8 fathoms). Dinghy can be hauled-out on N. shore where provision is made.

Facilities. A few local shops, and occasionally ice is available. Excellent restaurants, modern hotel on the point (baths and showers). Bus service to the city, also minibuses or shared taxis – a 20-min. journey.

Although there is little disturbance from passing steamers, the road traffic at night can be noisy.

Büyük Dere, used by many local craft, also provides good anchorage out of the current. This is the official port for entering and leaving the Black Sea. Yachts cruising to Bulgaria and Romania clear all formalities here but can get permission to stop in transit at the excellent new frontier harbour at Igneada.

Anchorage. Good holding on mud about 100 yds off Customs building in 3 fathoms. This is preferable to berthing alongside at the boat-steps or Customs office.

Facilities. Provision shops, fuel, water and ice are available. A good shipyard willing to undertake yacht work. Bus service to the city – at least 2 hrs. There is often much pollution here with oil as well as steamer wash from passing ships.

The Black Sea (Southern Shores)

Its water is nearly fresh, opaque green in colour, and very cold – about the same temperature as the North Sea. It abounds in fish which are caught mainly during the winter months, and the Turkish coast is dotted with artificial harbours, very well constructed, to accommodate the fishing fleets. These harbours, which are not much used during the summer, provide excellent berths for yachts for there is nowhere else a yacht can shelter from the prevailing winds. The wind-roses for June, July and August show a predominance of northerly winds increasing in strength as the summer progresses. A land breeze by night lasts until early morning.

The coast is attractive, resembling England with rolling downs, corn fields and woods. There are many excellent sandy beaches, most of them deserted, yet yachtsmen very seldom visit this area, and foreign tourists are rare. The local people therefore regard visitors as quite special and go out of their way to be hospitable and helpful.

The disadvantage of the area for cruising is that the coast is virtually one long straight line, so that one has to come back much the way one went.

Charts. The Turkish charts 111, 112, 113, 121, 122, 123 cover the coast from the Bosporus eastwards (29° E. to 36° E.). There is also a chart No. 1121 giving plans of certain harbours. These charts are much to be preferred to British charts which are of too small scale to be practical. They can be obtained from the Turkish Hydrographic Office on the Asiatic side of the Bosporus at Çubuk (see Chart 1198); it is about an hour in a ferry from the Galata Bridge. The charts are excellent, costing about one-third the price of British charts.

Earlier History. The Black Sea was formerly called the Euxine and until 1922 the villages and small towns were populated for many centuries by Ionian Greek colonists. The meaning of Euxine is 'Friendly to Strangers'; it is a pleasing thought to realize that the present Turkish population continues to show the same attitude towards the present-day visitors as their Greek predecessors in the past.

The west shore offers an alternative route via the Communist countries. On leaving the Bosporus one turns northward for about 85 miles and comes to Bulgaria. Although this country and Romania are willing to grant visas, their conditions are discouraging to yachtsmen. In Romania one must exchange into local currency 12 U.S. dollars per day per person. On the expiry of the visit, one is not permitted to take out nor to re-exchange any of the local currency so acquired. In Bulgaria yachts are restricted to the ports of Burgas and Varna. Entry to the Danube Delta is possible only for yachts with considerable power, preferably in the late summer when the spring current has eased.

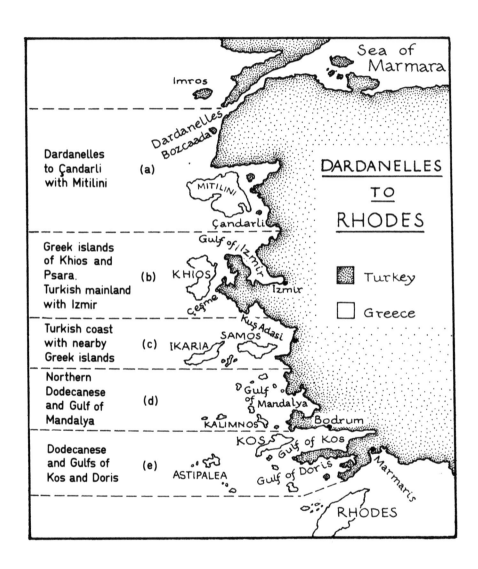

Dardanelles to Çandarli with Mitilini **(a)**

Greek islands of Khios and Psara. Turkish mainland with Izmir **(b)**

Turkish coast with nearby Greek islands **(c)**

Northern Dodecanese and Gulf of Mandalya **(d)**

Dodecanese and Gulfs of Kos and Doris **(e)**

Sea of Marmara

Imros

Dardanelles

Bozcaada

MITILINI

Çandarli

DARDANELLES

TO

RHODES

Gulf of Izmir

KHIOS

Izmir

Çeşme

Kuş Adasi

IKARIA

SAMOS

Gulf of Mandalya

KALIMNOS

Bodrum

KOS

Gulf of Kos

Gulf of Doris

Marmaris

ASTIPALEA

RHODES

Turkey

Greece

6a–e

Eastern Shores of the Aegean

This chapter includes a number of close, off-lying islands, some lying inside the Turkish gulfs, yet almost all are Greek; many are important, green and attractive, but as a result of political tension, which flares up at times, between Greece and Turkey, restrictions or prohibited areas on both coastal areas are sometimes imposed by both countries with little warning.

6a

The Dardanelles to Çandarlı

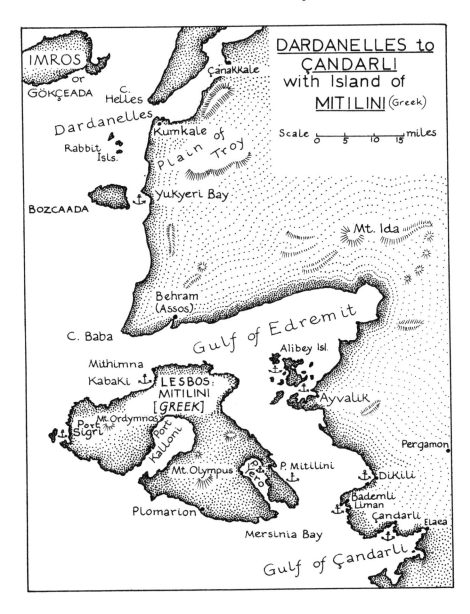

DARDANELLES to ÇANDARLI with Island of MITILINI (Greek)

Scale 0 5 10 15 miles

IMROS or GÖKÇEADA

Çanakkale

C. Helles

Dardanelles

Kumkale

Plain of Troy

Rabbit Isls.

BOZCAADA

Yukyeri Bay

Mt. Ida

Behram (Assos)

C. Baba

Gulf of Edremit

Alibey Isl.

Mithimna

Kabaki

LESBOS: MITILINI [GREEK]

Ayvalik

Port Sigri

Mt. Ordymnos

Port Kalloni

Pergamon

Mt. Olympus

Pero

P. Mitilini

Dikili

Bademli Liman

Çandarli

Elaea

Plomarion

Mersinia Bay

Gulf of Çandarli

TURKISH COAST	GREEK ISLAND
Island of Tenedos (Bozcaada)	Island of Mitilini (Lesbos)
The Port	Port Mitilini (*Port of Entry*)
	Port Kalloni
Beşika Bay	Plomarion
Yukyeri Bay	Mersinia Bay
Behram (Assos)	Port Yero
Ayvalık (*Port of Entry*) for	Scala Loutra
Pergamon	Mithimna (Molivos)
Dikili	Kabaki (Petra)
Bademli Limanı	Port Sigri
Çandarlı	
Aliaga	
Yenice (Yeni Foça)	
Çanak Limanı	

6a

The Dardanelles to Çandarlı

FROM THE DARDANELLES SOUTHWARD

Emerging from the entrance of the Dardanelles and turning to the southward a vessel passes the green valley of Troy and Beşika Bay, the anchorage where sailing vessels bound for Constantinople sometimes had to await a fair wind.

The small, flat and uninteresting island of Tenedos lies close off the Anatolian coast and, together with Imros in the north, form the sentinels guarding the Hellespont approach. Both were advance bases of the Allies in the First World War and are now the only Aegean islands held by the Turks. Whereas Imros (now Gökseada) is partly wooded and hilly, with two alternative partially sheltered anchorages, Tenedos is flat and rather bare with a small 2-fathom port, formerly defended by a well-preserved Genoese castle. Chart 1659.

Island of Tenedos (Bozcaada)

In Byzantine days when Constantinople was dependent upon its corn supplies from Egypt, ships frequently had long delays off Tenedos awaiting a favourable wind to blow them up the Dardanelles. To avoid this idleness of valuable shipping Justinian had a huge granary built to enable vessels to unload there and then return to Egypt for another cargo. Small freighters then ferried the grain up to Constantinople as opportunity offered. Nothing is left of the granary today; and the vineyards, which 200 years ago were so famous, have now dwindled, and though the quality of the grapes is good only a small amount of wine is produced for the home market. The harbour provides shelter for trading caïques, and a ferry-service to Odum Iskelesi, a small village on the mainland a few miles south of Troy.

Tenedos is a Military Area, but yachts proceeding to and from Turkish harbours may get permission to stay overnight.

The Port
Approach and Berth. Chart 1608 and plan 1880. The breakwaters are clearly to be discerned a mile off. Berth alongside. Though open to east, the harbour is quite comfortable in normal weather.

Officials. The island has a Governor, Customs and Police.

Facilities. Water on quay. There are a few provision shops and an excellent white wine can be bought.

One or two small deserted coves on the S. shore of the island also afford anchorage and shelter from the north, but they are not recommended.

On the mainland shore is **Beşika Bay** a favourite anchorage for the old sailing ships as well as modern men-of-war. It was here that Admiral Duckworth had anchored his squadron in February 1807 when H.M.S. *Ajax* of 74 guns caught fire and burnt out with the loss of 250 men. Nearly two years later Sir Francis Darwin on a visit to Tenedos described the melancholy sight of the wreck which had drifted ashore on this island.

For a yacht, however, there is a suitable night anchorage on the mainland shore at

Yükyeri Bay. Close under Kum Burnu where the spit extends much further than shown on the chart, one can normally find a good lee from the north wind in 3 fathoms on a sandy bottom.

Leaving this anchorage and pointing southwards down the straight Anatolian coast a sailing yacht, helped by the south-going current and a fresh north wind in the summer months, is quickly blown towards the impressive steep-to Cape Baba. Some 7 miles before reaching the cape one must be careful to stand well away from the coast. The shoal water at the mouth of the Tuzlu River extends much further westwards than charted. A decision must now be made whether to follow the Turkish coast towards the Edremiti Gulf (with Ayvalık and the Islands) or turn towards the island of Mitilini (Lesbos).

During the Meltemi season the wind off this headland now becomes westerly and again follows the Turkish coast into the gulf usually maintaining its strength until sunset.

Some 7 miles beyond the cape is the Bay of Sevrice on the eastern flank of which is the headland of the same name; it has shoal water close-off to the S.E. but in the N.E. corner is anchorage in about 5 fathoms. Good shelter from Meltemi but uncertain holding. This is the southern limit of the prohibited area of coast extending the whole way from the Dardanelles.

Behram (Assos), standing by some cliffs overlooking the sea, has little to show of its ancient past; but once it was a lovely city and according to Strabo, Aristotle settled here for several years. Anchor to E. of small boat harbour clear of reef. Poor holding, but good shelter from N.W.

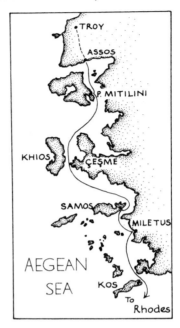

History. It was from here that St Paul embarked in A.D. 71. He had come here after visiting Troy and now started on his third missionary journey – described in the 21st chapter of the Acts.

He had been in Macedonia and having crossed by sea via Troy, St Paul embarked at Assos for the voyage to the Levant. This was at the period of the spring equinox; and as St Paul had left barely enough time to reach Jerusalem for the celebration of Pentecost, he had to hurry. He put in at Port Mitilini, Çeşme ('the point opposite Khios'), Samos, Miletus (now some miles from the sea), Kos, Rhodes, Patara, and thence to Tyre. Mostly rowing by day – the Meltemi would not have started so early in the season – and resting the oarsmen at night, speeds of at least 4 knots appear to have been maintained during the longer hops when sometimes 50 to 60 miles appear to have been made good in the day.

Towards the head of the Gulf are the resorts of Arcay with a short pier leading to a village, and Ören opposite.

Following along the southern shore towards the S.W. extremity is a group of islands, some with sheltered anchorage, and the small port of Ayvalik.

Ayvalık Limanı and off-lying islands

Chart 1627 shows two entrances leading into the Limanı (virtually a lake) of Ayvalık: (a) the main channel used by steamers is from the west via the Dalyan Boğazı leading into a well-marked canal (depth 16 ft), lit at night; (b) the shallow northern entrance of Dolap Boğazı closed by a causeway.

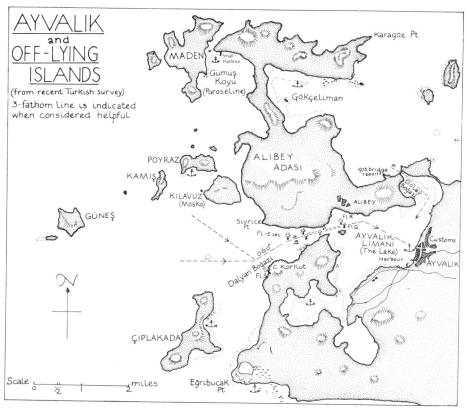

AYVALIK and OFF-LYING ISLANDS
(from recent Turkish survey)
3-fathom line is indicated when considered helpful.

Karagöz Pt.

MADEN

Gumuş Koyu
(Poroseline)

Gökçeliman

POYRAZ

KAMIŞ

KILAVUZ
(Mosko)

GÜNEŞ

ALIBEY ADASI

1976 bridge reported

Dolap Boğazı

ALIBEY

Sivrice Pt.

FL 15 sec

FL R

F IG

060°

AYVALIK LIMANI
(The Lake)

Harbour

Customs

AYVALIK

Dalyan Boğazı

C. Korkut

FL 3

ÇIPLAKADA

Scale
0   ½   1   2 miles

Eğribucak Pt.

Outside the approaches are nearly a dozen islands, largely barren and uninhabited except for the large Alibey Adası with its village by the 'lake'. Some islands afford temporary shelter with good anchorage protected from the prevailing wind. See map.

Madenada, the most northerly island, is almost joined to the large Alibey Adası where they form a large bay known in Greek and Roman days as Porosalene. Here Pausanias was an eyewitness of the spectacle of a tame dolphin that came at a boy's call and allowed him to ride on its back. Though confirmed by another witness this story still raises doubts as to its credibility, even though the dolphin was always regarded by the early Greeks as a friend and was not hunted. In 1981 a long mole was being built from the western shore of the bay. This together with the existing quay forms a safe little harbour.

Ayvalık, thrives on the export of high-grade olive oil and soap, also more recently on tourism.

Approach. Having reached a position half a mile N.W. of C. Korkut, steer for a light structure on a course about 060°. When close off, leave it to the northward, and passing between the buoys, steer a course of about 078° leading into the canal. A tidal stream may be felt.

Berth. Having entered Ayvalık Limanı, steer for the small harbour south of the town.

Officials. A Port of Entry: there are Health, Police, Immigration and Customs.

Port Facilities. Fresh fruit, bread and meat may be bought in the market and shops. There is a bank, a hotel, a cinema and a club. Ice and fuel can be bought. Market day Thursday.
    A steamer from Izmir calls weekly and buses to Izmir run three times a day ($3\frac{1}{2}$ hrs), A ferry runs to Port Mitilini weekly. There is a fine bathing beach on the S.W. side of the bay. On the surrounding hills and islands can be seen the ruins of some old monasteries.

Alibey. An attractive fishing/holiday village with many restaurants. Anchor just inside new mole to W. of village.
    On the south side of Ayvalık promontory is a summer anchorage off the open shore at Tatlı su Körfezi. Here are a few tavernas and some houses, all signs of a growing small summer resort.
    A car may be hired to drive to Troy and also the ancient city of Pergamon – an hour's drive and well worth a visit. There is also a bus service.

PERGAMON is splendidly situated standing upon a hill, and as the ruins gradually appear one is impressed by the vastness of this 'Athens of Asia'. Her port at this time – second century B.C. – was at Elaea, at the head of the Gulf of Çandarlı, where the river Caicus formed an artery of transport to the city.
    The modern Bergama, a substantial town, is built on the site of the former residential part of the great Greek and Roman cities. It lies at the foot of the Acropolis, on whose steep slopes stand the crumbling tiers of seats of the Greek theatre and the foundations of Greek, Roman and Byzantine walls. Seen from the top, in the light of the setting sun, the view across the ruins towards the green fertile plain beyond is magnificent. Not far down the hill are the ruins of the famous library. Its only rival was that at Alexandria, whither its whole contents were eventually dispatched by Antony. Here it survived until the 7th century when the Caliph Omar gave orders for its destruction.

Our word 'parchment' is derived from the name Pergamon. According to Pliny, the Ptolemies of Egypt, becoming jealous of the growing importance of the Pergamon library prohibited the export of papyrus from Egypt. This compelled the king of Pergamon to revert to the former use of animal skins for writing upon; but he demanded improvements in the technique, as a result the more delicate skins of calf and kid came to be used and adapted for writing on both sides. This eventually became known as vellum.

The famous Great Altar of Zeus, discovered in the 1870s south of the

Acropolis, was excavated by Humann and removed to the Kaiser Frederick Museum, Berlin. Carried off by the Russians after the Second World War this massive altar with its fine friezes was returned in 1958 and has been re-erected in the Pergamon Museum in East Berlin.

As well as the massive basilica of Hadrian's time there are, across the river-bed, remains of a Roman theatre and the more remarkable Aesculapium of the 4th century B.C.

Sailing southward, after some 20 miles, one reaches the little port:

Dikili, is a well-protected harbour much used by boats from tourist ships carrying passengers for visiting the ruins of nearby Pergamon; also by freighters.

Approach. One enters between the breakwaters, one extending in a S.W. direction, the other – far shorter – juts out from the shore westward.

Berth alongside at inner end of quay. Complete shelter.

Officials. Health and Immigration. A Port of Entry.

Facilities. Good water at dockside. Fuel from garage. Market on Tuesdays. Taxis available for Pergamon. Restaurants and banks. Ferry to Lesbos and Piraeus.

Sailing again southward one soon reaches the attractive inlet of Bademli Limanı and then the Gulf of Çandarli.

Bademli Limanı, a deeply indented inlet with well-sheltered anchorage 6 miles S.W. of Dikili, is well worth a visit. Chart 1617.

Approach. Leave Guvercin Rocks well to starboard and head for C. Pisa (Lt. with white sector). Round the cape more than 300 yds off to avoid submerged mole. Enter the inlet, making towards N.E.

Anchor close S. of factory ruins in 3 fathoms, mud. Excellent holding on mud and sand.

Facilities. None; a hamlet at head of inlet. Good bathing beach N. of lighthouse.

If leaving southbound pass between Kalemdası and the mainland – now reported minimum depth 17 ft at N. entry where channel was reported closed. Channel between islands now closed by sandbar at N. approach, but one may anchor at S. entrance on sandy bottom 2 cables within.

One can land for a pleasant walk on the S.E. shores where the fields are well cultivated. To the N. are olive groves, and at the head of the inlet, frequented by

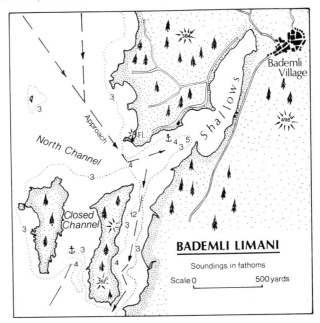

seabirds, one may land near a primitive taverna with a minor road leading to Dikili. A taxi can be hired in the village to drive to Pergamon.

The Gulf of Çandarlı has some interesting inlets and sometimes the diminishing ruins of Greek Ionian cities. The N. side's attraction is Çandarlı; unfortunately the south side of the gulf has been partly overtaken by industrial development. The winds in summer are nearly always westerly; an occasional N.E. wind may blow without warning, especially by night.

Çandarlı. Chart 1618. A peninsula of historic interest with suitable anchorage off a small attractive town dominated by a fine Venetian castle.

> **Approach.** The castle can be seen some miles off. Large yachts should make for the E. side of the peninsula, only small yachts for the west.
>
> **Berth.** On the E. side, open only to S.E. but beware of a rocky shoal close offshore 50 yds S. of the castle. On the W. side a small shallow harbour has been formed by building up the ancient mole once referred to by Strabo. Though shelter is good it is reported that a clear width of only 50 yds lies between the mole and a submerged rock, while the depth in the middle is only 8 ft.
>
> **Facilities** have recently been much improved with a number of shops, two restaurants, bars, taps and fountains of fresh water.

The present town, built largely of plundered material from ancient Pitani, has

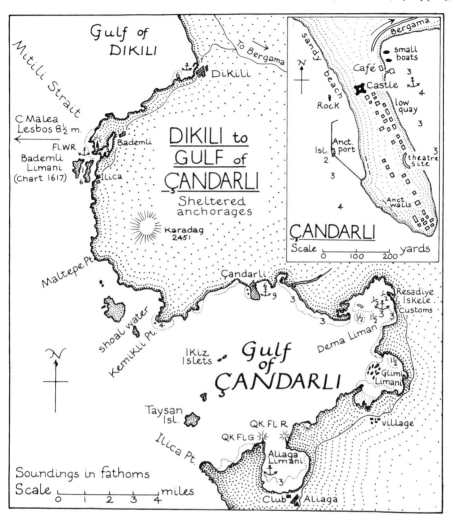

been restored and the old houses once again lived in, as well as the modern and not unpleasing ones recently built. The restored castle looks splendid.

History. The place continued to be of importance up to medieval times when the Venetians built the fine castle which is still in excellent preservation. At some later period the Turks modernized its defences, this being indicated by the presence of guns bearing the arms of George III.

About 5 miles east of Çandarlı is the site of Pergamon's seaport Elaea. Only a few mounds remain to show where city walls and the acropolis once stood: but the harbour mole consisting of large horizontal blocks running N. and S. can be seen, and show how well the port was protected.

On the southern shores of the gulf are some ruins of the ancient cities of Gryneum, Myrina, Aliaga and Cyme; but during recent centuries they have been greatly plundered to build new villages, and the original harbours have silted. An 'outer harbour' for berthing ships for the scrapyard has been proclaimed in the area between Tavsan Island and the capes of Tashburnu and Ilica.

Aliaga is a broad well-sheltered bay whose western shore has recently become a substantial oil refinery with a long T-headed pier for berthing large tankers. See plan, Chart 1618. The place no longer has any attraction for a yacht.

Close westward are two open bays: Nemrut (the ancient port of Cyme), and Horozgidiği. Close westward again are two bays partially sheltered against prevailing winds.

Yenice (Yeni Foça), a sheltered bay with a growing village lining the southern shore. A yacht may anchor 100 yds off the white building of the Club in 3 fathoms on a sandy bottom. A 50-yd mole extends from the E. shore and provides nearly 2-fathom depths to moor a few small boats. The bay is well sheltered from the prevailing wind. This former walled village was built by the Genoese in the 17th century for shipping alum then mined in the vicinity. When Captain Copeland made his survey in 1834 he shows on the chart that the village was then unaltered, but today the place has become a holiday resort with tourist development continuing along the western shore.

Çanak Limanı has anchorage at the head of the small inlet which is now deserted. Some ruined 'tower-houses' (Mani style) stand unoccupied close to the shore, but in 1981 military installations were being built.

'This noble and pleasant Island' STRABO

Island of Mitilini (Lesbos) (Greek)

This island (see plan, p. 114) is large and mountainous; now officially known as Lesbos. The eastern part of the island is green and wooded, but on the western side the land around the coast is poor and partially arid. With a population of 115,000 the island attracts many Greek visitors in the summer months, and is pleasant to visit in a yacht.

The countryside with its endless olive groves and some charming little villages is well worth a tour by car or bus; only in the south are there wheatfields.

In antiquity the island was made famous by Aesop who wrote many of his fables here, and by Sappho, who is believed to have been born at Eresos, a village on the S.W. coast; it was here she wrote her poems. In more modern times Mitilini was under the rule of Turkey for centuries, and reverted to Greece after the Balkan Wars in 1913, the populations being largely exchanged.

Port Mitilini, the capital, is a pleasant little town in a delightful setting of partially green mountains, with a port for caïques, fishing craft and the mail steamers from Piraeus.

Approach and Berth. Chart 1664. Enter the southern harbour and berth in the basin, stern to the broad quay at the yacht station.

Officials. A Port of Entry with Health, Immigration, Customs and Harbour Master.

125

Facilities. Water, fuel and ice; plenty of good shops for fresh provisions, and a palatable dry wine may be bought locally. There are some restaurants on the waterfront and two modest hotels. Clean hot baths and showers are to be had in a street leading off the Park. A museum. There are plenty of taxis. Mechanical repairs can be undertaken by Firestone. There is also an Esso station in the corner of the harbour. Ice from a factory S. end of the town. A daily steamer runs from Piraeus, and then sails for Khios; there is also a daily air service to Athens. A caïque runs to the Turkish port of Ayvalik.

In the town, apart from the Genoese castle and museum there is not much to see; but to offset this, a number of delightful drives may be taken into the country, passing through mountain forests and many olive groves from which the island derives much of its limited prosperity.

Port Kalloni on the south coast has an interesting mountainous entrance leading into a dull expanse of sheltered water.

Approach. Chart 1668. This is narrow, yet easy by day, for both good leading marks and buoys are now established. Certain lights are exhibited at night, but they should not be relied upon.

Anchorage. Apothiki Bay is well-sheltered from the Meltemi. The holding is good (mud) and the sea is cooled by fresh water from the river.

Facilities are non-existent. The few small cottages near the cove are partly deserted. Some fishermen are based here in summer.

Plomarion, lying between the two large gulfs, is a small port protected by two breakwaters.

Approach. Chart 1664. The entrance faces S.E. and the two moleheads are lit at night. There are 2–3 fathoms depth leading to the town-quay by the village square – and room for a medium-sized yacht to swing to her anchor; alternatively berth stern to the quay.

Facilities. Water at the quay. A few restaurants.

Mersinia Bay is an almost uninhabited cove; it lies 3 miles S.W. of the entrance to Port Yero.

Approach and Berth. Chart 1665. Proceed in direction of chapel, marked on chart, and anchor in 5 fathoms at the head of the bay. In the N.E. corner are the remains of an old pier of which the outer extremity (an 8-ft square standing in 9 ft of water) has ring bolts to which warp can be secured. The bottom is thin weed on sand. There is nothing here except a farmhouse with goats and a well of excellent drinking water.

Port Yero is more suitable for a fleet than for yachts. The approach and narrow entrance are attractive, and there are one or two coves here which afford convenient anchorage. The best one is

Scala Loutra, well sheltered, not attractive and now become very polluted.

> **Anchorage** is on the E. side off a taverna and shipyard in depths of 3–5 fathoms. Mud bottom.

> **Facilities.** Water, ice and basic provisions are obtainable. Bus service to Port Mitilini.

The adjoining cove to the S.W., quite deserted among olive groves and with fresh-water springs, is a very pleasant anchorage.

The harbour authority here is at Perama, a factory village on the W. side of the strait, with a ferry-service across.

The northern coast of Mitilini facing the Turkish hills 5 miles across the Muselim Strait is the most beautiful. Before reaching Cape Molivos a fine view of its castle suddenly appears through a gap and on rounding the cape is a small port:

Mithimna lies in an attractive setting with its very small harbour and village at the foot of a Genoese castle.

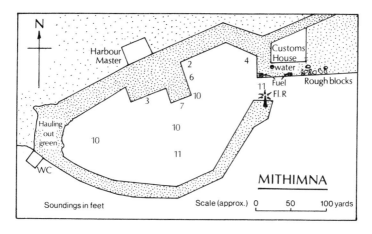

Berth and Anchorage. There are varying depths permitting a yacht up to 7 ft draught to enter the small and usually crowded port. Outside the harbour there is poor anchorage off the village almost under the shadow of the castle. Here the bottom is uneven and strewn with large rocks; it is open to the swell left by the afternoon breeze.

A good bathing beach extends round the bay with occasional protruding rocks. Hotel accommodation has now been provided.

A better alternative is to proceed $1\frac{1}{2}$ miles southward to the bay of

Kabaki (Petra). Here is a short mole extending in a southerly direction from the N. shore of the bay. In summer there is excellent shelter during normal conditions.

> **Berth** stern to the quay near its extremity, anchor laid to the eastward in $2\frac{1}{2}$ fathoms. Sand. (Ballasting at the quayside extends rather far underwater.) Clean for bathing. One or two pleasure boats are kept here.

> **Facilities.** The village, where basic provisions are obtainable, is 15 min walk. Octopus and ouzo are specialities. Mithimna's beach is 7 min by taxi.

The village of Petra is charming but being spoilt. One should see the Byzantine church with early frescoes and the old Turkish house. The place is very green with trees, flowers and running water.

Port Sigri, on the west coast, is a convenient place to shelter from the Meltemi and visit the petrified forest further S.

> **Approach and Berth.** Chart 1668 should be studied together with *Sailing Directions* giving a view of the approach which is sometimes difficult to find. The N. entrance is feasible by day when the sea can be seen breaking on the reefs.
>
> There is good protection from the N.E. wind and sea in the bay southward of Sigri village, when the old castle bears N.W. and the depth is 3 to 4 fathoms. The caïques also berth here, and in the event of northerly winds run a warp ahead to the rocks on shore, for the holding (thin weed on very hard sand) is poor. It appears that there is a hard layer of rock immediately under the sand, into which an anchor will not bite. There is better holding in the more remote N.E. corner of the bay, where the caïques often shelter in N.E. gales. A small quay has been built on the N.W. side of the promontory with depths of 5 or 6 m alongside. Untenable in northerlies because of the swell.

> **Officials.** Customs.

> **Facilities.** There is bus communication with Mitilini town every other day – 3 hrs.
>
> There are three restaurants (the best N.E. of anchorage) and provisions are obtainable.
>
> Water is piped to the village from a spring, and is good, but the few taps are rather far from the landing place.

6b
Gulf of Izmir to Körmen Adası

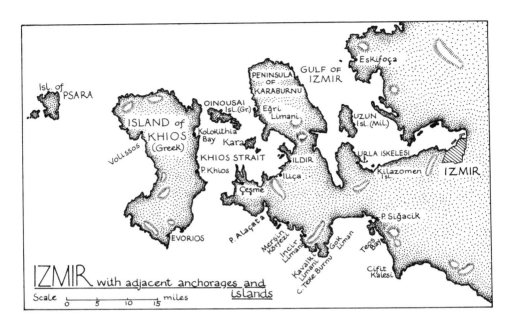

GREEK ISLANDS
Island of Khios
  Port Khios (*Port of Entry*)
  Kolokithia Bay
  Evorio
  Volissos

  Oinousai Islands (Spalmatori)
  Pasha Bay
  Mandraki
  Island of Psara

TURKISH COAST SOUTHWARD
  Eskifoça
  Uzun Island (Military)

  Izmir or Smyrna (*Port of Entry*)
  Urla Iskelesi

Urla Road Anchorage
Island of Kilazomen
Port Saip
Karaburnu Peninsula
Deniz Giren
Eğri Liman
Ildir Anchorage
Iliça (The Marina)
Çeşme (*Port of Entry*)
Eğriler (Ağriler) Limani
Mersin Körfezi
Incir Limanı
Kavalkı Limanı
Gök Liman
Siğacik
Teos Bay
Çifit Kalesi
Körmen Adasi

6b

Gulf of Izmir to Körmen Adası

GREEK ISLANDS

Leave battles to the Turkish hordes and shed the blood of Scio's* Vine.

BYRON

Island of Khios

This is relatively large and hilly with a bare mountain chain running along its spine. Formerly renowned for its shipping and exports of mastic, herbs and oranges, Khios' population, formerly declining, is now 54,000, but barely self-supporting. Early in the last century guidebooks described it as 'the most beautiful, most fertile, richest and most severely afflicted of the Aegean islands'. This has greatly changed and nowadays as one approaches along the east coast the island appears mountainous and barren; on landing it does not impress one either with its beauty or fertility, although inland there are some rich plains where agriculture still thrives. On the W. and N.W. coast the mountain slopes are still largely green with abandoned terraces where the vines were grown.

From the town one or two excursions are within easy reach by taxi; the most interesting is the drive over the hills to the Byzantine monastery of Nea Moni with its remarkable 12th-century mosaics. The 'School of Homer' with its rotund topped rock, and the poet's alleged birthplace 3 miles north of the town are of moderate interest; there is also the drive to Pyrghi with its medieval walls and some mastic groves nearby. The museum of Argenti, with its old maps and costumes, should not be missed.

Port Khios. A spacious sheltered port, with broad quays, and a busy town beside it. A Port of Entry.

> **Approach and Berth.** Chart 1568. The entrance is easy day or night. The yacht station is at the southern quay; a yacht should lay out anchor to N. and haul in the stern – 14 ft at the quay. Holding good, but slightly exposed to N. winds. Both quays have recently been extended.
> *Note.* Should the prevailing wind suddenly change and set in from a southerly direction, immediately a north-going current may be expected in the Khios Strait.

* The Venetian name of Khios in Byron's day.

Officials. Harbour authority, Customs, Police (Immigration), all by the quay.

Facilities. Water from a hydrant at the yacht station is hard, but good; fuel by hose. Ice at a store in S.W. corner of harbour. Provision shops in the street behind the waterfront. Many restaurants. The modern residential part of the town, Bona Vista, has grown up to the southward and is joined by a promenade; here are modern hotels, dining places, cabaret and tourist attractions. A shipyard on the N. side of the port is sometimes busy slipping and refitting local caïques. Mechanical repairs available.

The Piraeus steamer calls frequently on its circuit to Mitilini and Kavala and a car-ferry runs daily to Çeşme on the Turkish coast during the tourist season.

A heterogeneous trio slipped for repairs – Port Khios

Historical. During the past centuries the people of Khios aroused the admiration of a number of travellers largely on account of their marked ascendency over the inhabitants of other Aegean islands. In the 17th century it was recorded that after Constantinople and Smyrna, Khios was the most wealthy and civilized place in the Turkish Empire. Their women had the reputation of being exceptionally good-looking, and Lithgo, a Scot, writing at this period, records:

'The women of the Citty of Scio (its former spelling) are the most beautiful Dames or rather Angelicall creatures of all Greeks, upon the face of the earth, and greatly given to Venery. Their Husbands are their Pandors, and when they see any stranger arrive, they will presently demand of him if he would have a Mistresse: and so they make Whoores of their own wives. ... If a stranger be desirous to stay all night with any of them, their price is a chicken of Gold, nine shillings English, out of which their companion receiveth his supper, and for his pains a belly full of sinful content.'

At the beginning of the 19th century when the island was thriving on its valuable exports, many wealthy Greek families enjoyed the general high standard then prevailing. In the ill-fated year of 1822 the inhabitants were encouraged to revolt against their Turkish masters who, retaliating quickly, ruthlessly killed 25,000 people and carried off 45,000 inhabitants. The French artist Delacroix painted an imaginative picture of this gruesome event, which is now in the Louvre. Though this calamity wrecked the social structure of the island, vengeance soon came and the spirit of revolt revived when the Greek Admiral Canaris led a small naval squadron with two fireships into the harbour by night and destroyed two large Turkish warships, one with 2,000 men on board. General Gordon described this feat as 'one of the most extraordinary military exploits in history'. The statue to Constantine Canaris is in the park, and there are ships named after this modern Greek hero today. The most recent 'affliction' was a terrible earthquake in the 1880s when 5,000 inhabitants were killed.

Kolokithia Bay is also a sheltered anchorage, used by caïques, but has nothing much to commend it for a yacht.

Evorio, on the south side of the island, is a charming small cove lying between two hills and sheltered on three sides. A few cottages and a taverna have recently sprung up by the shore; ice comes every third day. Some vineyards and groves of mastic shrubs add to the attraction of this peaceful scene.

Approach and Anchorage. This small cove – 400 yds in depth – is unmarked on the chart, but it is easy to find. It lies close westward of Cape Kamari, which may be recognized, not by a 'monastery ruin' (shown on chart) but by a couple of modern stone huts. There are no lights. The bottom is of clear sand and runs out 300 yds to depths of 3 or 4 fathoms. There is a 2-fathoms depth about 100 yds off a small stone pier in the centre of the bay with barely room to swing – a warp ashore is recommended. The day breeze blows off the land. The cove is sheltered on the three sides and open only to S.E.

General. A British archaeological expedition dug some trenches here in 1955 and recovered certain Hellenic pottery now to be seen in the Khios museum. Skin-divers also made an exploration of the sea-bed.

Fishermen use the cove as a base during the summer months.

Volissos, a small cove, provides the only anchorage on the west coast of the island. The castle on the hill makes a clear distinguishing mark and *Sailing Directions* describes the approach. The very small boat harbour accommodates fishing craft and the ferry caïque for Psara; the village stands on the slope above.

The Growing of Mastic. For more than two thousand years there was great trade with the East in mastic. This is obtained by making incisions in the branches of these 6-ft shrubs and draining the sticky fluid into little cups – according to Pliny it is like 'Frankincense adulterated with resin'. That most highly praised was the white mastic of Khios which in later years had the entire monopoly for supplying the Turkish Empire and consequently brought much wealth to the Khians. The death-knell came when Turkish ladies ceased to chew mastic and other substances took its place in the paint market. Now the culture of these shrubs has declined and although it is still exported this, together with the recession in other industries, has brought some poverty to the island and induced considerable emigration to countries in the West.

The adjacent **Oinousai Islands** (Spalmatori) are barren and hilly. They project from the east coast of Khios and have some small bays on the southern shores where a yacht may lie for the night or ride in comfort during Meltemi.

Pasha Bay. Chart 1568. Here is a sandy bottom with good holding in 6 fathoms, and the adjacent coves are also claimed to be good for anchorage.

The only sign of habitation is a farmhouse, and some cultivation in the valleys where vines and figs are grown. The hilly slopes become dried up in summer but in the spring there is sufficient grass for grazing goats.

Mandraki. This is the only village in the group and has a thousand inhabitants, many of whom live here only part of the year. Two modern buildings, a naval school and a technical school, may be seen close to the shore.

> **Anchorage.** On the northern side of the cove is a landing pier with provision shops nearby. The anchorage off the pier is sheltered from prevailing winds, but the holding, being soft sand with boulders, is rather uncertain. A small yacht may berth at the jetty.
>
> The only officials here are Police.
>
> *Note.* A radio station has been set up upon the summit of a hill in position 38° 30 N., 26° 17.6 E. A white chapel already exists on a hilltop in position 38° 30.4 N., 26° 17.2 E. The cove S.S.W. of the chapel, a forbidden anchorage, but a yacht can anchor in the cove W.N.W. of it.

These islands form a splendid barrier and protect the Khios Strait from the lumpy sea caused by strong N.W. winds. As one runs southward the wind becomes more northerly.

Island of Psara, lying 10 miles west of Khios, is small and barren. The principal village is on the south side with a small, but recently extended harbour.

> **Approach.** Chart 1568, plan. The original mole extends northward from a point ½ mile N. of C. Trifilli. From the root of this mole a breakwater extending 130 yds eastward has recently been completed with a quay. There are 3-fathom depths near its extremity where a light Fl.R is mounted. Near here the Khios ferry berths.

> **Facilities.** Water is scarce. Provisions are basic. Communication by caïque to Volissos (Khios), bringing back passengers and ice. A simple restaurant.

The small village, built during the last century, houses most of the 600 inhabitants of the island whose young men nearly all go to sea in merchant ships. The villagers grow only enough produce for local needs and a few fishermen catch sufficient fish. Conspicuous among the small houses are the surviving walls of the fine 18th-century mansions of the great shipowners. These mark the prosperous period when 20,000 people lived here with an extensive maritime trade in the Mediterranean. The stump towers of several windmills standing on the high ground are also of this period when Russian corn was brought from the Black Sea and resold by Psariot merchants. When Sir Francis Darwin visited the island in 1810 he was impressed by the beauty of twenty-five ship models then hanging in St Antonia Church. This state of prosperity, however, came to an end early in the last century when Greek patriots rose in revolt against the Turks, and Psariot ships took a prominent part. Vengeance came swiftly when in 1824 a large Turkish expedition landed and completely destroyed the whole village and most of the people. It has never recovered; but Psara has not forgotten her great hero Admiral Canaris, the site of whose house is marked by an inscribed marble plinth.

TURKISH COAST

Approaching the Gulf of Smyrna (Izmir Körfegi) comes **Eskifoça** (**Foça** on Turkish chart), a thriving small town with a sheltered harbour at the head of a large bay.

Approach. Chart 1617 plan. *Sailing Directions* describe two wide bays, North and South, separated by a protruding cape and two islands. A yacht would normally wish to visit the southern bay with the village at its head.

A yacht should make for Büyükdeniz. No difficulty day or night.

Berth. Moor off the quay near harbour office. Alternatively, anchor close to the shore opposite near the Light in about 6 fathoms; here is excellent shelter from the day breeze. The seabed falls away rather steeply and a warp ashore may be necessary as the holding is uncertain. Küçükdeniz quay may also be used.

Officials. Harbour Master, Customs.

Facilities. Water and fuel close to Harbour Office. Fountains nearby with excellent pure water. Restaurants, cafés, provision shops, hospital, chemist, fibreglass boat-builder, mechanical repairs, hauling out slips and winter lay-up opposite harbour office. Good communication with Izmir.

The North Bay ('harbour' in *Sailing Directions*) is not recommended as an anchorage, the bottom being mostly weed on powdery sand and shelving too steeply to be reasonably sure of holding. Leading northwards over the shallow bank is an 8-ft passage frequented by small boats. A Club Méditerranée is situated on the shore north of the passage. If intent on anchoring here, the best place has been found to be in the N.E. corner in 2 fathoms.

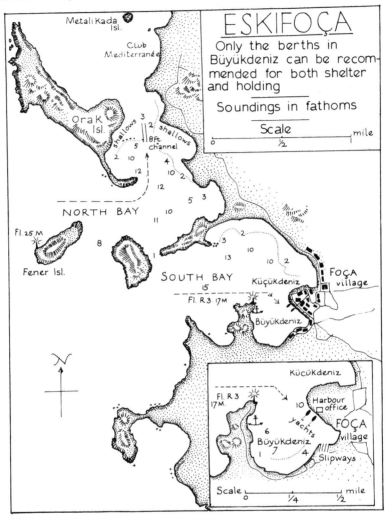

History. Eskifoça was the ancient Greek colony of Phocaea, being known for its navigators and the fast fifty-oared passenger vessels. With the Persian invasion they were driven from their country, some to become colonists in Italy, others fleeing to Corsica where they took to piracy. Eventually returning to Phocaea, they became busy traders and continued until modern times. Many were massacred at the end of the Balkan War and the colony destroyed nine years later when the inhabitants were driven out.

The remains of an ancient Mycenaean settlement, including those of a temple, were excavated here by Turkish archaeologists in 1953.

Uzun Island is a military area and yachts should keep well away from its shores.

IZMIR (SMYRNA)

Turkey's largest Aegean port, a city of 700,000 inhabitants, lies at the head of a large gulf. The objection to a visit by sailing yacht is that the return voyage beating against the daily Imbat or N.W. wind (similar to the Meltemi) can be tedious.

Many writers have described Smyrna as being among 'the more pleasant places on earth', and though one must concede certain advantages in its natural situation and climate – it was a city throughout historical times – few people today find the present town attractive. It has, however, many antiquities of interest, especially in the country around and for these a guide-book is essential.

During the last century the approach to the port was almost blocked by the alluvial deposit brought down by the Gediz Çay (Ancient Hermus) but in 1886 the river-bed was diverted to its present channel south of Eskifoça and thenceforth the navigable approach, though narrow, has been maintained. The new port on the north side of the town has relieved the hopeless congestion of the small port on the western side, which is now available for yachts.

Approach and Berth. Chart 1522. Yachts should make for the old port which the steamers no longer use. Berth stern to the quay, anchor laid out to the W.

Officials as for a Port of Entry. A British Consulate is established here under jurisdiction of Consul-General, Istanbul; NATO has a HQ in the city.

Facilities. Although away from the town centre, adequate supplies can be got quite near, and there are many hotels and restaurants. Before taking in water one should make careful inquiries about its purity.

History. From the time of Queen Elizabeth I until Queen Victoria came to the throne, Smyrna was of considerable commercial interest to Britain. The British Levant company maintained a high prestige in Turkey, and in London their position was so predominant that they used to nominate their own ambassador, consuls and the factors.

For many years a British naval guardship was stationed here, and a shore hospital maintained; the large Greek colony was a flourishing community and handled much of the Turkish commerce. When the 72-ton yacht *Gossamer*, R.Y.S., put in here in 1838 she found British, French and Austrian frigates in the port and the Royal Navy Hotel close at hand. At this time the population was only 90,000. After the defeat of Turkey in the First World War Smyrna suddenly became a focal point of world interest when the Greeks, encouraged by certain European statesmen, seized the opportunity to land a military force to invade Turkey. The Turkish army, however, unexpectedly rallied by Mustafa Kemal, soon routed the Greeks who, in September 1922, retreated in disorder and fell back on Smyrna. Here were scenes of terrible carnage when most of the Greek and American colonists had to abandon their homes and flee for their lives towards the harbour where already a number of allied warships and transports had been assembled. Meanwhile, to add to the confusion, the whole of the civilized quarters of the town, European, Greek and Armenian, had been set on fire and throngs of destitute men, women and children swarmed down to the quays hoping to board the waiting ships. H.M.S.

Iron Duke alone embarked 2,000 and during these few weeks an estimated quarter of a million refugees were rescued; among them was Aristotle Onassis and Sir Alexander Issigonis, Britain's outstanding automobile engineer. But there is little doubt that at least 100,000 perished.

The comparatively settled conditions today support a belief that the rich hinterland with an increasing agricultural produce and improved technique in mining valuable ores will ensure the port's prosperity. The modern centre of the town has been building up since the Great Fire of 1922 and in the last decade large buildings have been springing up everywhere.

Since the war a large modern Izmir called Karsicaka has been growing up on the northern shore of the gulf with frequent ferry services to the old port. At the head of the gulf there is much pollution, yet little shortage of fish.

Urla Iskelesi. A small fishing harbour on the corner of the Gulf used by a few Izmir yachtsmen, but of no interest to a visiting yacht.

> **Approach and Berth.** Chart 1617. The harbour, which is very small, is easy to find by day, for there is a large stumpy white tower on its extremity. (No harbour lights.) With nearly 3 fathoms in the entrance there is sufficient depth to berth stern to the outer extremity of the mole where shelter is all-round.

> **Facilities.** The village seems a poor little place and supports only a few fishermen. A bus runs to Izmir and ferry-steamers sometimes call.

When attempting to sail out of the Gulf northwards one may sometimes be confronted with a freshening N.W. day breeze which soon whips up a short steep sea. If wishing to find temporary shelter there are certain alternative choices:

(a) In **Urla Road** – depths of 3 to 4 fathoms.

(b) **Island of Kilazomen** (connected to the mainland by a causeway) was until recent years the quarantine station of Smyrna. In a wide bay on the east side of the island is good shelter and holding. By the shore are the extensive wings of a hospital; one need not be alarmed at the sight of the inmates for they are no longer detainees for quarantine, but patients with diseases of the bone.

In ancient times, when still an island, it was known as Clazomenae; but after the Persian invasion the causeway was built. Attributed to Alexander, it was referred to both by Pliny and Pausanius. Of the original port on the west side, only a few blocks of masonry are now to be seen on the N.W. corner – possibly the remains of a quay; there is also a short stretch of the ancient city wall. The shallow landing on the western shore now used by hospital boats is of modern construction. The island is sometimes referred to by the Turks as Klazumen.

On the N.W. corner of the gulf is the anchorage of

Port Saip formed under the shelter of the tall islands off the N.E. corner of the massive Karaburnu peninsula. The village of Saip can be seen above on the hillside. Though sheltered the anchorage suffers from strong gusts of wind off the mountainous surroundings.

The Karaburnu peninsula is tall and steep-to, but its northern slopes as far as the lighthouse are interesting to look at, being extensively farmed and growing vines on the terraced hillsides. About 6 miles southward of the lighthouse is

Deniz Giren, a cove mentioned in *Sailing Directions*, with a few small houses and fishing boats. This place has silted up and one can see the reeds growing where the anchorage used to be. The rocks extending underwater westward and S.W. from the promontory should be given a wide berth (half a mile off the headland), for in fresh westerly winds the seas break over them.

Eğri Liman. Plan on Chart 1617. This is a deserted inlet with excellent shelter and a good place to bring up for the night.

    Approach and Anchorage. A white cairn stands on the tip of the tall headland and helps one to avoid the $2\frac{1}{2}$-fathom patch about 250 yds to N.N.W. One can enter even in strong N.W. winds, and no swell penetrates inside. Anchor off a ruined house in 6 fathoms; plenty of room to swing for one medium size yacht. A white cairn also marks this low sandy point. Bottom is mud. With W. to N.W. winds, the breeze is N. The sides of this islet are very steep-to.

There is nothing here except a little cultivation on the E. bank; an occasional sponge-boat may put in.

On entering the Gulf of Ildir a yacht has the choice of making either for the deserted anchorage off the hamlet of Ildir, or proceeding to the S.W. corner of the gulf and berthing in the very modern marina in Ilica Bay.

Ildir Anchorage lies between the long Karabağ Island and Ildir village on the mainland, in deserted surroundings.

    The Anchorage (Chart 1645) is in 4 fathoms, sandy bottom with a light layer of weed. Excellent shelter. One must row in the dinghy some distance to land near the village.

Close southward of the anchorage one can see the village from which the Greeks were evicted after the First World War. Also to be discerned, with some difficulty, are the ruins of ancient Erythrae: city walls, theatre and acropolis, all much plundered by peasants for modern walls and small buildings during the last century.

    History. Erythrae, one of twelve Ionian cities, was surrounded by 3 miles of walls much of

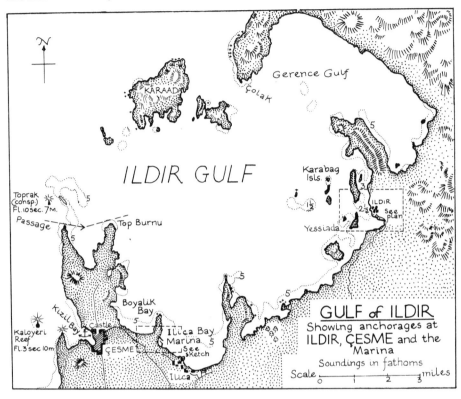

Gerence Gulf

ÇolaK

KARAAD

ILDIR GULF

Karabag
Isls.

ILDIR
see
plan

Yessiada

Toprak
(consp.)
Fl.10sec.7M.

Passage

Top Burnu

Boyalik
Bay

Kızıl Bay

Kaloyeri
Reef
Fl.3sec 10m

Castle

Ilıca Bay
Marina

ÇESME

See
sketch

Ilıca

GULF of ILDIR
Showing anchorages at
ILDIR, ÇESME and the
Marina
Soundings in fathoms
Scale 0   1   2   3 miles

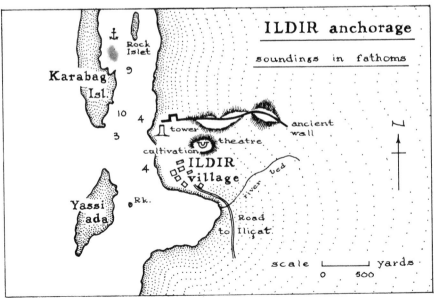

ILDIR anchorage

soundings in fathoms

Rock
Islet

Karabag
Isl.

tower

ancient
wall

theatre

cultivation

ILDIR
village

river bed

Yassi
ada

Rk.

Road
to Ilıçat

scale 0   500 yards

which can still be followed. In the 5th century B.C. it was a wealthy commercial city and as a member of the Delian League preferred to contribute ships rather than money. She had her prophetic Sibyl, but she was less favoured than her rival at Cumae in Italy.

The Marina (Golden Dolphin) (see plan p. 140) has a capacity for mooring 120 yachts and provides all-round shelter. On the shoreward side is a large modern hotel complex with shops, provision stores and cafés.

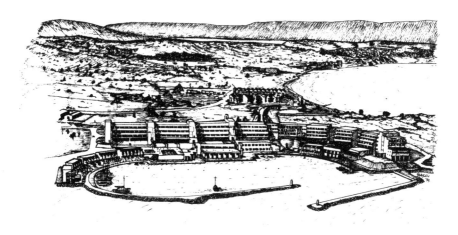

Approach. The curved breakwaters can be easily discerned and the extremities are lit. A yacht, on arrival, should secure to a buoy off the entrance to await instructions from the Harbour Master's launch.

Berth. Depths vary between 3 fathoms and less than one. Berths are allocated by the Harbour Master. Bow moorings are provided; anchoring is not permitted except in emergency and with official permission.

Officials. Harbour Master who can arrange formalities with Police, Customs, etc.

Facilities. Electricity, water, fuel, telephone. Showers are available. Arrangements can be made for slipping and limited repairs. Charges are made according to length, duration of stay, etc. The address is Golden Dolphin Marina, Çeşme; tel. 31 537 or 41 720.

This new marina lies midway between Izmir and Kuşadasi, some 65 miles southward. For those preferring an anchorage, Çeşme on the seaward side of the isthmus should be used instead.

When making for Çeşme, it is necessary to round Cape Üç Burunlar; on a clear day a yacht can pass safely inside the off-lying shoals. The islet of Topak is most conspicuous.

Çeşme is a bay, open to the west, with a small town overlooked by a Genoese

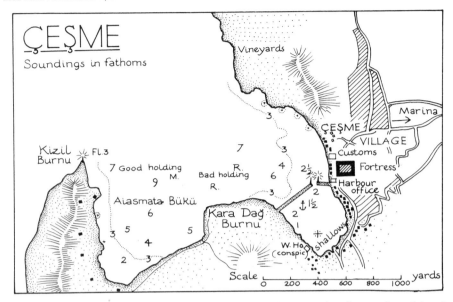

castle. Apart from Izmir this is the best place on this stretch of coast for taking in supplies.

Approach. Chart 1617 plan. The small harbour with pier and breakwater lies to the southward of the castle all of which can easily be distinguished. The entrance is narrow.

Anchorage is behind the long rough breakwater in 2 fathoms, splendid shelter in settled weather.

Berth stern to new yacht quay, outer harbour.

Facilities. A wide range of fresh provisions, including fish; the fruit and vegetables are remarkably good. Ice at the factory on the waterfront near the Customs. Water laid on, fuel at the pier subject to delay. Several good restaurants. A fast road leads to Izmir – bus and minibus service $1\frac{1}{4}$ hrs. Regular ferry to Port Khios during the tourist season.

History. The fine castle with two rings of walls and gun towers was originally built by the Genoese in the 15th century, and subsequently seized by the Turks. It protected the Roads where in the summer of 1770 the Turkish fleet had come to anchor. On 5 July they were attacked by three Russian squadrons and almost entirely annihilated. The Russians after refitting in England had sailed out from the Baltic to operate independently in the Mediterranean, and after seeking the Turks elsewhere in Aegean waters eventually found them here. The Russian victory was complete, and not without interest to the British, for on board the Russian ships were Admirals Elphinstone and Greig, while of the three fireships which caused such havoc, two of them had British captains. This was the period of Russian naval expansion when Catherine the Great had obtained British support to train and equip her navy with a view to its crushing Turkish sea power and thus enabling the Russian Black Sea fleet to break though the stranglehold of the Dardanelles and operate in the Mediterranean. At the time of writing, some two hundred years later, the Soviet Navy has recently started to operate Soviet warships in the eastern Mediterranean but this time without the assistance of a foreign power.

FROM ÇEŞME TO KÖRMEN ADASI

On leaving Çeşme a yacht proceeding southwards will round Ak Burun, and before reaching Teke Burnu (20 miles S.E.) must pass half a dozen inlets under the hills of the deserted Anatolian coast. Chart 1645 shows the choice of anchorages, but it may be noted that only two places have all-round protection, of which Incir Limanı is the best. For the first three ports plans are published on Chart 1568.

Except for Alaçata Limanı all are uninhabited and without cultivation; the hilly slopes are mostly covered with scrub.

Alaçata Limanı with a hamlet (often called Ağrıler) at its head is too large and uninteresting to attract a yacht. A plan is shown on Chart 1617.

Mersin Körfezi is a completely deserted bay with shelter from S. formed by the island at the entrance. Here the above-water rocks are conspicuous and a yacht can pass on either side.

> **Anchorage.** Best shelter is in N.E. cove; anchor in depths of 3 to 4 fathoms on a sandy bottom with plenty of room to swing.

> **Facilities.** See *Sailing Directions*. There are no fresh provisions; nothing to be had.

An unnamed cove midway between Mersin and Incir has a conspicuous beach at its head with summer camp equipment set up.

Incir Limanı provides excellent all-round shelter in South Cove for any size of yacht. Anchor in 4 or 5 fathoms on firm sand. Completely deserted.

Kavalkı Limanı, a long steep-to fjord without habitation, provides good anchorage at its head in 4-fathom depths, bottom of sand. Partial shelter from southward is provided by a small projecting point on the west side of the fjord. After rounding Cape Teke Burnu you enter the Gulf of Siğacik with the sheltered anchorage and village of Siğacik in the N.E. corner. One should put in en route at

Gök Liman, a charming well-sheltered inlet with anchorage in N. cove with room for a small or medium yacht to swing; and towards the head of the cove (silted) with warps ashore, there is room for a large yacht.

Siğacik is a small village within an old fortress. A small harbour has been formed by building a breakwater from the eastern shore to protect small craft.

Approach. Make for the end of the breakwater extending W.S.W. and berth stern to near to extremity in depths of 10–12 ft.

Facilities. A tap with plentiful pure water, two restaurants. Minibus or taxi to Izmir (1½ hrs).

One must land to see the ruins of ancient Teos; they lie in the middle of the isthmus, a mile from the landing place by the castle. This town of about the 3rd century B.C. originally extended from there to Teos Bay where the harbour quay can still be seen. Of the town itself the theatre, temple of Dionysos, the odeon and some paved streets are worth visiting. At Siğacik, the ancient mole can be followed underwater from the corner of the castle in a N.W. direction; near it is a curiously shaped block of stone of the same period, evidently lost during shipment; there are several others within this area, but the reason for cutting large blocks in a sort of cubist style is mystifying.

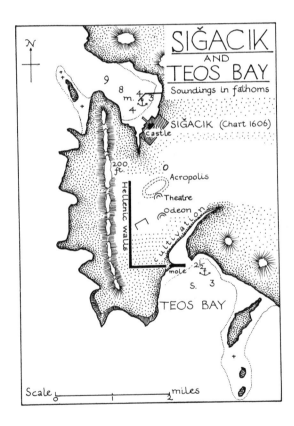

Teos Bay, lying on the S. side of the isthmus, is a better place to lie than Siğacik during strong N. winds.

Anchorage. Let go in 2½ fathoms about 150 yds east of the ancient mole. Bottom is sand and holding good. (S.W. of mole the holding is poor.) Land in the dinghy close to the wall of the ancient quay.

To visit the ruins it is best to make across the fields to the theatre, for from the top you get a fine view round the whole of the green isthmus with its many cultivated fields and a great variety of trees. The theatre itself is somewhat disappointing, for although the stage has been excavated and restored, the stonework from the cavea has completely vanished. Running down the coast for 8 miles one reaches a tall steep-to rocky islet joined to the coast by a partly submerged causeway. This is

Çifit Kalesi, 'Mouse Island', or ancient Myonnesus. In calm weather one can anchor off the causeway, but with fresh N. winds alarming gusts shoot down from this perpendicular wall of rock. On its northern face can be seen a number of ruins one of which is a remarkable section of Cyclopean wall. Passing on the west side is a great cleft which almost splits the rock in two. It seemed extraordinary that such a small islet could have attracted the attention of ancient writers; but Livy records an incident when a Roman galley fleet was chasing some pirates who had escaped and were defending themselves on the islet. The Roman galleys, while sheltering under the perpendicular cliffs, were so afraid of the prospect of lumps of rock being dropped on them from above that they abandoned their quest and set off for Teos instead.

Another mile southward is the islet **Körmen Adası** which helps to form a small sheltered inlet; but here again a yacht might need shelter from the N. wind, violent gusts make the anchorage untenable.

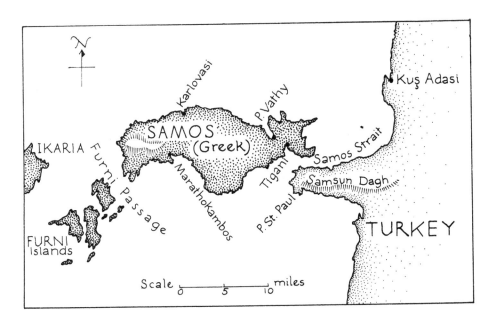

TURKISH COAST	GREEK ISLANDS

TURKISH COAST

Kuş Adası (*Port of Entry*) for Ephesus
The Marina
Sisan Bogaza (Samos Strait)
with Port St Paul

GREEK ISLANDS

Island of Samos
Karlovasi
Port Vathy or Port Samos
Pithagorion or Tigani
(*Port of Entry*)
Marathokambos

Island of Ikaria
Evdilos
Armenistos
Ayios Kirikos
Furni Islands

15 Izmir: the old port, still suitable for yachts

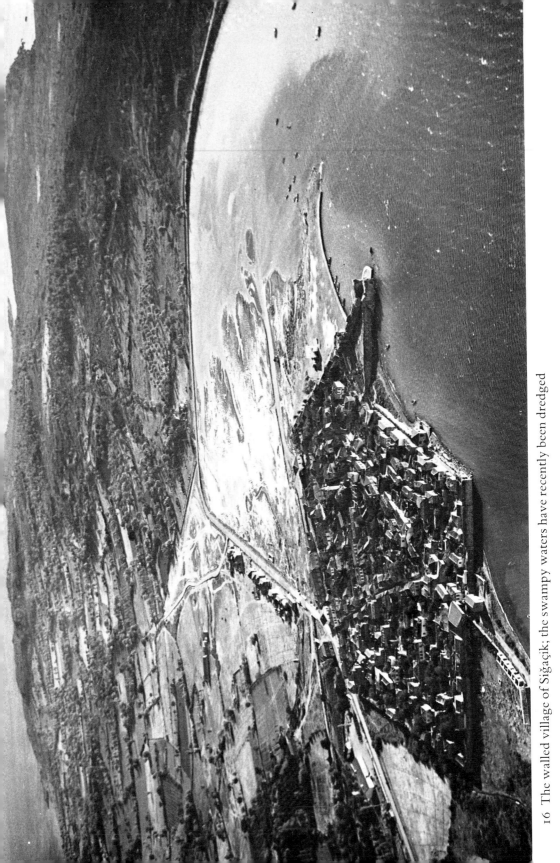

16 The walled village of Siğaçik; the swampy waters have recently been dredged

6c

Kuş Adası to Samos Strait

(with off-lying Greek islands)

TURKISH COAST TO PORT ST PAUL

Following the Turkish coast southward the first important place is

Kuş Adası. It is the most convenient port from which to visit Ephesus.

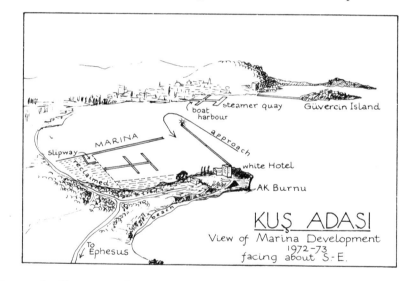

Approach. Chart 1546. If coming from the direction of Samos both Petroma Reef and Karakaci Bank should be carefully avoided.

The former island of Güvercin has been joined to the mainland by a causeway which also provides some shelter. The island with its fort was once a stronghold of Barbarossa and his corsairs, but has now become a nightclub.

Berth.
(a) The old harbour, on the S.E. side of the bay, provides berthing for tourist steamers and local craft. A yacht of modest draft can still berth stern to the stone pier inside the steamer quay.
(b) The large marina on the N.W. side of the bay. Pick up bow mooring as directed. Hauling out facilities by 60-ton Travel-Lift.

Officials. Customs, Harbour Authority and Immigration.

Facilities. Water and fuel, electricity. Provisions, restaurants, hotels in the town about a mile distant. Excursions by bus or taxi to Ephesus, Priene, Miletus and Didyma, mostly available in the square by the old harbour. Market day Friday.

Kuş Adası is a fast-growing tourist town. Many are employed in the olive oil industry and in agriculture, and an increasing number in the tourist trade. Much has been spent on modernizing the town which now has an occidental Riviera look. Even the old caravanserai has been restored and converted into a Club Mediterranée Hotel.

EPHESUS: the ruins of the greatest Roman city in Asia (with its former 250,000 inhabitants) can be reached by bus or taxi in half an hour.

The road follows the old course of the Cayster River, along which St Paul was rowed when visiting Ephesus nineteen centuries ago. Now completely silted, part of it has become meadows where the camels graze; but outside Ephesus where the old harbour has become a marsh the quays can still be traced. From here a broad street, perfectly preserved and paved with marble, leads up to the city and the large theatre, estimated to hold an audience of 25,000.

Historical. It is easy to re-create here the historic occasion of the demonstration by the silversmiths after St Paul had been preaching here for some months. Summoned by their leader, Demetrius, they met together to protest against the ruin of their souvenir trade in selling small silver goddesses to the Roman tourists. They became infuriated against St Paul and a riot ensued. Rushing into the amphitheatre they shouted 'Great is Diana of the Ephesians'. (*Acts of the Apostles* 19.)

Even in Greek and Roman days this 'largest emporium of Asia Minor' had its difficulties in keeping the river navigable for its essential sea-borne trade. Strabo writes: 'The mouth of the harbour was made narrow by the engineers, but they, along with the king who ordered it, were deceived as to the result – for he thought the entrance would be deep enough for large vessels ... if a mole were thrown up at the mouth which was very wide. But the result was the opposite, for the silt thus hemmed in made the whole harbour as far as the mouth more shallow. Before this time the ebb and flow of the tide would carry away the silt and draw it to the sea outside.'

But whatever steps were taken by man to keep open the ancient Greek ports on the west Anatolian coast, subsequent silting throughout the centuries has proved that the forces of nature predominate. Other examples of these city ports may be seen at Priene and Miletus, both of which are well worth visiting from Kuş Adası. (See p. 168.)

Following the Turkish coast southwards towards the 4,000-ft Çan Dağı mountains one is soon in the Samos Strait; the large and equally mountainous Greek island of Samos lies close to the west.

On the Turkish coast there is no anchorage other than a very small deserted sandy bay at the southern entrance to the strait. Only recently our hydrographer has discarded its traditional name – St Paul; but close under the lee of Nero Islet a

Turkish Customs launch may often be seen lying in perfect shelter from the Meltemi in this little bay. (39° 39.2N., 27° 0.5E.)

History of Port St Paul. After the battle of Salamis, some of Xerxes' galley crews which had escaped from the action were resting ashore in this cove and at an adjacent inlet when they were attacked and mostly destroyed by some of the Spartan ships.

The origin of the name is obscure, but by tradition St Paul on one of his voyages down the Anatolian coast put in here for a night's shelter to rest the oarsmen.

GREEK ISLANDS

Thus all their forces being joined together, they hoisted sail towards the Isle of Samos and there gave themselves to feasts and solace.

PLUTARCH, writing of Antony and Cleopatra

Island of Samos (Sisam)

This large, wooded and mountainous island, separated by barely a mile from the Turkish mainland, is one of the most attractive in the Aegean. Since the days of Polycrates it has been famous for its forests and vineyards. Today there are 42,000 inhabitants in Samos distributed among a number of hill villages as well as at the three major ports.

Samos produces a dry white wine most of which is now exported to Germany, France, Holland and other European countries; it can however still be bought locally, but is more difficult to obtain than the less palatable sweet wine. The best pinewood for caïque construction is grown here and there are still three or four small building yards but their activities are declining. Tobacco is grown and processed for export, and an unusual species of sweet olive is also shipped to America. Notwithstanding these assets the trade of the island is barely holding its own. The pottery for which Samos was famous in Hellenic days is no longer produced. It should not be confused with the dull-red 'Samian Ware' sometimes dug up by archaeologists on Roman sites in England. This pottery, though it took the name from Samos, was imported into England by Roman merchants in the 1st century A.D. and was actually made in France. Samos was the centre of Ionian culture. At that time her science, arts and crafts were of world repute. As well as providing a temporary home for Antony and Cleopatra, Samos became the winter residence of the Emperor Augustus. After the Middle Ages the island fell under the suzerainty of Genoa and Venice but when conquered by Turkey she avoided the destruction suffered by other islands in the last century by becoming more or less an independent principality. Ruled by the wealthy land-owners who elected themselves princes, the island prospered; her commerce and agriculture flourished. Not until after the second Balkan War in 1913 did Samos become part of Greece.

On the north coast of the island is the rather dull port of

Karlovasi which has been repaired and dredged.

Approach and Berth. Chart 1568, plan. There is no difficulty day or night. Berth near the Customs House but clear of the steamer quay which is in daily use. Holding is poor, but the port is well protected by its long breakwater against the prevailing N. winds.

Facilities. Water by tap close to Harbour Office. Restaurant on the waterfront. A few shops for basic provisions. Bus service to Vathy. Three caïque building yards, repair shop and a floating crane. Piraeus steamer daily in summer.

The small village with a church on a pinnacle rock makes a pleasant walk from the port, and the mountainous country behind is impressive; the oldest church on the island lies in the next bay to the westward. Otherwise there seems little inducement for a yacht to call here. Today, even the old tanneries are derelict.

The mountainous coast from Karlovasi eastwards towards Port Vathy is one of the most beautiful in the Aegean. Terraced slopes with carefully tended vineyards alternate with pine forests on the mountainsides, while here and there are villages of red-roofed houses tucked into the green valleys above.

Port Vathy (Port Samos), the capital of the island, lies at the head of a wide inlet bordered by wooded hills. Protected by a short mole where the steamers berth the port is subject to a disturbing swell in Meltemi conditions. This is a Port of Entry, but it is not a safe place to leave a yacht unattended.

Approach and Anchorage. An above-water rock not shown on the chart extends for about 100 yds N.N.W. of Cape Kotsikas whose light structure cannot easily be discerned. The mole light is Lt.Fl. (R). A yacht can anchor about 100 yds E. of the mole and run out a mooring ring on the waterfront (5-ft depths). Alternatively berth stern to the steamer quay close to the root of the mole (10 ft); but in this berth a yacht can be endangered by the screw wash when the Piraeus steamers are berthing. In 1981 the whole waterfront on N.E. side was built-up.

Officials. Harbour Office near the mole. British Pro-Consul on seafront. A Port of Entry.

Facilities. Water is sometimes in short supply. Ice can be delivered daily. Provision shops at the town centre; dry Samos wine can be bought close to the mole. A few tavernas, and hotels. The archaeological museum in the town is worth visiting, also the Byzantine museum in the Mitropolitis and the portrait gallery above the Post Office. Daily air service (weather permitting) to Athens, and in summer also a daily steamer (16 hrs.). A ferry service operates to Kuş Adasi during the tourist season.

The town is attractive and the views across the mountains are beautiful. Mountain excursions can be made by car and bus; a pleasant half-hour's drive is to the monastery of Zoodochos Pigi, or further afield to the more interesting Brontiani above the village of Vourliotes.

Pithagorion (Tigani) is a well-sheltered little port of great antiquity beside a pleasant small village lining the waterfront.

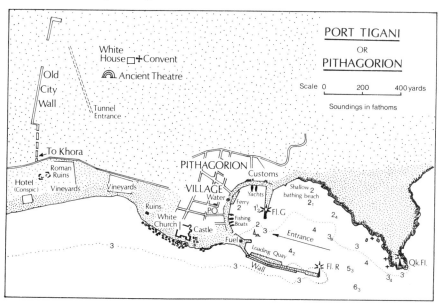

Approach and Berth. Chart 1568, plan. When passing through the Samos Strait there is the probability of a 3-knot W-going current with tide-rip, and during Meltemi conditions very strong gusts will be experienced from the high land of Samos. It is sometimes wise to lower the mainsail. The outer harbour is easy to approach day or night, the breakwater extremity being marked by a Lt.Fl. (R). The inner harbour which is frequently dredged has an average depth of about 14 ft – off the quays about 10 ft. Care must be taken to keep in the centre of the entrance channel, i.e., pass midway between a white port-hand beacon and the extremity of the mole. A yacht may berth comfortably off the Customs House where there are several mooring rings, and a water hydrant is within reach. Although a few gusts of wind may be experienced in the port, they are relatively mild compared with those outside. In winter the southerly gales occasionally surmount the breakwater, but recently this has been strengthened and in 1981 heightened for half its length.

Officials. As necessary for a Port of Entry.

Facilities. Fresh-water taps and two hydrants on the quay but water often uncertain. Ice at corner of quay by main street. Provisions by the quay. Several hotels, tavernas on quayside shaded by eucalyptus and mulberries. Air service daily to Athens; car-ferry to Kusadasi. Bus service to Samos town.

In 1945 the Greek Government decided to rename Tigani (which it had been called for some decades) Pythagorion (spelt Pithagorion on the chart) in honour of the great mathematician's birthplace; but it is even more famous for the 'great works' of Polycrates, still to be seen today. At the time of Herodotus it was considered to be one of the most important cities in the world. In the port itself, the inner harbour is much as Polycrates built it, and on the hill above can be seen his walls, about 14 ft thick, which encompassed the old capital. A number of drums of columns and some capitals from the buildings of the old city have been plundered from the ruins and brought to the port for use as bollards. The famous water-tunnel, now 2,500 years old, is interesting to explore and in 1981 was cleared for its whole length of 3,600 ft. (The drop at the Pithagorion end is 26 ft.) Electric lighting now installed the whole way.

The village has much charm, and in the coolness of a summer evening it is pleasant to be on the waterfront enjoying an evening meal under the mulberry trees.

New roads have been under construction over most of the island including one to the mouth of the tunnel.

There is rich farming country in the broad valleys on either side of Pithagorion, vines, tobacco and corn being grown extensively. An interesting drive leads along the coast to the temple of Hera, and another excursion takes one to the mountain hamlet of Koutsi where a small hotel has been built beside the mountain stream.

Marathokambos is yet a fourth harbour lying on the south-west coast, but it is very little used partly on account of storm damage, and because of the violent squalls off the high mountains which, during the summer months, strike across Marathokambos Bay. The principal shipyard of the island is here.

Island of Ikaria

A long, tall and largely barren island lying only 5 miles west of Samos. Its main village of Ayios Kirikos has hotels and bathing beaches, and also radioactive springs which in summer entice many sufferers from rheumatism from the Greek mainland.

On the north side of the island are two small places where during the summer months the Meltemi frequently causes disturbed conditions.

Evdilos with a small hamlet and port formed by a mole (projecting northwards and then E. for 160 yds) at the head of the bay. The mail steamer calls when the Meltemi permits.

Armenistos is similar but without breakwater protection.

Ayios Kirikos on the S.E. side of the island is a summer resort with a new but poorly sheltered harbour. The breakwater protrudes eastwards; it has a quay off which the mail steamer berths. Despite a recent extension to the breakwater, shelter is unsatisfactory and few yachts call.

> **Approach.** A large blue-domed church in the village is a good landmark. The recent extension of the breakwater is marked on its underwater extremity by a buoy. (Fl.R.)
>
> *Note.* The mail steamer when berthing at the mole uses a wire hawser which completely blocks the port entrance.
>
> **Anchorage.** Let go close to the local craft in 4–5 fathoms with the church bearing W.N.W., poor holding on boulders and weed. Open from N.E. to S.E.
>
> **Officials.** Harbour Master.
>
> **Facilities.** Provisions, hotels, ice at fish shop, Post Office.

The island derived its name from the legend of Icarus, son of Daedalus, who, having incurred the displeasure of Minos, made wings of feathers and wax for himself and his son so as to escape from Crete. But, rising too high, the sun melted the wax of Icarus's wings and he fell into the sea near this island.

Furni Islands

Lying between Samos and Patmos these islands are barren, rocky and indented with several coves. Together with Ikaria they are administered by Samos. Their few inhabitants live on the main island close to the narrow strait, which is shown on Chart 1568 (plan) together with details of some deserted sandy bays – ideal places for anyone wanting complete isolation.

A small cove close N. of Marmara is said to be the most sheltered anchorage.

> **History.** The Furni Islands were formerly a lair for pirates, one of whose captives, an Englishman named Roberts, writing after his escape in 1692 states: 'They go to Furnes and lie there under the high land hid, having a watch on the hill with a little flag, whereby they make a signal if they see any sail; they slip out and lie athwart the Boak of Samos, and take their prize.'

Today one may walk up this hill and enjoy the same view across the strait towards Samos.

6d

Northern Dodecanese

and Gulf of Güllük (Mandalya)

Kovela (Ancient Gulf of Latmos)

GULF OF GÜLLÜK (MANDALYA)
  Kukurcuk
  Skropes Bay (Altınkum) for Didyma
  Kuru Erik Limanı
  Akbük Limanı
  Kazikili Limanı
  Saltaluthea
  Asim Körfezi
  Asim Liman, Port Isene (Anct. Iassus)
  Güllük (*Port of Entry*)

Sheiro Bay
Varvil Koyu (Anct. Bargylia)
Salih Adasi
Kuyucak Harbour
Güvercinlik
Ilica Bükü
Türk Bükü
Büyük Farilya Bükü
Gümüsslük (Myndus)
Karabakla Islands with Yassi Islet

(*For Bodrum see* 6(e))

6d

Northern Dodecanese and Gulf of Güllük (Mandalya)

Greek Islands : Introduction

The Dodecanese, which lie so near to the Turkish gulfs, are described simultaneously with the Turkish coast of similar latitude in Chapters 6d and 6e.

The 'Twelve Islands' with their mountainous formation, rugged grandeur and indented coastline, make an attractive sailing area for a yacht. Also called the Southern Sporades, these islands appeared to the early Greeks as 'lean wolves'. So close are they to Anatolia that their extremities sometimes jut into the Turkish gulfs.

After being under Turkish rule for many centuries, these islands were ceded to Italy after the First World War and handed back to Greece after the Second. Kos and Rhodes still reflect the recent influence of Italian occupation, the other islands are sparsely populated but offer some delightful, solitary anchorages, each different from the other in size, shape and character.

The Dodecanese are under the central administration of Rhodes (described in Chapter 7) and have separate Customs regulations from the rest of Greece, whereby many foreign imports are allowed to enter either free or with very little tax.

The Turkish coast opposite these Greek islands has some attractive deserted inlets. The summer winds being suitable, it is recommended to cross over between respective Ports of Entry and then return to Greek waters to top up with water, fuel and provisions. One must bear in mind, however, that although they are more cordial towards a visiting yacht, Turkish officials are usually very bureaucratic and exacting with their lengthy procedure which may mean wasting the best part of a day before obtaining clearance. Some yachts prefer to pay the local agent to overcome the difficulties and thus save much time and irritation.

THE DODECANESE
with adjacent
Turkish Coast

PORTS OF ENTRY

Greece	Turkey
KOS	GÜLLÜK
RHODES	BODRUM
(Mandraki)	MARMARIS

NORTHERN DODECANESE

Close southward of the Furni Islands lies

Island of Patmos

Nearing this island from the eastward a vessel passes some rather forbidding rocky spurs, and enters the large sheltered bay; thence a long inlet leads to the Scala, the little port buildings, in modern Italian style, to be seen in the distance.

On the hill behind lies the principal village, Chora, dominated by what appears to be a medieval stronghold. It is, in fact, the Monastery of St John the Divine.

The Harbour

Approach. Chart 1669, plan. Sailing into the inlet one should make for the modern ex-Italian buildings on the waterfront.

Berth. Extensive harbour improvements now provide 750 ft of quay space for cruise ships. Yachts have been allocated a quay close northward. See plan. Lt.Fl. (R) S. of jetty.

The former anchorage at the head of the bay has now been fouled by sewage discharge.

General. The island is beginning to be spoilt by tourism; the islanders remain most friendly.

Facilities. Water (sometimes ferried in drums) and fuel are available at the quay N. end of bay where it is also convenient for shopping. Ice can no longer be obtained. A good hotel with baths is near and some modern restaurants, also a Post Office.

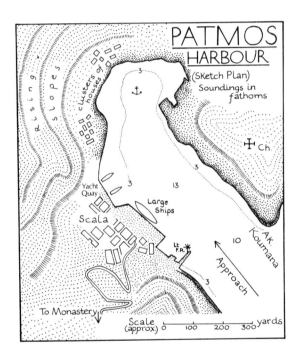

On account of the monastery and the island's biblical associations, many tourist ships enter the anchorage, berthing at the quay for a few hours' stay.

Close to the Customs House, a bus or taxi is available to climb the new, well-graded road that spirals up the hill. Half-way is a small shrine built around a grotto, where St John is said to have written the Revelations after having been condemned by the Emperor Domitian in A.D. 96 for preaching the Gospel.

Crowning the hill immediately above the small village is the fortress-like monastery built in the 11th century – a complicated structure with chapels, treasure room, museum and library beneath asymmetrical roofs and 'bellcotes' at different levels. At one time it was full of treasure, some of which, during the last century, found its way to London, Leningrad and Vienna; the most valued asset remaining today is the thirty-three leaves of St Mark's Gospel, written in the 5th century on purple vellum, called the Codex Porphyrius, but there are many other treasures.

The superb view from the roof of the monastery must not be missed. Looking towards the Anatolian coast the massive mountains of Asia can be seen in the far distance behind the outlying islands of the Dodecanese. An easy walk through the village and then downhill soon brings one back to the harbour. There is nothing remarkable about the village, but when the French traveller Tournefort came here two hundred years ago he expressed surprise at finding twenty women to every man.

Anchorages outside the port. Chart 1669. Unless one wants to stay in port close to the shore amenities it is more pleasant for a yacht to come outside the harbour and anchor at one of the following coves on the N.W. shore of the large Patmos Bay:

Meloyi Bay, the nearest to the harbour has room for two or three yachts.

Anchorage is off the sandy beach in 5-fathoms depths, weed on sand. Two small houses, and tamarisk trees line the shore.

Livadhi Bay, slightly more attractive, is better sheltered and attracts a few bathers who come from the port by small ferry-boats. Anchor as convenient off the beach.

Kambos Bay is more populated with one or two summer villas, a jetty, taverna, shop for basic provisions. An hourly ferry-service with the port. Anchorage as convenient off the sandy beach.

All the above coves are connected by road to the village. There are also other small coves on the eastern side of Patmos not described, but easy to discern on the chart.

Island of Arki

This lies among a small group of barren islands east of Patmos. It is long and narrow with some attractive sheltered coves suitable for small yachts. Normally only a few local fishermen make use of them. The three main coves are on the S.W. side of Arki:

The principal anchorage, Augusta, is recommended by *Sailing Directions*; the second cove southwards, **Avgous** or Stretto, has uncertain holding but is better for swinging room. **Campo** also affords anchorage.

Augusta Bay affords 2-fathom depths well beyond the elbow where the inlet turns westwards.

> **Anchorage.** On anchoring it is well to run a warp ashore to steady the bow of a yacht during Meltemi when, except fot the gusts, shelter is excellent. In mid-channel the bottom is sand and the water clear. The depths are actually greater than shown on the chart.

Half-a-dozen fishing boats berth at the head of the inlet, some of them being crawfish boats which sell their catch at Patmos. The headman of the island lives in a house on the shoulder of the hill separating Augusta and Avgous inlets. In summer a small tourist steamer calls twice a week.

For a large yacht there is good anchorage with plenty of room in less attractive surroundings on the opposite shore from Arki at the adjacent

Maratho Islet, where a sheltered sandy bay opens only to E. with convenient depths on a sandy bottom. The bay can be recognized by the white church on the hill and two small houses.

About 150 people live on these islands in two or three scattered hamlets. Though nothing is produced for export, the inhabitants grow enough to live on; an occasional caïque runs to Patmos with fish and returns with stores.

Island of Lipsi, lying to southward of Arki, has a small port on the S.W. side. The depths behind the new and insignificant breakwater are not enough for a yacht of medium draft to anchor, and outside the holding is bad. Fortunately, farther out and close under the land to the westward, holding is better, though strong gusts from the Meltemi sweeping down the hills, spoil the tranquillity of the anchorage.

The small village adjoining the port is uninteresting and rather poor, though very recently it has been improved with a new quay and concrete roads.

There are two unimportant islands off the Turkish coast:

Island of Gaidaro (Agathonisi) is small and barren. Barely 200 people live here, mostly at the head of the large cove on the south coast where comfortable summer anchorage may be found for a medium-sized yacht.

> **Anchorage** can best be found about 150 yds from the head of the cove in 5 to 6 fathoms on a bottom of sand and mud with a thin layer of weed. Good holding and room to swing. Meltemi gusts from the hillside. Open only to south.

Most of the inhabitants live at the top of the valley above the head of the cove where there is some sparse cultivation. Cattle, including goats, sheep and cows, are bred for export and the inhabitants grow sufficient to live on. Water is collected by some catchments visible on the hillsides. On the waterfront are only a couple of fishermen's houses whose inhabitants invariably welcome a visiting yacht. The local people, who have known no other but this simple way of life, appear to be a happy community. Some have never been away from the island, and their only link with the outside world is the weekly caïque, a small steamer and Radio Athens. There are two tavernas.

Island of Pharmako, lying to the southward, has gentle slopes and is partially covered with green scrub. It is not worth a special visit. There are four small coves on the eastern coast, sheltered from the prevailing northerly wind; the north-westerly cove is the most convenient.

> **Anchorage and Approach.** This cove can be recognized by a small white church on the hill above and by four arches of a Roman villa close by the water's edge. The sea-bed shelves to form a sandy anchorage close offshore in 3 fathoms. Though satisfactory in summer, this temporary anchorage is completely exposed to the eastern quadrant.

The island is largely barren with only one small inhabited cottage. Among some Roman remains may be seen the foundations of two or three villas, and underwater there is the rubble of a former jetty; at the southern part of the island there are further remains. Today the only visitors are Greek fishermen who spend the summer months here. They keep their boats under the shelter of the loggia of a Roman house, and at night poach the fish from the nearby Turkish coast.

> **Historical.** It was here that Julius Caesar spent many weeks in captivity. In 77 B.C. at the age of twenty-two, he was on the way to Rhodes to finish his education when pirates captured him at sea off Miletus and brought him to Pharmako. Here he was kept a prisoner, and a ransom of 22 talents was demanded by the pirates. Meanwhile, Caesar, apparently maintaining an ascendancy over his captors, expressed disgust that his life should be assessed at such a low value, whereupon the pirates raised their price to 50 talents (about £60,000). His many weeks of captivity were well occupied and we are told he wrote poems and speeches, took exercise, and jested with the pirates, assuring them they would eventually be hanged. The ransom from Rome was sent to Miletus and thence to the pirate camp at Pharmako. Caesar, on being released, soon raised a punitive expedition, captured the pirates and had them sent as prisoners to Pergamon, where they were condemned to death by crucifixion.
>
> It is said that, bearing in mind their humane treatment of him during captivity, Caesar had their throats cut before they were nailed to the cross!

Island of Leros

With the advantage of its sheltered anchorages, this island sprang into importance before the Second World War when Mussolini built a small naval base at Lakki as part of the Mare Nostrum campaign for hegemony in the Mediterranean. The island's population today is 8,500.

The island is largely barren, although in the valleys the slopes are green and cultivated. To the north-west of this rugged coast the long island of Arkhangelos forms a shield against the prevailing winds and provides shelter in the bays of the Pharios Channel. See Chart 1669, plan.

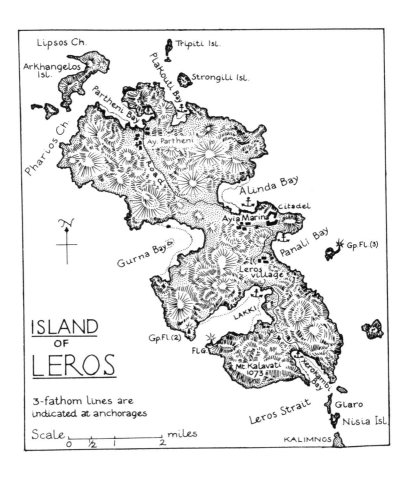

Plakouti Bay provides a useful anchorage in deserted surroundings, but requires careful pilotage. Well sheltered except from north. A small settlement is at the head of the bay. See *Sailing Directions*.

Partheni Bay, completely landlocked, affords perfect shelter in suitable depths. The village of Ay. Partheni lies at the head of the bay.

17 Island of Samos: view of the harbour

18 Island of Patmos: view of the monastery

Approach and Berth. Chart 3926, and plan on Chart 1669. There is anchorage with convenient depths of 4 fathoms in the middle, shelving gradually. Some large mooring buoys have been laid out inside the entrance to the bay, making an approach by night most hazardous.

Alinda Bay on the eastern coast is easily distinguished from seaward by the imposing Venetian Castle on the high Cape Castello. Off the attractive village of **Ayia Marina**, on the southern side near the head of the bay, is a short mole protecting a 70-yd quay facing N.W. but it is exposed to the north wind which makes it uncomfortable. A further quay facing S.W. has decreasing depths.

Berth. Chart 1669, plan. In settled weather a yacht may berth stern to the quay, but with a north wind it is better to anchor off. In event of fresh to strong N. winds shelter in Panali Bay is better.

Port Facilities. At the shops in the port there is a limited choice of fresh provisions, but at Leros village on the saddle of the hill there are better supplies. There are some freshwater taps near the quay and one or two modest tavernas. Taxis are available.

An interesting half-an-hour's drive by taxi from Ayia Marina leads up the hill through Leros village and then down to Lakki. There are fine views across the hilly unproductive country of the island.

Over the saddle S.E. from Ayia Marina is

Panali Bay with a small fishing village affording convenient anchorage sheltered from the prevailing wind.

Anchorage. Off the centre of the sandy beach in 3- to 5-fathom depths, on a bottom of light weed and sand. Open only to south.

Facilities. Plentiful provisions can be bought at Leros village, 15 min walk up the hill. A modest taverna by the shore sometimes provides fish and ice.

Local fishing boats land their catch on the beach whence it is carried by lorry to Leros village on the saddle above the hamlet. In late afternoon the setting sun provides an impressive sight when it shines on the Venetian castle towering on the tall promontory above the colourful fishing boats and the small houses of the hamlet.

On the south coast is the inlet of

Xerokambi with a small fishing hamlet, without particular interest; a convenient anchorage for any sized yacht – light weed on sand. Open only to the south.

Lakki is the former Italian naval base. Since its destruction in 1944 the buildings of the village have been repaired and an attempt has been made to turn the place into a Greek summer resort.

Berth. Plan on Chart 1669. The yacht station is in an exposed position at the N.E. corner of the harbour. Here the mole had been extended a further 70 yds in its original easterly direction, and a further 100 yds in a southerly direction. The steamer berths alongside the latter extension. A better berth is on the W. side, away from the promenade.

Facilities. Fuel at the yacht station. Water tap at the root of the mole. Ice factory E. of the village. Provisions, including plenty of fish usually available. There are a number of cranes, a slipway and a repair yard.

The planting of shady trees on the promenade and redecoration of the houses has given the place a new look, the bathing beach and Ayia Marina being attractions.

Recent History. During the Second World War, after the surrender of Italy and the capture of Sicily in 1943, the British decided to operate against the Dodecanese. The plan was to prevent the Germans from reinforcing their key point at Rhodes.

After securing the islands of Kos and Samos, Leros was next occupied; but the Germans soon reacted with an attack on Kos followed by an assault on Leros on 12 November.

Dive-bombers and destroyers supported a landing at the N.E. end of the island and at Panali Bay; parachutists were dropped later to reinforce the earlier landings. The island being without an airfield and divided topographically into three separated mountain areas it was extremely difficult to defend against a growing scale of attack. On 16 November the British garrison was compelled to surrender. 'A bitter blow to me,' wrote Churchill.

The small War Cemetery lies on the eastern side of Leros by the shore of Ayia Marina Bay. Protected from the salt spray by a line of tamarisks it contains the graves of 183 soldiers, seamen and airmen. Flowering shrubs, jacarandas, roses, oleanders and some tall cypress trees form a colourful environment.

Island of Kalimnos

A narrow, well-marked strait separates Leros from Kalimnos immediately southward. The beautiful scenery along the west coast of this mountainous and largely barren island should not be missed, and there are some delightful anchorages here sufficiently sheltered against the prevailing winds.

Port Kalimnos is an interesting small town with a large and recently improved harbour. Many of the small houses are still colour-washed in blue, said to have been a ruse of the islanders for irritating their former Italian masters by flaunting the Greek colours.

Approach and Anchorage. Chart 1669, plan. Considerable improvements have been undertaken in the port. Land has been reclaimed at the root of the mole, and the mole itself has been widened with broad quays, affording deep water alongside. The mole has been extended a further 550 yds (1977). Yachts are expected to berth stern to the southern mole near its landward end. In strong northerlies this is uncomfortable and the holding is poor. In such conditions it is preferable to anchor near the northern shore between the two moles.

Facilities. There has recently been marked progress in raising the standard of the local amenities. No longer is the port the squalid place it was; a broad road with flowering shrubs now leads from the new quay towards the village where there are some modest hotels, tavernas, cafés and provision shops. Steamer communication with Piraeus and Rhodes daily. A large shipyard which can haul up a dozen caïques, it builds most of the local sponge-boats.

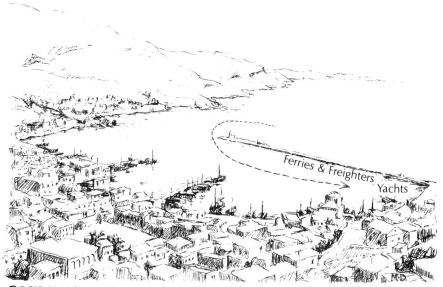

PORT KALIMNOS - yacht berths at new quay on the right

The inhabitants have been renowned over the centuries as sponge fishermen. Until recently, after the Greek Easter scores of men in perhaps eighty sponge boats would set forth for the shores of Africa. In recent years this has changed and sponges must be sought in Greek waters. The method of diving, too, has changed more than once. In the last century a diver would go down unaided except for a marble slab; then came the diving rubber suit and helmet. Now the diver, wearing only his mask and a small emergency air bottle, is towed by a wire over the seabed and supplied with air through a tube from the boat. Danger of the airtube being cut by the boat's propeller is overcome by fitting a guard.

Many of their sponges, after local processing, find their way to the American market. During the Second World War when sponge-fishing was denied them, many men from this island, fearing starvation, escaped in their boats, together with their families, to Turkey.

History. At the beginning of the last century Kalimnian divers were taken to Kithera where in 1802 they retrieved the Elgin marbles, then lying in a wreck in 60 ft of water. (See p. 8.)

The island can barely sustain its population of nearly 13,000. It was denuded of trees during the long Turkish occupation, and now only the valleys and a few inland plains are cultivated; this however is sufficient. The island also attracts a few tourists mainly for the radioactive springs. The port, relatively large, is sometimes a busy place accommodating one or two modern freighters and perhaps fifty caïques.

Other anchorages on the east coast:

Vathy, a deep fjord with a hamlet at its head and suitable moorage for one or two small yachts at the entrance.

Approach and Berth. On entering the fjord one can see to starboard the mouth of the Grotto Dhaskalio and also a quay where a couple of small yachts may berth. One may walk 3 km to Platanos to see Cyclopean walls and a delightful small Byzantine chapel.

On the west coast is temporary anchorage at

Borio Bay. It has a small hamlet and offers the choice of two coves for anchoring. Off the hamlet is a stone pier to which a yacht can run out a stern warp. There is a simple taverna and basic provisions.

Telendos Island. There is anchorage off the village, in convenient depths, at the foot of the tall mountain, with impressive views along the rugged barren coast. The island appears to have been inhabited since earliest times, for there are some massive stone blocks of a Cyclopean wall, as well as some Greek and Roman ruins, and the remains of an abandoned monastery.

Linaria Bay has a few summer villas and a partly sheltered anchorage; a road leads to Port Kalimnos.

On the south coast is

Ormiskos Vlikhadia, a cove open only to S., providing sheltered anchorage on a sandy bottom. With only a few summer villas and a taverna at its head, it is a pleasant place to bring up for the night.

Island of Pserimos is of no particular interest, and its only sheltered cove is on the S.W. coast; this is used by the Greeks from Kos as a summer resort.

Approach and Anchorage. There is no difficulty by day, but a yacht should beware of a rock awash to the southward of this cove. The sandy bottom in the cove rises conveniently to 3 fathoms, but there is a rocky ledge running across which protrudes about 2 ft above the sand. The Meltemi brings in a lively swell. There are some landing steps on the north side of the cove where tourists from neighbouring islands are landed from caïques. In 1980 it was reported that a short protecting mole was being built.

General. There is a good bathing beach; but apart from a few summer bungalows built close to the shore, no other dwellings can be seen except the small taverna.

TURKISH COAST TO KOS STRAIT

Kovela lies close southward of the present mouth of the Menderes River.

The Ancient Gulf of Latmos together with the Menderes River have undergone many changes throughout the centuries; this has accounted for the abandonment of important Ionian, Greek and Roman cities whose ruins may now be seen many miles inland.

> *The face of places, and their forms, decay;*
> *And that is solid earth that once was sea;*
> *Seas in their turn retreating from the shore,*
> *Make solid land where ocean was before.*
>
> Ovid's *Metamorphosis XV*, DRYDEN, trans.

The present mouths of the Meander or Menderes River can be seen on Chart 2682, but in early Greek times the waters of this river emptied into the spacious Gulf of Latmos, some 20 miles further eastward. On its shores were the cities of the Ionian Greeks, inherited later by the Romans. Miletus, a prosperous commercial city with its four harbours – 'one large enough to accommodate a fleet', wrote Strabo – was famous for 'its men of destiny, talents and sublime genius'; the best known today is probably Thales, the philosopher and astronomer. Although largely destroyed by the Persians and later conquered by Alexander, Miletus did not actually begin to decline until the silting of the port in the early centuries of our millennium, and during Byzantine days its importance was waning rapidly. In A.D. 52 St Paul came here by sea. Today the extensive ruins of the city are well worth seeing; among them is the theatre, the largest in Asia Minor.

Opposite Miletus on the north side of this former spacious gulf was Priene, a carefully planned city by Alexander's architects – now called Gülbahçe. Its port, as Strabo records, had already silted in his day, and in the 1st century A.D. a channel had to be dredged through the mud to enable shipping to operate. German archaeologists have excavated much of the old city including a theatre, council chamber, and nearly 400 houses. Myus is another of the twelve Ionian

cities; there is also Heraclaea, and Magnesia, lying on a tributary of the Meander – most of these places are easily accessible by motor-car from the more sophisticated anchorages mentioned in this chapter. But the waters of the gulf have vanished: 'Furrows take the place of waves, and goats leap where once the dolphins played.' The river-bed has continued to silt and the only part of the original gulf still to survive is the inland lake of Bafa; being connected to the sea, a profitable fishing industry has developed, the majority of the fish being cured locally and exported abroad.

Kovela. The present village of Kovela on the eastern shore is poor and squalid, and the shores having silted, there is no longer shelter at the anchorage; it may be used only in settled weather and not in the Meltemi season. If wanting to see the ruins of Didyma, a yacht should make for Skropes, lying inside the Gulf of Mandalya. This is a better alternative, although the guard-post there may have to call by telephone Police and Customs from Kovela before permitting foreigners to land.

Formerly the ancient port of Panormos, Kovela handled the commerce of Didyma with which it was linked by a road bordered by sphinxes. Today there are practically no remains, but it has port officials and is the headquarters of a coastguard detachment: here one may land in fine weather to visit the ruins, not only of Didyma, but also Miletus (8 miles) and Priene (17 miles). Take a taxi from Yeronda.

Gulf of Güllük (Mandalya) (Chart 2682)

This large gulf has an exceptional number of inlets worth visiting in a yacht. Some of them are remarkable for their attractive mountainous surroundings, others for their ancient ruins, and some for both. They mostly afford good sheltered anchorage for medium-sized yachts. During the summer months the Meltemi blows into the gulf from a direction W. to W.N.W. starting in the forenoon, freshening after 1100 and easing off before sunset. Occasionally the hot Voyras (N.E. wind) sets in for a couple of days. Inside the inlets the wind sometimes follows round the contours of the coast and also blows off the nearer mountains in hard squalls. At night there is a light land breeze, each inlet creating its own quite independently. Customs guards frequently come off and demand Ship's Papers; it is therefore essential to have made an official entry in order to satisfy these officials with the necessary papers.

In contrast to Greece where every sheltered anchorage has a few small houses, one or two caïques and some small fishing boats, in Turkey this maritime atmosphere is entirely lacking. Only at a commercial port one may find a caïque loading timber or charcoal, but apart from the sponge-boats hardly any local craft are to be seen.

Kukurcuk, close east of the Cape Tekağaç are two sandy bays sometimes used by sponge fishermen in the summer months. They have good holding on a sandy bottom and occasionally afford a useful night anchorage when sheltering from the Meltemi.

Since the survey was made for Chart 2682, sand bars have appeared across the mouths of both these bays and the depths are barely two fathoms where the chart shows $3\frac{1}{2}$. The water is unusually clear.

Skropes Bay (Altınkum), a comfortable sandy anchorage and useful for a yacht when visiting Didyma. Recently a large modern hotel and restaurant have been built, and the place is becoming a summer resort.

Approach and Anchorage. One should give Skropes shoal a wide berth and approach the anchorage from the E.S.E. This shoal is now only partly under the surface, usually showing above, and may be seen by the discoloured water. Let go 300 yds to the eastward of the small Customs shack in $2\frac{1}{2}$ fathoms, on a sandy bottom. Both holding and shelter are good, the bay being open only to the southward.

Officials. A Customs post examines passports and recently omitted the usual formalities, but they may refer them to the authorities in Kovela which can mean some delay.

The village of Yeronda is 3 miles distant by a new road; taxis are available but bargaining is necessary. Beside this village are the extensive remains of the Ionian temple of Didyma.

Historical. Towering above the village the surviving columns of the temple stand 100 ft above the ground and all around lie the drums of many more where they were felled by the earthquake at the end of the 15th century. Though nothing remains of the earlier temple destroyed by Xerxes after Salamis, these are the ruins of its successor, the vast temple put up by the Milesians. The scale was so great that even after 150 years' work and despite the subsequent efforts of the Romans, it was still unfinished. Had it been completed it would probably have ranked as one of the Wonders of the World. It was approached by a sacred way from Panormos from which Newton, the archaeologist, recovered some seated figures and sphinxes of the 6th century B.C., now to be seen in the British Museum. (See also map on p. 168.)

The following inlets on the northern shore are worth a visit:

Kuru Erik Limani, a pleasant anchorage off Talianaki.

Anchor in 4 fathoms in N.W. corner, or alternatively enter Talianaki Cove where there are 2-fathom depths in the western arm and also 2 fathoms on the east side of the entrance.

Akbük Limani, a somewhat open bay with a hamlet which provides basic supplies.

Anchor in 3 fathoms W.S.W. from the hamlet. Good holding on a mud bottom.

Kazikili Limani, an attractive cove at the head of a bay with nearly all-round shelter.

Anchor in 3 fathoms off a conspicuous ruined house; bottom is mud, excellent holding.

The village which is quite large lies a couple of miles inland and can barely be seen from the anchorage. On the eastern shore are some ruined houses, but the western side is wooded and green, the large pine trees coming down to the water's edge. Inside the woods are some scattered Roman ruins.

Saltaluthea in the open cove at the northern corner of the gulf of Alan Gül Körfezi is an attractive anchorage. The shore is wooded down to the water's edge.

Asim Körfezi (gulf) is the most important of these inlets on account of the Iassus ruins and the Port of Entry at Güllük.

At the head of this inlet is the Iassus Promontory with the crumbling Venetian fortress easily distinguishable at a distance. On its western side is the landlocked bay of Asim Liman (Port Isene) suitable for medium-sized yachts, and on the east is Asim Bükü (Isene Bay) suitable for large yachts.

Asim Liman, Chart 1606, plan, which also shows the archaeological sites (Iassus).

> **Approach.** Keep close to the small ruined tower as a sunken mole projects from the western shore opposite, reaching more than half way across the entrance. This obstruction does not show at all on a dull day with a breeze, although it is only 3 ft underwater.
>
> **Anchorage.** Let go as convenient towards the head of the bay which shelves gradually from 5-fathom depths at the entrance. Bottom is mud.
>
> **Officials.** They may appear from the ore-port of Güllük, but usually there are none.
>
> **Facilities.** The hamlet of Kuren at the head of the bay has supplies of fresh fruit, bread etc. and a bar.

The Venetian castle is prominent, and, among the ancient ruins, can be seen the Greek theatre with its Roman additions, including the proscenium. Part of the classical walls remain (with Byzantine restoration) but much was torn down to build quays at Constantinople harbour during the 19th century. The early Carians once lived here, but the subsequent history of Iassus is complicated and was often disastrous for the inhabitants. Strabo attaches his dolphin story to Iassus – of the boy who called it by playing the harp.

Güllük, the only Port of Entry in the Gulf of Güllük, consists of a very small town at the head of a bay with a substantial stone pier for berthing freighters.

> **Approach and Berth.** The houses can be seen from the cape, and at night a red light is exhibited on the extremity of the new loading pier. This extends in a N.W. direction from the centre of the bay for about 100 yds and has 25-ft depths at the steamer quay. A yacht requiring pratique should anchor in about 3 fathoms on the N.E. side of the pier, good holding on sand, but after the prevailing day breeze this anchorage continues to be uncomfortable. Only when calm can a yacht haul in her stern to the pier. In the S.E. corner a small basin has been built with a mooring-buoy in the centre, and a quay on the W. side. Though shallow it has been reported as suitable for a medium-sized yacht and preferable to the open anchorage in the Roads.
>
> **Officials.** Health, Customs, Immigration and Harbour Master who board the visiting yacht soon after arrival. Their offices are close to the inner basin.
>
> **Facilities** are primitive, but fruit, bread and fish usually available. Water of doubtful purity. Ice sometimes available. Motel-restaurant on the coast just outside the hamlet.

Güllük sends away shipments of emery only when sufficient ore has accrued at the dump in the hamlet; it is brought in from the mines, some distance away, in small quantities. Timber and logs are shipped by caïque to Istanbul. The little

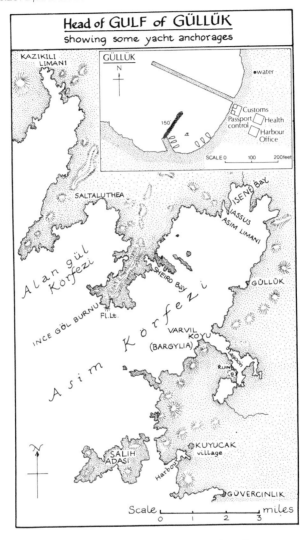

Head of GULF of GÜLLÜK
showing some yacht anchorages

town is without interest, but now expanding with hotels to attract local tourists.

Sheiro Bay on the N.E. side of the gulf opposite Güllük is the place to make for if the port should be found untenable.

Varvil Koyu (anc. Bargylia) is worth a visit for the scenery and the Hellenic ruins, but it is not as sheltered as one could wish. Half-a-mile inside the entrance the bottom comes up very quickly.

    Anchorage. About 200 yds off a square, ruined house on the S.W. shore (where the Chart shows 3 fathoms there is in fact 2). Bottom is mud. A swell comes into the cove during the summer day breeze. Land in the dinghy at a wooden jetty, half-an-hour's row across the lagoon.

On the top of the hill are extensive Hellenic and later ruins, very overgrown and difficult to discern. Although unexcavated, the agora, temples and theatre can be found. The view over the marsh is very fine.

Salih Adasi is an island with two pleasant anchorages for small yachts on its eastern coast. At the northern end of the channel is a small cove with a hamlet and jetty at its head and a very restricted anchorage is close off. At the S. end of the channel is a better anchorage, also a small cove with wooded shore where one can anchor in 2–3 fathoms on a sandy bottom.

Kuyucak Harbour (opposite Salih Adası). A very small, yet completely landlocked harbour with the ruins of a monastery on the isthmus and a formerly Greek village where the river enters.

> **Anchor** in the centre of W. arm of the harbour in 3 fathoms – mud and sand. The N.W. arm has become shallow and foul, and it is reported to be plagued with mosquitoes.

Güvercinlik, lying at the head of the gulf, is an uninteresting place. The modern Turkish hamlet stands back from the coast; the former Greek settlement was by the waterfront, and recently the place is developing.

> **Anchorage** is in convenient depths of about 3 fathoms off the port. Land in the dinghy at the ancient mole.

Much forestry work has recently been put in hand on the nearby mountain slopes. There is a bus service to Bodrum.

Torba, lying at the head of the north-facing cove of Turfanda Bükü, has recently had a substantial breakwater built on the W. side of the cove – said to afford shelter in all weather and a useful place to shelter if Bodrum is full.

Ilica Bükü is an almost deserted little cove surrounded by pine forests with a very deep anchorage on sand and weed. The head of the bay is attractive and quiet, and you can walk over a good path to the marsh.

Türk Bükü is a cove with a small village at its head. A breakwater extends westwards for 100 yds off the small peninsula from the position immediately below the anchor shown on chart 2682.

Yachts sometimes prefer to anchor close inshore on the E. or S. side of the buoy to avoid the violent wind gusts; alternatively anchor inside the islands on the W. side by the entrance. (Local knowledge necessary.)

Facilities. Basic provisions and excellent fresh fish. Good fish restaurants. A modern wood repair yard.

One can make an interesting climb up the hill on the S.E. leading to anc. Madnasa ruins. A fine view from the top.

Anchorage. The bay is normally sheltered from the prevailing N.W. wind, but the new breakwater now provides shelter from N.E. and is used by local fishing craft anchoring in depths of 10 ft or less and running out a warp to the breakwater.

Facilities. At the village one may buy basic provisions, but there is nothing to see.

Büyük Farilya Büku has nothing to recommend it other than the shelter in the S.W. corner; but considerable depths force one to anchor inconveniently close to the shore.

Leaving the Gulf of Güllük off the Sandama Peninsula, one follows this rocky coast southward:

Gümüsslük, as the Turks now call Myndus, has little to show of the ancient city beyond some foundations of the old walls: but it provides a pleasant landlocked harbour suitable for a medium-sized yacht.

The harbour entrance is tricky and narrow – during the Meltemi it is almost impossible to enter under sail though the bay is entirely sheltered inside.

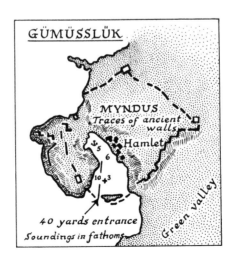

Approach and Anchorage. Though Chart 1604 is not clear, *Sailing Directions* gives a good description. As the 40-yd wide channel of entry reaches its narrowest point, an underwater ledge (part of the ancient wall) extends from the W. entrance point. About 150 yds N. of the E. entrance point is the submerged rock referred to in *Sailing Directions*. An examination of the sea-bed in 1968 fixed its position: E. entrance point bore 190°, W. entrance point bore 235° (true); there was about 3 fathoms depth above the rock. By keeping about 30 yds off the western shore it was found that the depths of the channel exceeded 50 ft. A yacht having passed through the narrow entrance should steer a northerly course in the direction of a large restored house until reaching the anchorage. The only difficulty for a sailing yacht arises when entering in a Meltemi; strong gusts sweep down from the high land, but once inside the wind is fairly steady and cooling, coming in from N.

Anchor in the N. corner of the harbour in about 5 fathoms on a sandy bottom, or nearer the hamlet in 6 fathoms and take a warp to the stone pier (5 ft at its extremity).

Facilities. A simple restaurant, a café, and daily bus service to Bodrum.

The harbour is occasionally used by caïques seeking shelter from the Meltemi when working up the Turkish coast. The former Greek houses on the waterfront are now restored and the valley behind, extending towards Bodrum, is well populated and very green with orange groves and market garden produce. The cattle are well fed and cared for: many cows, donkeys, horses, Oriental fat-tailed sheep and camels. The latter may be seen on the sandy shore close to the anchorage being given seabaths and a scrub every morning.

Close southeard of Gümüsslük is a group of small rocky islands of which **Karabakla** is the largest. On its eastern side is a bight close to a low-lying isthmus. This provides convenient anchorage in 4 fathoms on a sandy bottom with patches of rock. Shelter here is claimed to be good, even in southerly winds. The island is uninhabited. Close S.W. of Karabakla is the islet of **Yassi** where the hull of a Byzantine ship was recently excavated (see p. 188).

The coast continues southward towards Hussein Burnu where it then turns to E.S.E. forming the northern shore of the Gulf of Kos (Kerme Körfezi). See Chapter 6(e).

6e

Southern Dodecanese and
Gulfs of Kos and Doris

GREEK ISLANDS

Island of Kos
  The Port
  Kamari Bay (Kefalos)

Island of Nisiros
  Mandraki

Island of Yali

Island of Tilos
  Livadhi Bay

Island of Astipalea
  Scala
  Analipsis (Maltezana)
  Port Agrilithi
  Vathy

Island of Symi (Simi)
  Port Symi
  Pethi Harbour
  Panormittis
  Small yacht anchorages

TURKISH COAST

Gulf of Kos (Kerme Körfezi)
  Aspat Bay
  Gumbet Bay
  Bodrum (*Port of Entry*)
  Keramos Bay
  Akbük
  Gökova
  Gelibolu Limani
  Sehir Adaları
  Söğüt Limanı
  Canak Limanı (Kesir Cove)
  Inğiliz Limanı (Deremen)
  Guzlemek
  Balisu Bay (Gerenlikli Limani)

  Yedi Adaları
  Cape Krio with Büyük Limanı
Gulf of Doris (Hisarönü Körfezi)
  Palamut Bükü
  Datça
  Miliontes Bay
  Kuruca Bükü (Kocini Bay)
  Göktas Bay
  Bençik (Penzik)
  Thiaspori Cove
  Keyif Cove
  Keçi Bükü (Port Kiervasili)
  Port Dirsek
Gulf of Symi (Simi)
  Bozburnu Limanı

6e
Southern Dodecanese and Gulfs of Kos and Doris

(Charts 872 and 1604)

GREEK ISLANDS

Island of Kos (Chart 1898)

A long and partly mountainous island with a well-sheltered small port adjoining a modern resort. As with most of the Dodecanese certain sections of the coast are prohibited in Kos and all the mountainous country inland. Patrol boats and guards give warning of illegal approach.

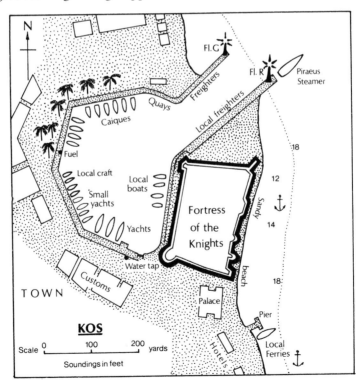

The Port was reconstructed in 1980 with improved quays.

Approach and Berth. Chart 1616. The harbour entrance, which has recently been considerably widened, is easy to approach day and night. The fortress can be clearly distinguished and one passes between the mole-heads with the new steamer quay to port and the freighter quay to starboard. The wider entrance permits a limited swell to enter the port during strong N. winds and in winter the harbour has recently proved to be unsafe.

The entrance is also apt to silt and must be continually dredged to maintain the uniform depths of 18 ft found elsewhere. Berth off W. quay; anchor eastward; larger yachts off the quay at the head of the harbour. Large ferries berth by the castle (repaired in 1979).

Occasionally larger yachts anchor outside where shown on the chart, but they should keep clear of the steamers which also sometimes anchor off.

Officials. As for a Port of Entry. Offices are on the quay. Embarking crew for Bodrum may prove difficult here.

Facilities. Water may be obtained from a hydrant on the quay by the steps – apply at town hall. Fuel is available. Limited repairs. There is an excellent market and many modern shops, a number of hotels and restaurants. Early closing Thursdays. Ice can be ordered at a shop next to the Post Office in a street at right angles to the quay; the factory is 1 mile outside the town. Taxis and bicycles are available. Piraeus steamers call twice daily in summer, and there are also ferries to neighbouring islands. Daily air communication with Athens.

Both town and harbour were reconstructed by the Italians after the 1933 earthquake. Most places of interest adjoin the port. The flowering hibiscus and oleanders which border the streets do much towards enhancing the look of the town.

One must see the 18th-century mosque incorporating Hellenic and Byzantine columns, the 13th-century castle of the Knights of St John, the museum, the old plane tree which, according to Hacke writing in 1699, was then so 'vaste that its branches would shade a thousand men'; the local guide explains that Hippocrates used to teach under this tree in the 5th century B.C. but foresters maintain that no plane tree can live for more than 500 years. There are also some of the more recent Greek excavations on the fringe of the town.

About 3 miles outside the town is the Asclepeion, the medical school and hospital of Hippocrates, which has been rather over-restored by the Italians; from here the view across the Strait towards the Anatolian mountains is magnificent. One may hire bicycles for this expedition and for exploring some of the villages. Platanion, one with a small colony of Turks who, retaining their Muslim faith, took Greek nationality when the Italians left. The population of the island in 1978 was 16,000; in the town 8,140.

Today Kos is a gay little port with plenty of activity; the quays constantly busy with the arrival and departure of small freighters and caïques, and the daily crowd of jostling passengers being embarked and disembarked from the mail steamer. As far as tourists are concerned Kos might be styled a younger sister of Rhodes; but its economy also rests on agricultural produce and honey, fish being sent to Athens and canned tomatoes to the United States.

History. Kos town, famous for its wine and silk, was founded in 366 B.C. and became almost immediately a great maritime power. When St Paul put in for a night's rest on his third missionary journey from Macedonia to Jerusalem, he probably came to the same harbour as exists today. It silted up in medieval times, but this did not prevent it from being used by pirates. It was occupied in turn by Alexander, the Ptolemies, Romans, Genoese, Knights of St John, and the Turks who conquered it in 1522. A picture of the place at the end of the 17th century when under Turkish rule is given by Hacke: 'Here being seven half galleys each carrying three hundred men, forty-eight oars, four guns and everyman's small arms. They also have brigantines each carrying seventy men, twenty-eight oars, six patereoes, and small arms each man. These are governed, owned and commanded chiefly by one man who has his commission from the Grand Seigneur; and for retaliation he gathers tribute of the Isles yearly, and by which he is no loser, imposing on rich and poor what he pleases and forces them to pay. And in his progress he takes many Christian slaves.'

The Turks held Kos for almost four centuries until 1912, after which the Italians occupied it until 1941. It was restored to Greece after the war.

Recent History. In the Second World War, following the Italian surrender in 1941, the British occupied the island. It had a poor airfield capable of operating only single-seater aircraft. When the Germans, on 3 October, launched a strong seaborne attack supported by paratroopers, the British garrison was eventually forced to surrender, many men being killed or taken prisoner. Kos remained in German hands until the surrender in 1945. The British soldiers buried in Kos had their graves subsequently transferred to the large cemetery at Rhodes.

Towards the western extremity of the island's barren south coast is a tall promontory forming the western arm of an open bight:

Kamari Bay (Kefalos) where there is excellent shelter in strong northerly winds.

Approach. Chart 3925. Kefalos village stands conspicuously on the hill, and as one nears the head of the bay both Paleo Kastro and the mole of the small port can be seen.

Anchorage. In strong N. winds it is recommended that a yacht should anchor close west of Paleo Kastro in depths of 3 to 5 fathoms on a sandy bottom; good holding and a steady wind.

With fair weather the small port is suitable. Lay out an anchor to the northward and haul in the stern to the extremity of the mole by the light tower (Lt.Fl.R.) Holding is sand, but the depths decrease rapidly towards the shore. At the mole-head there is nearly 3 fathoms.

Facilities. None at Paleo Kastro. At the port is a small taverna and a water tap. Fruit and bread can be brought at a store near by. A new hotel has grown up.

Small freighters often call to collect the ore (pyrites) which is quarried on the hillside above the port. A Customs Officer is stationed at the port. A few fishing craft are based here to supply the village of Kefalos (2,000 inhabitants). Bus communication.

Opposite Paleo Kastro is a ruined basilica of the 6th century which has been recently exacavated.

Island of Nisiros (Chart 3923)

Nisiros is square-shaped and largely green with two harbours. The population is barely 1300. The land rises in terraces towards a ring of hills in the centre, surrounding a depression with volcanic craters, last active in 1885, and hot sulphur springs. Unlike Milos, the volcanic soil is fertile, the island is wooded, and there are almond trees and olive groves on the hillsides. The three small villages are very primitive and the two mountain ones are almost depopulated. The island lives on tourism, the export of pumice, and the money sent home by relatives in the United States and Australia. There is a shortage of water because the volcanic rock is porous, thus preventing the sinking of wells: huge cisterns have been built on the high ground and water is piped down to the village.

Mandraki has been dredged to a uniform 23 ft, the mole extended to 90 yds and a broad quay built, but the harbour is still open to a heavy swell. Yachts lie stern to the quay, steamers alongside the mole.

> **Officials.** Harbour Master and Customs on the quay.

> **Facilities.** Basic provisions, mostly imported from Kos and Rhodes, local fish. Post and Telegraph office on the quay. Five small pensions, others building in 1978. Two excellent fish restaurants on the quay, one in the village. Steamer once a week to Piraeus, twice to Rhodes, once to the northern Dodecanese, once to Kavala and Alexandroupolis: caïque twice a week to Kos. The monastery church inside the Venetian castle is well worth a visit; it has a remarkable library. Interesting excursion by minibus to the craters, and the beautiful but almost empty villages of Nikia and Emborio.

Just east of Mandraki there is a conspicuous white spa building on the beach, open from June to September for hot sulphur baths. E. of this are buoys and a tip where small freighters lie to take off the pumice quarried in the hills above. This is exported to the United States and Japan.

Two miles E.N.E. of Mandraki is

Pali, a small fishing harbour open to N.E., being dredged to 2 fathoms (1980) to provide shelter from prevailing swell.

> **Approaching** the rectangular harbour from E. a conspicuous white church can be seen to the W. and ruins opposite.

> **Berth.** A small yacht may berth 20–30 yds inside the mole. Heavy swell in onshore winds.

> **Facilities.** Several good fish tavernas.

Three miles to the N.W. is the

Island of Yali distinguished by the extensive pumice quarries in the hillside; here under Meltemi conditions shelter can be found at the centre of the island near the tip and by some buoys used by freighters. There are a few houses on shore for the workers, mostly from Santorini, who quarry the pumice. The northern half of the island has obsidian (hence the name of the island, meaning glass) and was leased to a British company in 1968.

This small island, though unattractive and without permanent habitation provides a useful anchorage for a yacht in need of shelter from a strong northerly blow. It was used by Admiral Canaris during the War of Liberation.

Island of Tilos (Piscopi, formerly Episcopi) is a dull little island with an anchorage in **Livadhi Bay** close to the main village.

> **Anchorage.** Chart 1898. Let go in about 7 fathoms off the entrance to the small boat harbour. Here the bottom is sand; open to north-east, a swell often comes into the bay.

> **Facilities.** The village, 20 min walk along the shore of the bay, is uninteresting but can provide basic fresh supplies. A steamer from Piraeus calls once a week.

There are three villages on the island, whose agriculture has deteriorated; now the only export is goats. The island has never been of historical importance, but during the period of the Knights its security depended upon signalling warnings of enemy approach to Rhodes from a number of watch-towers – hence the name Episcopi, which is also said to have been derived from once having had a bishop.

Island of Astipalea (Stampalia)

This is the most westerly of the Dodecanese; its twin mountain peaks make it appear in the distance as separate islands. Chart 1666.

From seaward this sparsely populated island appears barren and forbidding, but it affords a choice of good anchorages for even large yachts. Its pleasant little port of Scala offers certain amenities.

Scala lies at the head of a cove with its white houses lining the waterfront and ascending the ridge to a ruined Venetian castle on top. There is anchorage for half-a-dozen medium-sized yachts or caïques to swing.

> **Approach and Anchorage.** Chart 1666. Both the ruined castle and the light structure (Lt. Qk. Fl.) are conspicuous. Yachts berth stern-to on the W. side of the new 100 yds quay which has

been built out on the S. side of the bay. The steamer goes alongside on the N. side. With normal summer weather shelter is good and the gusts referred to in *Sailing Directions* are no more alarming than elsewhere. In event of southerly weather shelter should be sought in Analipsis.

Facilities. Bread and fresh provisions; water at jetty (caution when berthing), ice at the electricity works. Two tourist hotels with restaurants have been built on the waterfront and a large number of summer villas. The Piraeus steamer calls three times a week.

Officials. The harbour Office is on the terrace close by.

Only a few hundred people live at the Scala which has great charm. The castle was built by the Quirini family who governed the island for 200 years before it was taken by the Turks; the family coat of arms still survives on a plaque by the castle gateway.

Analipsis (Maltezana). Chart 1666, plan, provides nearly all-round shelter.

Anchorage. A patch of sand in 3 fathoms close westward of the white obelisk has good holding, but elsewhere it is undependable and poor.

There are no habitations by the shore, but a road passes leading to Scala.

Port Agrilithi, $2\frac{1}{2}$ miles west of Cape Poulari, affords excellent shelter, in a deserted creek.

Anchorage is in a small cove on the east side of the creek in 5 fathoms on a bottom of sand.

There are no facilities here. The only sign of life is when a caïque arrives with workers for a small quarry on the west side of the creek. The land to windward is relatively low-lying and in strong north winds the gusts are mild.

Vathy. Chart 1666, plan, although Chart 3922 gives sufficient detail. This landlocked basin with its barren and uninviting shores appears to be a secure anchorage, but the holding has been reported as being uncertain and the place subject to strong gusts.

Anchorage. After passing the 2-fathom bar turn to port and anchor off some small houses in 2 to 3 fathoms. Bottom is weed on mud, but the water is cloudy. A quarry with power plant has recently been set up close above the shore and two or three cottages were being built in 1969 for the workers.

In Roman days, after the suppression of piracy, warships were sometimes stationed at Astipalea to maintain the safety of shipping. Pirates also used these natural shelters in the later centuries, and in 1812 one of H.M. ships having captured a pirate galley reported:

Yet she rowed fast, possessed a swivel and twenty muskets, and with forty ferocious-looking villains who manned her might have carried the largest merchant ship in the Mediterranean. The pirates had just captured a Turkish boat with five men, four of whom were massacred and the fifth, a Jew, had merely been deprived of an ear!

Apart from the interesting approaches to these natural harbours, this island hardly merits a special visit. Even the mussels, whose quality was praised by Pliny, are no longer cultivated. The population has dwindled to about 1,000.

Island of Symi (Simi)

Rugged, mountainous and largely barren it lies on the eastern extremity of the Aegean within the mouth of the Turkish Gulf of Doris. Today the island has a flourishing tourist trade, several steamers arriving daily with holidaymakers from Rhodes. Most of the population live in the port.

It has two main harbours: one, Panormittis, on the western side of the island, affording good shelter in depths of 3 fathoms; and the other on the east side, Port Symi, lying in a deep inlet surrounded by pleasing little houses. Close beside it is the well-sheltered bay of Pethi.

Port Symi lies at the head of a bay with its colourful houses rising up the hillside towards a line of windmills – now dismantled – standing on the ridge above. Approaching the port one can see that although a few houses have been abandoned some of the more substantial ones have been restored and painted in various delicate shades giving one the impression of a small Italian rather than a Greek port.

> **Approach.** Chart 1669. A concrete quay has been built south of the light tower to enable the Rhodes steamer to berth and land her passengers.
>
> **Berth.** The depths are considerable until reaching the head of the bay which becomes shallow and is cluttered with small craft; but there is room to berth in $2\frac{1}{2}$ fathom depths in furthest S.W. corner of harbour. A suitable berth can be found on the south side towards the head of the bay with anchor laid to the northward and stern hauled in to a short projecting quay.
>
> **Facilities.** A small modern hotel stands near the light tower. Nearby is the modest local yacht club with a quay which is too exposed for a visiting yacht to berth there. Provisions and ice are obtainable. Restaurants in the N.E. corner of the port.
> A small shipyard still builds the trehandiri sponge-boats and could probably help with repairs.

Some thirty years ago Port Symi had a population of 7,000 people, many of whom were employed in the sponge fleet. Today there are only 2,500 of whom only about fifty men go away sponge-fishing in the summer months.

On the front wall of one of the houses is a plaque recording in the English and Greek languages the surrender of the Germans in the Dodecanese in 1944.

A mule-track leads over the mountains from Port Symi to Panormittis: this passes through a wood of pines and cypresses, but it is rough going and takes at least four hours. Also, a walk of one hour takes one to Roukoumiotis monastery with a 5th-century church under the Byzantine one.

Pethi Harbour is a well-sheltered inlet, but rather deep for a yacht wishing to swing to her anchor.

> **Anchorage.** Let go in 8 fathoms in S.W. corner of the inlet; weed on mud. Alternatively a yacht can anchor to seaward off a stone pier (6-ft depth at extremity) and haul in the stern. Gusts are apt to sweep down the hillsides even with light winds.
>
> **Facilities.** Although nothing much can be bought locally it is only 20 min walk over the hill to Port Symi.

Panormittis. A delightful, enclosed, natural harbour in mountainous surroundings with a monastery by the quay.

> **Approach and Anchorage.** Chart 1604. On the N.E. side of the entrance is a ruined windmill painted white, which stands out conspicuously to the westward visible at least 5 miles, and by night a light (Fl. R.) is now exhibited. The shore generally is steep-to.
>
> It is convenient to anchor half way between the S.W. headland of the entrance and the southern extremity of the monastery, in 3 fathoms on a sandy bottom. About 30 yds south of the monastery tower is a short stone pier which also has a quay; at the head of the pier are depths of 8 to 9 ft diminishing towards the shoreward end. Though a yacht could berth with her stern to the pierhead for a short while, it is well to know that caïques frequently call here, as well as the Rhodes steamer. In Meltemi weather the best shelter is in the N.E. corner of the harbour about 25 yds from the shore in depths of 12 ft. A warp can be run ashore. There is a slight swell caused by the day breeze.
>
> **General.** Fresh water is limited, being collected in winter and stored in the monastery cistern; a small general store is in the monastery where tinned provisions and vegetables may be bought; there is also a taverna. Bread can be bought and ice can be ordered by caïque from Symi. On the southern shore of the anchorage is a small restaurant. The modern monastery has a charming bell-tower and in its courtyard a 12th-century church, with some interesting carving and icons.

Only a few monks live here, but many Greek visitors stay a few days and eat at the café; there are a few private rooms with showers. In front of the monastery is a memorial to the late abbot who was shot by the Germans in the last war. The custom of ringing the monastery bell as a sign of welcome to a strange vessel (including yachts) is still continued.

Other anchorages for small yachts off Symi

On East Coast:
An unnamed little sandy cove lies close northward of the entrance to Pethi Bay.

An islet off the N. shore of the cove provides adequate shelter for a small yacht; the anchorage being open only through a narrow sector to the east.

Marathouda Bay, lying about 3 miles S. of the southern side of Pethi Bay, has a small sandy cove at its head.

> **Anchorage** is off a quay in 3 fathoms on a sandy bottom; it is sometimes necessary to run out a warp when mountain gusts sweep down. Partly open to east.

> **Facilities.** Only a few vegetables to be bought locally, but a 20-min walk brings one to Panormittis where there is a wider choice of fresh provisions.

On West Coast:

Cape Kephalo. East of this peninsula is a very small peninsula (almost an islet). Here is the monastery of Ayios Emilianos, and beneath it a small sandy cove with 2-fathom depths, open only towards the Symi coast.

TURKISH COAST : GULFS OF KOS, DORIS AND SYMI

(Chart 1604)

Gulf of Kos (Kerme Körfezi)

This deep inlet extends eastwards for 50 miles, reaching Gökova, a small trading port lying at the mouth of a mountain stream, at its head. The day breeze blows into the gulf from west reaching a strength of 4 or 5 on an average summer's day. The steep, barren, northern shores gradually become more precipitous towards the head of the gulf with mountains rising from the cliffs to heights of 3,000 ft. The last fifteen miles is green and wooded on both shores. On the southern side are some attractive anchorages shown on plans of Chart 1533. These places were completely deserted until recent tourist caïque invasions.

On entering the gulf from the northward a yacht should be careful to avoid the rocky shoals lying half a mile off Hussein Point and beyond. Although Bodrum is the one major port close at hand there are some pleasant coves where according to the wind one can conveniently bring up for the night:

Aspat Bay. Here a yacht can anchor in 5 fathoms on a sandy bottom near some cottages. The peasants take their produce by boat to Bodrum daily.

Gumbet Bay is within close walking distance of Bodrum and is sometimes preferred by a yacht, when that port is too crowded.

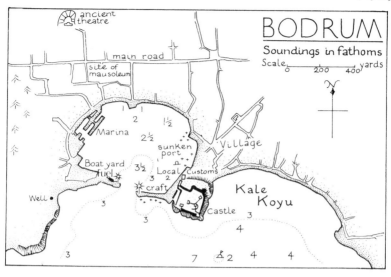

Bodrum

The ancient Halicarnassus, former capital of Caria. Its sheltered port is still protected by the original Greek breakwaters.

The site of one of the famous Wonders of the World – the Tomb of Mausolus – is close beside the harbour on the bare rising ground, but today apart from the recent excavation of the foundations, not a stone remains. The only objects of interest here are the Castle of the Knights with its museum, and the market on Fridays.

Approach and Berth. Chart 1606 shows the dangerous rocks off Khator Point which are unmarked but just awash. Otherwise the entrance is well marked. Yachts should make for the marina where Customs and police are located.

Although in summer the harbour is considered to be well-sheltered, in winter S.E. gales make the harbour unsafe, and a number of yachts laid up at the marina have suffered damage. Slipping a yacht at the yard of Erol Ağan, some 3 miles E. of the town, has recently been reported as being performed efficiently. A 60-ton Travel Hoist. English and French are spoken and the atmosphere is friendly.

Officials. See above.

Facilities. Fresh water at the marina is chlorinated but drinkable. Ice, soft drinks. New fuel station to port of entrance. Mails should be addressed: c/o Yat Limani, Bodrum. Improvement in facilities, under construction 1982: provision of showers, laundry, restaurant and bar.

Note. Owing to winter storm damage the marina will in future be closed from 15 November to 15 April.

The modern Turkish town, mostly built by the former Greek colony, is only of particular interest on market day (Friday), when peasants from outlying villages wearing colourful national costume come in with their wives bringing with them country produce.

View across the marina towards the castle

The Castle. On the east side of the harbour standing on a rocky eminence are the well-preserved walls of a large medieval castle built by the Knights of St John. During its construction fragments of the Mausoleum were torn down to embellish the castle and some of them remain embedded in the walls today. The English tower with the coats of arms of Plantagenet Knights still stands, despite a hard knock from a British cruiser's bombardment in the First World War. Among the scattered pieces of masonry one notices a plinth, a jamb or an architrave to a doorway, a marble capital lying on its side, carved with a heraldic device.

The famous Amazon frieze which, in 1856 Newton* with the Royal Navy's help, removed from the walls of the castle (where the Knights had placed it as decoration) was carried away by H.M.S. *Siren* together with the 9½-ft statue of Mausolus – 'the tall handsome man ... formidable in War!' Both statue and frieze are well displayed in the British Museum.

The castle was used by the Knights for many years, as a base for making sorties against the Turks, and as a sanctuary for escaping Christian slaves. Today much of the stonework has been repaired by the Turkish government and the castle restored to become a great attraction for tourists. Within the walls are exhibited many of the more interesting early Greek finds – sculpture, pottery, etc. Also very well displayed are the underwater exhibits of the joint Turkish–Pennsylvania Museum archaeological expeditions, led by George Bass and Peter Throckmorton. There are pieces of the hull and parts of the cargoes of a Byzantine period ship which sank about A.D. 620 off Yassi Ada, in the Karabakla Group north of Bodrum, and of the wreck of a Bronze Age ship which went down about 1200 to 1300 B.C. off Cape Gelidonya.

*C T. Newton, British archaeologist and at that time appointed British Consul in Smyrna. Some captured Turkish reports described him as the 'mad English Consul digging holes in the ground at Cape Krio'.

Continuing along the northern coast one comes to some deep and somewhat open bays, where the steep-to mountains cause strong gusts of wind at the anchorages beneath them. Towards the head of the Gulf are:

Keramos Bay, rather too deep for a small yacht; the hamlet is close to the shore with a taverna. The ruined Dorian city of Keramos which lies above the plain, formerly gave its name to this gulf.

Akbük affords a pleasant anchorage in wooded surroundings.

> **Anchorage** is in the western corner of the bay, 120 yds off the beach in 7 fathoms on a bottom of thin weed on mud.

There are several peasant houses and a good deal of agricultural activity. At the head of the gulf is

Gökova (Port Giova) where there are two loading jetties (depth alongside 12 ft) where small freighters load chrome ore. Here are port officials and a small hamlet where a bus or taxi is available to go to Marmaris.

On the S.E. shores the coast is well indented, hilly and wooded. See Admiralty Chart 1533 for plans of anchorages which are all quite close together. The first from eastward is

Gelibolu Limani, the most open and least attractive inlet of the four.

Sehir Adaları. Plan on Chart 1533. It provides a delightful anchorage between two small low-lying wooded islands with interesting Greek archaeological remains.

> **Anchor** as convenient in 3 fathoms in the S.W. corner of Castle Island Bay: sand on rock. Good shelter. A sand bar stretches some 50 yds from the mouth of the stream.

The sand is not of the original site but, according to Professor Tom Goedike, originates from the African coast. It is said to benefit those suffering from rheumatism.

The Hellenic ruins on Castle Island are well worth visiting. Best of all is the charming Greek theatre looking across the close-lying islets towards the tall mountains on the opposite shore. The theatre is nearly intact, and probably seated about two thousand people. Nearby are fluted drums of temple columns, many well-preserved sections of the citadel walls and some underground passages. It seems amazing to think of this small island as a fortified stronghold

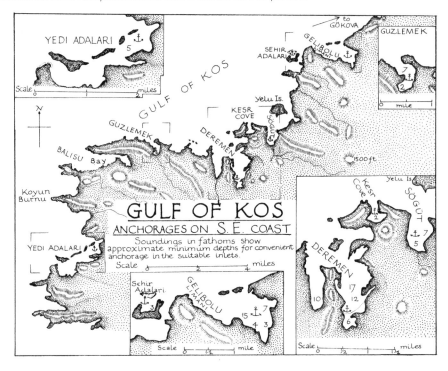

enclosing buildings worthy of a large city; one must assume that the adjacent country was then highly populated. Now, only a few peasants graze their goats and look after the olive trees.

Söğüt Limani is a pleasant bay with a good anchorage towards the mouth of a stream at its head.

Çanak Limani (Kesir Cove) is a deserted wooded inlet with all-round shelter at the head, but suitable only for a small yacht.

Ingiliz Limani (Deremen). Chart 1533 (plan). A large deserted fjord with densely wooded banks and attractive anchorages in superb surroundings.

> **Anchorages.** The creeks to N.E. and N.W. are preferable to the 'admiralty anchor' though it may be necessary in the former to put a warp ashore. Perfect shelter. Unfortunately N.W. creek is now less attractive owing to the destruction of the woods by fire.

> **Facilities.** Two small restaurants on the eastern shore – where simple food can be obtained and water is available (hose to the boat).

Guzlemek, a deep winding fjord, the sides densely wooded, with anchorage for only a small yacht at its head.

Balısu Bay (Gerenlikli Limanı), a pleasant bay, but shallow at its head.

Yedi Adaları is an interesting long lagoon formed off the coast by a row of small islands.

> **Anchorage.** There is a choice of two places. The safest alternative is S.W. of 7-fathom mark in Götağac Bay. Here the sea-bed rises gently to the beach behind which is a lake. The sea-bed is weed on mud, there being convenient anchorage in depths of 5 fathoms. Good shelter though within the lagoon is a fetch of 2 miles towards N.E. Anchorage inside the winding creek is impossible, but a small yacht can anchor in the little inlet to the N.E. taking a line ashore. Behind this anchorage is a most attractive valley well worth exploring.

There is no sign of habitation, and a yacht could spend a pleasant day or two underwater fishing.

On the southern shores of the Gulf from Yedi Adaları as far as its mouth are some open coves; but no further anchorages are worth mentioning and one follows the northern coast of the great Dorian Peninsula for 30 miles towards its western extremity. Here at the N.W. tip of a small cliff-bound peninsula is Cape Krio; a low, sandy isthmus joins it to the tall mainland range (1,800 ft). This cape, dividing the Gulf of Kos from the Gulf of Doris, forms on its S.E. side a most useful port of shelter (see p. 197).

Cape Krio with **Büyük Limani** affords shelter to local craft in this very windy corner of the Aegean. This anchorage is sheltered from the Meltemi by the low narrow isthmus, and from the Sirocco by the two ancient moles – 'carried to a depth of nearly 100 feet', wrote Captain Beaufort during his survey 150 years ago, 'one of them is almost perfect, the other which is more exposed to the S.W. swell can only be seen under water.'

> **Approach and Berth.** By day this is easy, and a vessel may pass in deep water 20 yds off the extremity of the S.W. mole. Keeping in the centre of the bay, the sea-bed rises slowly to 3 fathoms with a bottom of heavy weed on sand and sometimes boulders. It is extremely difficult to get a plough anchor to hold. Though there is perfect shelter from the sea, strong gusts blow from N.W. by day and from N.N.E. by night during Meltemi periods. Off the Cape itself very violent gusts make it advisable to lower sails before entering harbour.
>
> **General.** There is an outpost of a dozen Turkish soldiers who may insist on seeing ship's papers.
>
> **Facilities.** Watertap by jetty at head of the bay. Three tavernas each with frail jetty. Excellent crayfish but too many tourist caïques.

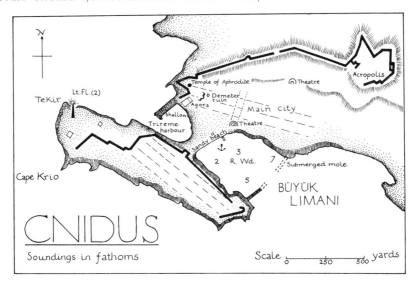

ANCIENT CNIDUS. Round the harbour are the terraced walls of large stone blocks often rising from the water's edge to the ridge above. Nothing except the lower theatre can be seen from the anchorage, but one must land to explore the ruins on the north side of the harbour.

Near the top of the ridge stands part of the large theatre, more than half having collapsed. Westward of its base is the ruined temple of Demeter, one of whose statues was carried off by the archaeologist Newton (with the help of the Royal Navy) in the middle of the last century, and brought to London for the British Museum. The most exciting excavation in recent years has been by the Americans who found on the slope overlooking the isthmus the podium of the Temple of Aphrodite. They also found the base of a statue which they have reason to believe was made for the famous Aphrodite by Praxiteles – described by Pliny as being 'not only the finest of Praxiteles' works, but the finest in all the world'. Close above the harbour is another theatre for about 8,000 people.

On the south side of the harbour there is not so much to see, but near where the lighthouse now stands, Newton dug out a fine 12-ton lion – the symbol for valour – which now stands proudly aloof in the British Museum. It was probably a naval war memorial, and one likes to think that it was this lion which inspired Thucydides to write these words:

> *The whole earth is the tomb of heroic men*
> *and their story is not graven only on stone*
> *over their clay but abides everywhere*
> *without visible symbol, woven into the stuff*
> *of other men's lives.*

The Scots chose this inscription for their war memorial at Edinburgh.

The ancient trireme harbour described by Strabo as 'a station for 20 vessels' has silted, and is now too shallow to serve any purpose today.

Gulf of Doris or Hisarönü Körfezi (Gulf of Fortresses)

See Chart 1604 and note that many hilltops are marked with the ruin of some early defensive work.

Entering the Gulf near Cape Krio (Iskandil Burnu) a vessel should follow the tall, barren Dorian promontory towards the wooded shores at its head. The mountain ridge (with a rough road from Cape Krio at its foot) slowly descends to the Plain of Datça. There is very little traffic in the Gulf – the occasional trading caïque or sponge-boat may be seen. Much of the countryside is deserted.

Palamut Bükü, lying 7 miles east of Cape Krio and west of the north end of Baba Islet, has a small but shallow harbour completed in 1955. (36° 40′N. 27° 32′E.). The main breakwater extends from a wall on the beach in a S.E. direction for 170 yds and then turns N.E. (parallel to the shore), for nearly 300 yds. The entrance to the harbour is between the extremity of this mole and another short mole projecting from the shore. Depths are less than 8 ft, but silting inside the short mole has already taken place and a vessel having entered should follow close along the outer mole in a S.E. direction.

> **Approach.** The new breakwater extending S.W. from the point of the promontory has caused silting under its lee.

> **Anchorage.** This is at the head of the cove where there is improved shelter from the N.N.W.

Hayit Bükü is a small pleasant cove with partial shelter.

> **Anchor.** E. of short mole in 3 fathoms, sand, slight W. swell.

> **Facility.** Only one small taverna.

Datça. A sheltered anchorage at the head of a cove with a substantial village standing on the hillside.

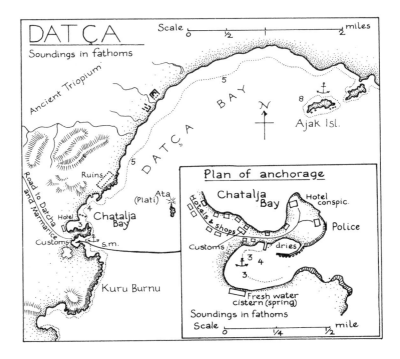

Approach and Anchorage. Since the building of the breakwater the whole inlet has silted – anchor to S.W. of jetty or restaurant in 3–4 fathoms and haul in stern by a long warp! (Depth at jetty head 4 ft.) Fresh water flows through the cove from a large cistern on the shore. Should the wind shift to the eastern quadrant, a yacht should make for Acak Adası, 4 miles to the N.E. and anchor behind the islets where shelter is good.

Officials. Customs, police. Harbour master.

Facilities. Fresh water at a tap on the quay or on application to 'bureau' at the head of cove; pensions and hotels and shops in the hamlet including a bakery. Local market Saturday.

Datça was the original capital of the Cnidian Peninsula. The ruins of the acropolis stand on the hill by the shore about one mile north of the castle. After the Persian invasion in the 4th century B.C., the Cnidians again settled down but, because of the recent increase in sea trade, they realized the importance of the strategic position of Cape Krio, and built their harbours and the new city there. By doing so they abandoned the agricultural plain supporting Datça, but the sea-trade compensated for the arid land adjoining the new city.

The present modern hamlet has been tidied up and the place is much visited by Turkish tourists. The village of Datça lies 1½ miles inland on the hillside and is approached by road. A minibus runs daily to Cnidus and Marmaris.

Miliontes Bay, which is attractive and sheltered, lies close southward; unfortunately the depths are too great for convenient anchorage.

Kuruca Bükü (Kocini Bay) is a sheltered anchorage in pleasant wooded surroundings but recently invaded by tourism.

> **Anchorage.** Let go off the N.W. beach in 5 or 6 fathoms on a mud bottom, being careful to avoid patches of heavy weed. It may be desirable to run out a warp to the shore. Basic provisions are available.

Göktas Bay, on the west of Kezil Head, appears to be worth exploring.

Bençik (Penzik) is a winding narrow inlet, wooded and well-sheltered.

> **Approach.** *Sailing Directions* give warning of a sunken rock ½ mile before head of the inlet.
>
> **Anchorage** is at the head in 4–7 fathoms, shortly before reaching the marsh where it narrows; a warp ashore may be desirable. Mooring is forbidden off the Government Solar Research Institute on E. side of entrance.

A few scattered farmsteads can be seen from the anchorage. The only objection to the place is mosquitoes and occasional visits by sharks!

When Commander Graves was making his survey for the chart in 1844 he discovered traces of ancient cuttings in the rocks where evidently an attempt had been made to dig a canal across the mile-wide isthmus which marks the end of the Cnidian peninsula. In a description of this excavation written by Herodotus twenty-three centuries earlier there is mentioned that, at the time of the threatened Persian invasion, the Cnidians set to work to dig a defensive canal; but the diggers, being continually wounded and cut in the eye by flying chips of rock, began to wonder if their work was really necessary. Accordingly, priests were sent to consult the oracle at Delphi and returned with the following answer:

> *Dig not the isthmus nor build a tower,*
> *Zeus would have made an island had he wished it.*

The undertaking was abandoned, and later when the Cnidians were attacked they surrendered to the Persian invaders.

Thiaspori Cove (N. of islet) is entered by the eastern channel.

Anchorage is in N.W. corner in 5 to 7 fathoms, good holding and excellent shelter in attractive surroundings, but owing to deep soundings one must anchor close in.

Keyif Cove, the westernmost of two coves near the head of the gulf (36° 47.3 N, 28° 4.5 E) provides a pleasant anchorage in fine scenery among wooded surroundings.

Anchorage. Let go off the centre of the beach in 5 fathoms, on a bottom of mud and thin weed.

At the head of the beach is a waterhole which attracts wild boar at night and roaming cattle by day. A short climb through the maquis takes one to the top of the ridge. Here, especially in the cool of the evening, when surrounded by a variety of sweet-smelling shrubs (rosemary, rue, thyme, sage, bay-leaves and myrtle), one can enjoy the view across the Gulf of Kerme.

About 2 miles eastward is the head of the Gulf, with a small river mouth. Nearby is a Customs Post and on the hilltops can be seen the ruins of ancient defences.

Along the south-east shore of the gulf the coast continues to be green and indented, but usually the heads of inlets are inconveniently deep for anchoring. This applies to the inlets of Port Losta and the anchorage under the islets of Karamea and Kaloyere.

Keçi Bükü (Port Kiervasili) is a narrow sheltered inlet with a hamlet one mile from its head.

Approach. A mile inside the inlet you pass an islet crowned by a ruined fort. There were reported to be 9-ft depths between the islet and the western shore.

Anchorage. A small shallow draft yacht may anchor close under the islet in $1\frac{1}{2}$ fathoms, but a larger yacht should anchor at the head of the creek in depths of 6 fathoms where shelter is better.

The valley is cultivated with scattered farmsteads. At the hamlet, half-an-hour's walk, one can buy small quantities of fruit and vegetables. The fort on the islet is interesting to visit, also the theatre and temple near Arin Dağ – a long walk. Mini buses convey one to Marmaris, a frequent service, taking 40 minutes.

Port Dirsek, an attractive sheltered inlet with an anchorage at its head in depths of 4 to 7 fathoms. A warp led ashore is sometimes advisable.

In the adjacent cove eastward (marked 'well' on chart) there is also a lovely anchorage off the beach with a deserted farmhouse. Fish and a few provisions may be obtained from local fishermen.

Turning into a large 'bay' opposite the Greek island of Symi is a gulf of that name: there is a suitable port but not of much interest.

Bozburnu Limanı is a small boat harbour by a hamlet. A mole recently constructed enables a yacht to berth off the quay in 10-ft depths with all-round shelter. Alternatively, anchor in the remote N.W. cove but if crossing from one berth to the other care should be taken to avoid the shoal which appears to have extended.

Although there is no longer activity in the port, it was formerly the centre of the Turkish sponge-gathering industry; their Greek rivals were established at Symi. Nowadays a few fishing boats are built here.

Officials. Port Captain and Customs.

Facilities are few: a couple of poor shops and some modest restaurants.

Körköy. A harbour of refuge N.E. of C. Krio in position 36° 46.2′N., 27° 39.2′E. (See Chart 1604.)

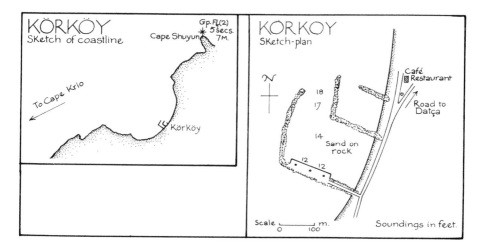

Approach and Berth. Enter from the N. between two rough, unlit moles and berth stern-to a quay, bows northward. The quay, 4 ft high, has bollards and rings, but the bottom has clusters of debris.

Facilities. Fresh water from a well below the café is of uncertain purity. Crayfish sometimes are available from fishermen.

Turning southward along the coast one leaves the Gulf of Symi and comes to Cape Alobi Burnu when the coast turns eastward forming the northern side of the Rhodes Channel.

7

Eastern Gateway to the Aegean

TURKISH COAST
Marmaris
    and convenient anchorages

GREEK ISLANDS
Island of Rhodes
    Mandraki
    Lindos
    Other anchorages:
        Cape Istros
        Cape Vigli

Island of Alimnia
Island of Khalki (Halki)

Island of Karpathos
    Pigadia (Port Karpathos)
    Tristoma
    Other anchorages:
        Amorphos Bay
        Foiniki

Island of Kasos
    Ofris
    Makronisi

Kasos Strait

7
Eastern Gateway to the Aegean

There are three broad channels between the Turkish coast and Crete: Rhodes Channel, Karpathos (or Scarpanthos) Strait and Kasos Strait.

Coming from the east one could be held up by strong westerly winds, making it desirable to shelter on the Turkish coast to await favourable opportunity for entering the Aegean or to obtain clearance.

At the northern corner of the Turkish coast is the attractive port of

Marmaris (Marmarice). This small port, with 6,500 inhabitants, has now become a popular tourist resort. It lies in a delightful green mountainous setting and in summer there is usually sufficient shelter at the quay for a yacht to berth.

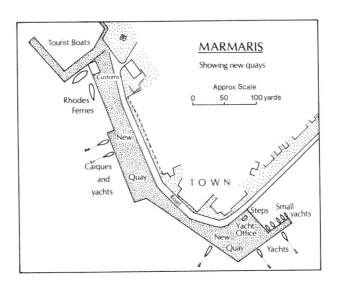

Approach. If entering by the W. Channel, watch for the rock visible above water in the centre of the fairway. (Chart 1545.)

Berth. Although a new quay has been built from the S. it affords only limited shelter. Many berth here stern to the quay during settled weather, but squalls sometimes sweep down from the mountains, when it may be advisable to anchor in the N.E. corner off the castle. A marina is planned in the area between the stone pier and the incense trees.

Officials. A Port of Entry with Immigration, Health, Customs and Harbour officials.

Facilities. Water, fuel and electricity at quay. Market day Friday, provision shops, restaurants, hotels, etc. Port of call for mail steamers and cruise ships; daily ferry for tourists to and from Rhodes all the summer months. Daily bus to Izmir, Istanbul, and to Fethiye. Details of the port and surrounding country are given in *The Ionian Islands to the Anatolian Coast.*

Proceeding southward towards the Rhodes Channel are half a dozen anchorages with varying degrees of shelter – Turunc Bükü, Amos, Çiftlik Bükü, Arap Adasi, Bozuk Bükü, all described in *The Ionian Islands to the Anatolian Coast.*

Rhodes Channel between C. Alupo (Turkey) and the N.E. tip of Rhodes (C. Zonari) is 9 miles wide and usually has a west-going current not exceeding one knot, except close off C. Zonari when it has been known to be north-going even against a contrary wind.

Island of Rhodes

This larger, green mountainous island is of great historical interest – the capital of the Dodecanese (Chart 1667).

Mandraki (Chart 1666, harbour plan), the yacht harbour of the island, is invariably crowded with yachts – large and small. Adding to the general confusion during berthing movements is a number of local ferry-boats which also operate from here.

Approach. Entering the approaches to Mandraki harbour, the extensive medieval walls of the old city come into view as well as the modern pseudo-Venetian buildings close to the quayside.

By day there is no difficulty in the approach. By night, however, if coming from southward along the coast caution is necessary to ensure clearing off-lying shoals, and on no account should the port be entered in strong southerly winds.

The light on Fort St Nicholas can be clearly distinguished from afar; but the weaker light marking the extremity of the dangerous, rocky point on the north side of the approach has, on a number of occasions, been washed away by winter gales and subsequently replaced. The last time it was washed away was before the loss of the yacht *Trenchemer* (Robert Somerset) in a S.E. gale during darkness on the night of 27 February 1965. The light was eventually set up on a safer site a few yards further inshore and was still in position in 1980. Its present characteristic: Qk. FL. G. shows over the arc of the approach and red through an arc towards west. Characteristics of the other lights can be found in *The Light List.*

The summer wind is from N.W., and along the W. coast it is deflected to W.N.W. With strong E. to S.E. winds a yacht is strongly recommended not to try and enter Mandraki; instead she should anchor off the beach in Trianda Bay, 3 miles W. of C. Zonari.

Berth. Large yachts berth at the head of the marina, others off the quay by windmills, where the water is often rather foul. Although completely enclosed there can be a surge in the harbour during winter gales from S.E. when seas have been known to surmount the breakwater.

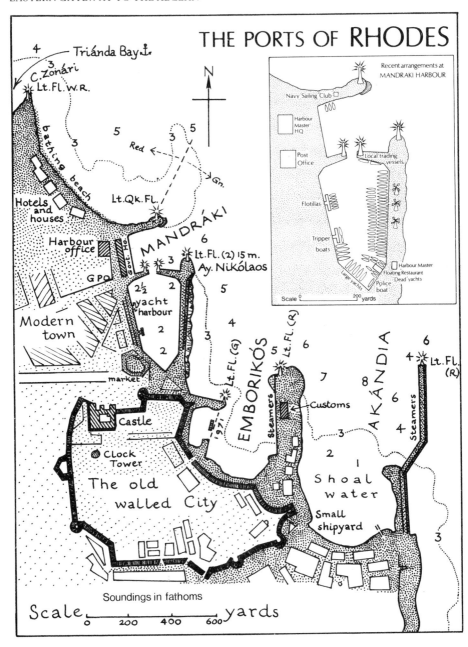

THE PORTS OF RHODES

Trianda Bay
C. Zonári
Lt.Fl.W.R.

Recent arrangements at
MANDRAKI HARBOUR

Navy Sailing Club

Harbour
Master
HQ

Post
Office

Local trading
vessels

Flotillas

Tripper
boats

Large yachts

Harbour Master
Floating Restaurant
'Dead' yachts
Police
boat

Scale 0 — 200 yards

Red
Gn.

Hotels
and
houses

Lt.Qk.Fl.

MANDRÁKI

Harbour
office

GPO

Modern
town

2½ 2
yacht
harbour

Lt.Fl. (2) 15 m.
Ay. Nikólaos

market

Castle

Clock
Tower

The old
walled City

Lt.Fl.(G)

EMBORIKÓS

Steamers

Lt.Fl. (R)

Customs

AKÁNDIA

Steamers

Lt.Fl.
(R)

Shoal
water

Small
shipyard

Soundings in fathoms

Scale 0 — 200 — 400 — 600 yards

Officials. Health, Customs, Immigration and Harbour Master, this being a Port of Entry.

Port Facilities. Water is laid on by a hydrant near the root of the jetty: its supply and a hose can be arranged by the Harbour Master. Petrol and diesel fuel are available at the Fina Filling

Station. Many shops are close at hand, especially at the white, octagonal market. There are numerous modern hotels, several restaurants of various standards, a number of banks, and wine in the old town near the harbour gate.

Fast steamers from Piraeus run many times a week (about 20 hrs) and berth in Emborikos Harbour. An air service to and from Athens several times a day; and air communications with Cyprus once a week.

Repairs and Laying-Up. The boat-yard Nereus undertakes yacht work. Travel-lift (capacity 60 tons) has been installed and storage space provided for more than 100 yachts. Gardienage can also be provided for yachts berthed in Mandraki Harbour (Nereus, Odos Australia 19, Rhodes. Tel. 22.717). For laying up in winter a concrete hard has been built, but bearing in mind the climate of Rhodes it is recommended that wooden yachts should lay up afloat at the yachtyard moorings. In 1981–2 local authorities raised some difficulties.

Mandraki – fifty years ago

The Town. Rhodes has had many conquerors during its remarkable history. The modern resort of today was started by the Italians during their domination between the two World Wars. Not only did they erect the pseudo-Venetian buildings of the new town and lay out the avenues of flowering trees, but they restored the medieval city. The architecture of the Knights of St John of the 14th and 15th centuries is to be seen everywhere in the Old City, where almost until the First World War the old Turkish custom still continued of tolling a bell every night at sunset to denote the closing of the city gates. Only Turks and Jews might then remain within, while visitors from the west had to be content with accommodation provided outside in a little Greek inn. In half a century things had completely changed and instead of the one 'Hotel des Roses' of the 1920s, Rhodes has become one of the principal resorts of the Mediterranean with 150 hotels (1981).

No one can visit Rhodes without noticing the large stone balls which have been neatly stacked in piles near the city walls. Many of them are believed to be the missiles used in the siege of 305 B.C. when Demetrius Poliorcetes of Syria hurled these monsters from the catapults of his fleet at the city's defences. As the siege was responsible both for these missiles and for the Colossus, a brief account extracted from the history by Diodorus Siculus is of interest:

Historical Note. Known as the Besieger, Demetrius, a claimant to the Empire of Alexander, had already had success in battle against Ptolemy and Cassander. He wanted to consolidate these conquests and realized that Rhodes with its great trading fleet lay astride the main sea route to the Aegean: since it could at any time threaten Demetrius's communications, he decided to destroy this little 'maritime empire'. A vast expeditionary force of 200 warships and nearly as many transports was prepared, and with 50,000 men they set off for Rhodes.

The most remarkable vessels in the expedition were the 'Great Tortoises' or huge monitors, carrying large catapults and high towers intended to overshoot and destroy the Rhodian defence towers guarding the moles of the port. The siege was a tough one, and the Rhodians, although outnumbered, held their fortress. Reluctantly forced to withdraw, Demetrius returned to Antioch and having redesigned his equipment, again returned to the challenge.

This time his new attacking craft was the Helepolis described by Diodorus Siculus as having a large square base and a huge nine-storey tower – higher than any Rhodian watch-tower, and fitted with enormous catapults and drawbridges. Manned by 3–4,000 men, it was supported by 'tortoises', and when sighted by the Rhodian look-outs, it must have presented a formidable appearance. This was the master siege-weapon of all time, and it is known that catapults at that period could hurl stones weighing more than half a ton.

The result of the siege depended very much upon the effectiveness of the Helepolis which, despite repeated assaults on the harbour and defences, was only partially successful. Meanwhile messages from Syria demanded the immediate return of Demetrius. Reluctantly obeying, he was forced to make terms with the Rhodians; abandoning siege weapons and equipment, he agreed that a colossal war memorial should be built with the proceeds to commemorate this great event. Hence, there came about the erection of the great Colossus cast in bronze and 105 ft high dedicated to Helion, only to be overturned half a century later by the destructive earthquake of 227 B.C.

Afterwards the broken metal lay in the shallow water for nearly nine hundred years, and it was in this state when Pliny, impressed by its immensity, wrote: 'Even lying on the ground it is a marvel. Few people can make their arms meet round the thumb, and the fingers are larger than most statues'.

Now all is gone, the scrap metal, bought by a Levantine Jew, going back to Syria where it was first moulded: but among the piles of huge stone balls still lying by the city walls, some perhaps are the remaining relics of this great siege.

For some centuries local people thought the great statue stood *astride* the harbour entrance, as shown on the tourist post-cards; but there is no evidence of this from the early descriptions. In Roman days many distinguished citizens came here to study, including Scipio the younger, Caesar, Brutus, Cassius and Sulla.

The fine medieval walled city built by the Knights of St John more than six centuries ago is largely intact. After they had been driven from Palestine at the end of the 13th century, the Knights captured this island from the Byzantines and soon began to build their city. With the support of the Venetians and the Genoese they were established in a key position to plunder Turkish shipping and exercise control of commerce in Levant waters. The building of fortresses at Halicarnassus, Kos and Kastellorizo, helped them in these activities which lasted more or less continuously until 1522, when the Knights, having withstood two sieges from the Turks, finally capitulated. They were however treated with great consideration, being allowed to evacuate the island with their arms and belongings, sailing first for Cyprus and finally after a period in Tripoli, making Malta their ultimate home. The best of the Knight's architecture remaining today is the Street of the Knights, and the 14th-century hospital, now the museum. Most remarkable too are the very broad walls, more than 2 miles in length and surrounded by a moat 50 ft deep, hewn from the rock.

On leaving the town, the sight of the green countryside with its pleasant villages soon restores the feeling of being in Greece. Lindos, 20 miles down the S.E. coast, should not be missed, nor should the Hellenic city of Kamiros and the Castro of the Knights on the north-west coast. The scenery, particularly in the southern part of the island, is very fine.

Lindos, one of the three Hellenic cities, lies at the top of a high headland whose sides fall abruptly into the sea. Beneath it is **Port Lindos**, a sheltered summer anchorage where one may land to visit the acropolis.

> **Approach.** See plan on Chart 1666, which is not entirely accurate for depths or under-water delineation. There are no harbour lights, so that except under a bright moon and with previous knowledge, entry by night would be difficult.
>
> **Anchorage.** Let go in about $2\frac{1}{2}$ fathoms in the centre of the bay with St Barbara chapel bearing S.E. A warp ashore is necessary. The nature of the bottom varies, being in some places mud or sand on flat rock and occasional ridges of weed which afford poor holding. There is a good shelter except between E. and S.E.
>
> **Facilities.** A path leads up to the village which has several lodging houses, a restaurant, and a few provision shops, tavernas, cafes, post, telegraph and bank. There is bus communication with Rhodes.

This place is well worth a visit, and it makes a pleasant day's sail from the town of Rhodes and back during the Meltemi season when there should be a broad reach and smooth water both ways. The acropolis of Lindos, set on a rock high above the sea, is one of the most spectacular sites in Greece. Here is evidence of the whole history of the island, dramatically and lucidly displayed; there is the classical Greek colonnade which caps the high platform of the acropolis with the temple of Athena Lindos, the ruined Byzantine church, and the castle of the Knights. Even the Turks have left a fortification to round off this long tale.

The citadel opens on weekdays 0800 to sundown (Sundays and holidays 1000 to sundown). Coaches bring tourists from Rhodes who overrun the place most of the day. If landing from a yacht it is therefore advisable to land early or late.

Beneath the citadel is the modern village formerly celebrated for its pottery and its weaving. There are still two houses with working looms and four which exhibit the old plates, together with the poor modern copies which are for sale. The church should be visited because of the frescoes; though of a late period they are complete and traditional, and give an impression of how the Byzantine churches must once have looked. It is pleasant to wander among the little white houses which, unlike most Greek villages, are all still lived in and well-preserved. Many of them incorporate Venetian windows and masonry, many have the Arabic dirt roof and all have the black and white pebble courtyards. The square has a beautiful fountain and shading trees.

Note: By night a restaurant on the beach at Port Lindos dispenses loud music, and to avoid this inconvenience yachts have reported a preference for the small bay south of the citadel inside Cape Apostoli – suitable in calm weather.

> **Other Anchorages.** *Sailing Directions* refer to a number of places in open bays off this coast suitable according to the weather. The south-east coast of Rhodes, which is mostly steep and hilly, provides some sheltered anchorages under a good lee during summer conditions. Among them are:

Cape Istros with a jetty on the S.W. shore. Caïques sometimes anchor here.

Cape Vigli, recognized by its ruined tower, has a good anchorage on sand S.W. of the point.

When leaving Rhodes to cross to Karpathos and Crete it may be necessary to anchor and wait for the weather to moderate. There are two convenient coves with excellent shelter and holding close to the southern cape of Nisos, where a vessel can await the opportunity for crossing. It is also necessary to bear in mind the impeding short sea that is sometimes whipped up over the shallow bank extending south-westward from the extremity of Rhodes.

The two small islands N.W. off Rhodes: Alimnia and Khalki, though of limited interest themselves, are worth a visit for the view of the castles of the Knights perched in prominent positions on the Rhodian coast:

Island of Alimnia has a well-sheltered bay rather deep for anchoring. In unsettled weather there is a choice of two convenient coves where, with a warp ashore, a small vessel can lie in a hard blow from any direction.

> **Approach and Anchorage.** Chart 1667. There is no difficulty by day, though it would not be advisable to enter at night. At the head of the bay a slight lee is provided by the remains of a breakwater extending from a small projection of the shore on which is built a little church.

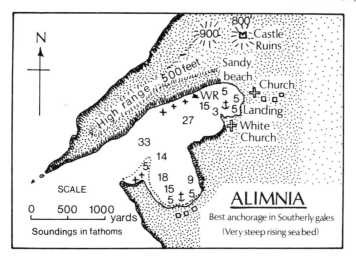

In a southerly gale the caïques, seeking shelter, prefer to anchor in the small square bay, the south-east corner of the harbour, but the bottom shelves steeply and one should run out a warp to the beach.

General. Although the castle is in ruins, the view from the hilltop is magnificent. Only twenty-five people live in this little hamlet and they communicate with Rhodes by caïque, landing sometimes at Castella.

Island of Khalki is mountainous with the partially sheltered Emborio Bay and a village at the water's edge.

Berth. Chart 1667. The mail-boats berth at the new pier; but caïques and visiting yachts berth at its extremity or off the pierhead by the centre of the village with a stern warp ashore. This is not a desirable place to bring up in a yacht except in very settled weather. The holding is poor – mud with stones.

The Castle of the Knights stands in a dramatic setting on a peak, 2,000 ft up, behind the village which in 1978 appeared to be deserted. The houses are in a state of disrepair and though the island once had a population of over 3,000, agriculture seems now to be abandoned. Communication is maintained with the main island of Rhodes by caïque which runs to Longonia on the opposite coast.

Karpathos Strait, 24 miles broad, separates Rhodes from Karpathos. Usually there is a moderate S-going current.

Island of Karpathos (Chart 2824)

Long, mountainous and narrow, it lacks an adequately sheltered harbour suitable for a yacht in the summer months. There are some indentations, but strong gusts of wind off the mountains sweep down upon the S.E. coast during the Meltemi season. Tristoma, the only well-sheltered harbour in Karpathos, lies on the north-west coast. It is closed all the summer and autumn months because of the dangerous sea breaking at the mouth. The port-of-call is Pigadia on the south-eastern shores.

The tall mountain range, rising to nearly 4,000 ft, forms the spine of the island; it runs from end to end and causes hard gusts to sweep down to the S.E. shores, thus limiting the places where landing is possible. In addition to Pigadia there are some small, well-sheltered sandy bays on the S.E. end of the island, where the land is lower and the valleys are more fertile, and there are signs of cultivation. At **Makri Yalo** the adjoining cove, Amorphos, is the more suitable for temporary anchorage.

Pigadia, also known as Port Karpathos, the principal village of the island, has a small inadequately sheltered port.

> **Approach and Anchorage.** Chart 2824 shows the anchorage. The mole, 100 yds long, runs in a N.W. direction from a small projection on the north side of the town; its extremity has a Lt. Fl. (R). It does not provide shelter against the prevailing mountain gusts which drive a vessel hard against the quay. It is advisable for a yacht to lay out an anchor and to make use of warps to hold her off. Depths of $2\frac{1}{2}$ fathoms until near the root of the mole, and the bottom is mud. Shelter is poor and there is often a swell. In the N.W. corner of the bay are yellow cylindrical buoys marking the position of submarine pipelines.
>
> A yacht should bear in mind that when the steamer calls she takes up most of the space alongside the quay.
>
> **Facilities.** There are a few provision shops, spring water in some of the houses, a restaurant, some small hotels, cafés and one or two tavernas. The mail boat calls twice a week. A small airport for connection with Rhodes.

Only a few hundred people live in the village around the port, but nearly 6,000 on the whole island, and although so close to Rhodes, life here is surprisingly primitive. A large number of the men receive remittances from England, the United States, Italy and elsewhere, where they have worked for most of their lives. Summer tourism is creeping in.

Tristoma is an attractive and out-of-the-way harbour with half a dozen houses, 3 hours by mule from nearest village. It cannot be used during the Meltemi season or during strong onshore winds.

Approach and Anchorage. The plan on Chart 1666 gives detailed information. In offshore winds very strong squalls blow out of the harbour between South Islet and Tristoma Bluff, making entrance under sail impossible. Under engine-power one may use the northern entrance (50 yds wide) keeping in the middle.

Note. (a) The ruined church shown on chart, north of Church Point, no longer exists;
(b) a flashing light has been established on South Islet.
    Anchor as suggested in Admiralty plan on Chart 2824, bearing in mind the possibility of strong squalls during onshore winds.

Facilities. There are no shops, but small quantities of bread, milk, fruit and vegetables may be bought locally.

Other Anchorages on Karpathos. (a) A good lee during strong N.W. winds is to be had in a sandy bay near the southern tip of the island; this is much used by small vessels on passage to Crete. (b) Good shelter has also been reported in **Amorphos Bay** where Cape Volokas bears 100° and the little white chapel on the tip of the promontory bears 220°. Here is good anchorage in 2½ fathoms, but open between S. and E.; it is also exposed to mountain gusts during the Meltemi. (c) There is also Foiniki, a shallow small fishing-boat haven on the west coast.

Foiniki, a small cove on the W. coast, lies about 2 miles N.E. of C. Theodorus. A short breakwater trending S.S.E. from the W. point of the cove affords some protection to small craft berthed at a concrete quay; here, among half a dozen fishing boats, a couple of small yachts could also moor.

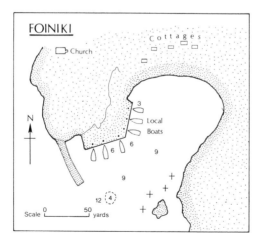

Approach. Keep near the breakwater side of entrance, the E. side being dangerous. There is only a small hamlet by the harbour; the ruins of Palio Kastro, reached by road, are one mile south.

Island of Kasos

This small island, mountainous and barren, lying between Karpathos and Crete, has half a dozen hamlets and, since 1962, a very small port at Emborikos. This serves the main village of Ofris which has only a boat harbour.

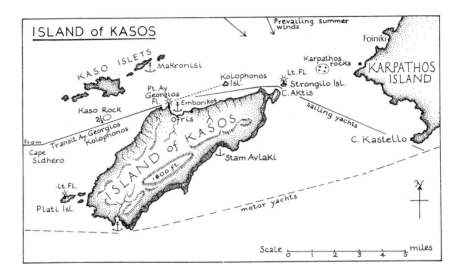

The Port. Emborikos lies 1½ miles east of the village and is very small, protected by a mole extending in a W. direction about 130 yds. Alongside the quay the mail steamer berths with difficulty even in settled weather.

> **Approach and Berth.** A large white church by the shore is easy to distinguish. The molehead is lit (Lt.Fl.G). The mail steamer berths at the outer parts of the quay and yachts near the steps at the bend in the mole in 2½ fathoms. A road follows the shore to the village. In the event of a strong Meltemi the steamer anchors on the lee of the island about 4 miles S.W. of Strongilo Islet (between Stam Avlaki and Phira Rocks) and communicates by boat with the shore.

The main village of Ofris built round the shores of the bay, accommodates most of the island's 1,350 inhabitants and today can boast of small hotels, a bakery, a few shops and cafés. Little more than a hundred years ago the population was more than five times as large and, though then without its own harbour, Kasos shipping could be seen in many ports of the Mediterranean. Egypt attracted many of the young men, 5,000 of whom left the island and emigrated at the time of the construction of the Suez Canal. It is claimed that the pilot of the leading ship in the procession at the opening of the Canal was a sailor from Kasos.

The north coast of the island is entirely exposed; if caught by bad weather, and

19 Lindos: battlements on the acropolis

20 Crete: Sitia, a pleasant harbour on the north-east coast

21 Crete: Grabusa, the solitary anchorage

there is no room in the harbour, caïques sometimes shelter under the lee of the islets north of Kasos. The low-lying islet of **Makronisi** is claimed to be the best choice; here shelter is good and there are convenient depths on a sandy bottom. If approaching from the south-west the transit of Cape Ayios Georgios light with Kolophonos Islet clears the Kaso rock.

The Kasos Strait, Chart 3679, between Kasos and Crete is 25 miles across; there is occasional Levant and coastal traffic. If seeking shelter under the east coast of Crete, the safest place to make for is Kolpos Grandes – see Chart 1677. Though open to east Dhaskalio anchorage or those recommended by *Sailing Directions* are safer to approach than Sidhero Cove (Ayios Ioannis) which should only be attempted by day and during calm weather (see Chapter 8, p. 215-plan of N.E. Crete.)

8

North Coast of Crete

(Charts 3677, 3678, 3679)

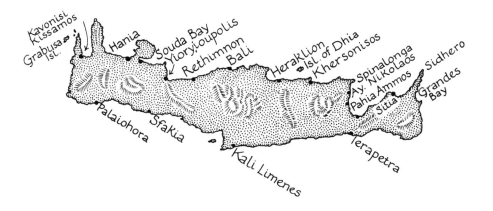

Sidhero
Dhaskalio Bay }N.E. corner,
Erimoupolis }Grandes Bay
Yioryioupolis
Pahia Ammos
Ay. Nikolaos
Spinalonga Bay
Spinalonga Islet
Khersonisos
Island of Dhia

Heraklion (Iraklion)
Bali
Rethimnon
Souda Bay
Hania
Kavonisi Kissamos
Island of Grabusa

8
North Coast of Crete

Knossus, her capital of high command;
Where sceptred Minos with impartial hand
Divided right . . . ;

ODYSSEY XIX

Known as *Kriti* to the Greeks, this island was once the centre of the western world and the home of the first European civilization. It has a population of half a million.

It is Greece's longest and tallest island, being 140 miles in length; Mount Ida is in the centre of the great chain of high mountains (rising to more than 8,000 ft) forming a spine through which half a dozen valleys provide the only communication between the north coast and the south.

Crete at the peak of the Bronze Age was the leading maritime power. According to Diodorus 'Crete lay very favourably for voyages all over the world' (i.e., the Greek world of the eastern Mediterranean). At the time of the disastrous Santorini eruption about 1500 B.C., the eastern half of the island suddenly became depopulated and the Minoan hegemony declined almost overnight. Recent geological surveys have proved that the whole surface of eastern Crete was coated with a layer of pumice powder which had been blown by the prevailing wind from Santorini; it had destroyed all cultivation and compelled the population to abandon this part of the island for many years to come.

Rich finds of early Minoan and Mycenaean civilization are admirably displayed at Heraklion, Knossos and Phaestos. The medieval architecture still surviving is Venetian, and the houses and streets of the larger towns are partly the legacy of the Turks. They held the island for two and a half centuries, having wrested it from the Venetians after the twenty-year siege of Heraklion in 1669, and they ruled it until 1898 when it became autonomous; in 1913 Crete was handed back to Greece. Since then some good roads have been built and the towns have been improved with many modern hotels and houses.

The country scenery is grand; although more than half the island is impossible to cultivate, the northern slopes of the mountains and the elevated plains are rich with vines, olives and farm produce. There are areas of forests, but almost no rivers; the rain water runs away in torrents.

213

Early History of Crete: Minoan Palaces. Those interested in Minoan culture should not fail to visit one or more of the Bronze Age ruined palaces at Knossos, Phaistos, Zakros or Mallia. Originally built about 2,000 B.C., then destroyed some 300 years later and afterwards re-built only to be destroyed once more. All are different in their situation and purpose. Much has been learnt from the deciphered Linear B tablets which proved to be of a later Mycenaean language from the mainland.

The most vivid remains of these palaces today are those of Knossos, largely because of its partial restoration by Evans early this century; Phaistos on the south side of the island is perhaps the most elegant and remarkable, especially from its situation with commanding views in every direction; Zakros on the east coast was also an important trading port, and Gurnia standing above the Mirabella Gulf was a town.

At the same time one should study in the famous Heraklion Museum the magnificent collection of Bronze Age artefacts including beautiful specimens of design and craftsmanship all imaginatively displayed.

It has recently been ascertained that the Mycenaeans from the mainland had displaced the Minoans and taken possession of Crete about the year 1450 B.C.

The half-million inhabitants who live in the villages and small towns, mainly on the northern coast, differ slightly from the mainland Greeks. Though St Paul complains of their being 'always liars, evil beasts, slow bellies', these people today are certainly in a different category and though very independent by nature are pleasant to strangers visiting Crete.

Winds off Northern Crete. During the summer months north-westerly winds may be expected generally.

From the eastern end of Crete as far as Heraklion winds are almost invariably N.W., but in the Souda Bay–Hania area they become north; and in the Kithera Channel westerlies predominate with periods of N.E.

Although the northern shores are open to the prevailing wind all the summer there is sufficient shelter for a yacht at most of the ports listed.

Prohibited Areas. Off both the north and south coasts of Crete there are large areas used for military purposes, marked on the charts. Some of these are only firing or bombing ranges and when in action are referred to by their code name in the Notices to Mariners broadcast daily on the First programme (radio) in Greek; and in English from coastal radio telephone stations at Athens, Heraklion, Corfu, Patras and Rhodes at times stated in Introduction (p.xxii).

Yachts are warned that the west side of the Sidhero Peninsula and the Souda Bay area with its approaches are Prohibited Areas, and they should keep well clear of the coast.

When approaching the N.E. corner of Crete from the direction of Rhodes with the normal summer wind (W. to N.W.) sheltered anchorage may be found if necessary on the S. side of Cape Sidhero (see plan below).

Sidhero (Ayios Ioannis on some Admiralty Charts) is a minute 2-fathom cove close under Cape Sidhero affording shelter in all weather except S.E. but if Wreck Rock cannot be seen it is advisable to make for

Dhaskalio Bay is about a mile to the S.W. Alternatively in bad weather, especially N.W. winds, a yacht should make for

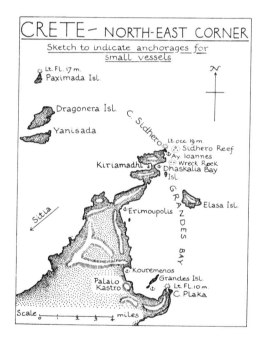

Erimoupolis and anchor in good shelter off a sandy beach.

On the west side of C. Sidhero is

Sitia, a pleasant unspoilt little town adjoining a small unfinished harbour.

Though reasonably sheltered from prevailing summer winds it is frequently uncomfortable.

Approach. The village and ruined fort can be seen in the distance and the harbour should be approached on a westerly course. There is a choice of two berths, each off a mole. A stranded wreck 700 yds S.S.E. of pierhead. (Chart 1677.)

Berth. The North Mole, some 250 yds long, lies north of the village. It has a high protecting wall and broad quay, depths of 40 ft at its extremity which is lit (Lt. F.G.). Here mail steamers, freighters and traders berth, as well as, sometimes, yachts at the root. (A fuel pump near the root for trawlers only.) The South Quay and projected small harbour is 500 yds south of the North Mole and close to the village. There are depths of more than 2 fathoms for most of its length and on its extremity is a Lt. F.R. The quay is apt to be crowded with small fishing boats, but yachts are always instructed to berth here on the south side. To form the eastern flank of the small harbour a mole has been planned to project from the shore close south of a watercourse in a direction N.N.E., but by 1978 only about one-third of the planned length had been built up to sea-level, work being now discontinued. This extremity is lit by a hurricane lamp.

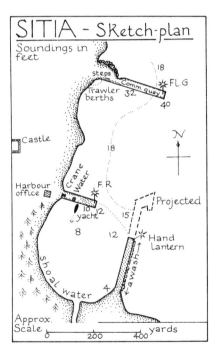

Officials. Harbour Office at the root of the South Quay.

Facilities. Electricity and water available half way along the South Quay. A 2-ton crane at the root. Fresh provisions at the shops in the streets parallel to the waterfront, ice obtainable and excellent local wine; workshops and a small-boat builder. Many hotels, tavernas and cafés. This is the best place in all Crete to provision, being little affected by tourism. Buses to Palaikastro,

Ierapetra, Ayios Nikolaos and Heraklion and in summer to Var and Erimoupolis (Itamos). Excursions to Toplou (see Palaikastro).

Yioryioupolis is a pleasant little place at the mouth of a very shallow river estuary. Chart 1658, plan and Greek chart 097 reproduced below.

Approach. The white houses by the river are conspicuous in the distance and also the ruined fort standing 450 yds inside the river. Following the coast from westward there are 3–4 m depth close to the headland. Approaching from the east one should keep outside the 5-fathom line and steer towards the white church at the foot of the bold headland of Ayia Kiriaki, passing 350 yds north of the white church on the Ay. Nikolaos islet. When Ay. Nikolaos church is in transit with a large solitary hotel on the shore, course may be altered towards the extremity of the short mole at the river mouth. One should keep very close to its quay because the bottom slopes up steeply to half a metre: then berth alongside before reaching a ramp near the bridge. Perfect shelter. Trawlers drawing 2 m also berth alongside. Local fishermen are often helpful.

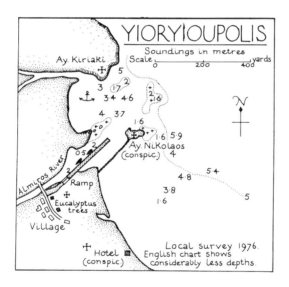

This place could hardly be recommended except in calm weather when all hazards can be seen. A small yacht prepared to trust the local survey might attempt to reach the river.

The little hamlet with its 100 inhabitants is attractive. The main square shaded by large eucalyptus trees has several shops, workshops and tavernas. Plenty of local fruit and vegetables, fish from small local boats. Several buses connect with Hania, Rethimnon and Heraklion.

Proceeding westward one soon comes to the Gulf of Mirabella, with the choice of four anchorages: Pahia Ammos, Ayios Nikolaos, Spinalonga Bay and Spinalonga Islet.

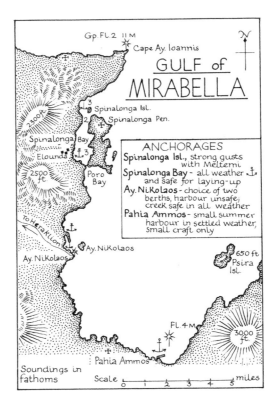

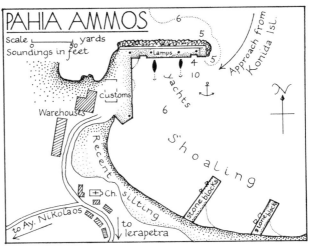

Pahia Ammos is a very small summer harbour at the head of the Gulf of Mirabella.

Approach. In settled weather one should approach the molehead from Konida Islet (distant 7 cables) on a S.S.W. course. The molehead must be given a wide berth.

Berth. Stern to the quay in depths of 7–10 ft, but keep clear of a rocky patch by some steps near the mole's extremity. A slight swell comes into the harbour with the prevailing westerly wind, but a yacht may ride more comfortably in the deeper water south-eastward. The harbour is constantly silting and has to be periodically dredged; in winter it is untenable in N.E. gales. Quay is lit at night.

Facilities. Simple provisions, bread brought from Ierapetra, small hotels, tavernas, cafés. Local olive oil of high quality. Buses to Ay. Nikolaos, Heraklion and Ierapetra.

Ayios Nikolaos, a former fishing port, has now become a tourist resort.

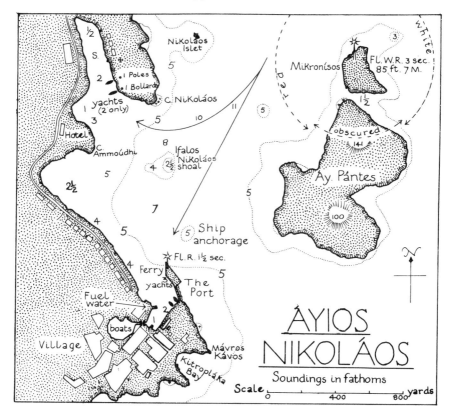

The Port

Approach. Chart 1677 fails to indicate that the shore is lined with hotels and houses. A mole runs from the N.W. eminence of Mandraki Point in a direction W.N.W. and then N.W. for nearly 100 yds. Its extremity is marked by a red flashing light. There are depths of 5 fathoms at the entrance and deep water all along.

Berth. Yachts are advised to berth near a ramp at the root of the mole, usually alongside. During a strong Meltemi shelter is inadequate in the harbour and vessels generally move to the shallow cove 6 cables N.N.W. It is well-sheltered and a pleasant place to moor with the stern to some bollards on the N.E. shore, the depths being slightly more than those marked on the English chart. Small yachts have reported wintering here quite comfortably in recent years, but today it is usually occupied by local yachts.

Facilities. Water and fuel laid on at the quay on the west side of the harbour; ample provision shops, banks, hospital, hotels and restaurants and tavernas. Bus service to Heraklion, Sitia, Kritsa and Ierapetra. On the jetty in the S.E. corner of the harbour is a 2-ton crane.

Ayios Nikolaos is now the capital of the Lassithi province, though until the latter part of the last century it was not even a settlement. It has become the most important place in modern Crete and, as a result of tourism, is still expanding. A car may be hired to drive to the excavated Minoan town of Gurnia, the Byzantine church at Kritsa and the monastery of Faneromeni – off the main road near Pahia Ammos.

Spinalonga Bay Anchorage. Following the shores of the Mirabella Gulf northwards, after 2 miles one reaches the large bay of Poros. This is wide and open to the E. and S.E. – a suitable steamer anchorage. In the N.E. corner is a large white block of hotels with a boat harbour off which a yacht may anchor exposed to easterly weather.

Continuing into the corner of the bay is a shallow boat canal (depth 3 ft) leading into the lagoon of Spinalonga, a spacious 4-fathom bay protected by an island. Its entrance in the north has depths of at least 2 fathoms increasing to 4 fathoms inside the bar. The deepest channel across the bar has been found to be about one-third the distance from the eastern shore.

Anchorage. There is suitable anchorage off Skisma 6½ cables W.N.W. of the shallow boat canal. Perfect shelter, a safe place to lay up; permission to do so must be sought from Harbour Master at Ay. Nikolaos. Boat harbour at Skisma.

Facilities. Provisions, pensions, car hire, buses to Ay. Nikolaos and Elounda which is worth a visit.

Spinalonga was used by Imperial Airways during the 1930s for seaplanes routed to Egypt and India. There is now a small hamlet at 'Turkish Cemetery' with a daily bus service to Ay. Nikolaos. On the island of Spinalonga (Lepers' Island) the old Venetian and Turkish buildings remain, but the island is uninhabited.

Spinalonga Islet Anchorage lies 3 miles S.S.W. of Cape Ay. Ioannis, east of Spinalonga Islet (distinguished by its ruined fort). There is anchorage in 2–3 fathoms with good holding, although there is nothing here to see, shelter is good except for the strong gusts off the high cliffs by the cape – a useful anchorage, if westbound when waiting for the Meltemi to relent. The leper colony on the islet came to an end after the Second World War.

Khersonisos. A small and very shallow little harbour adjoining a village; suitable for a small yacht in settled weather but with N.E. gales seas surmount the breakwater.

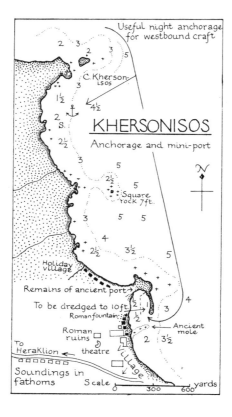

Approach. A white church, marked as an 'anc. fort' on the chart, is conspicuous. The new mole which has a short arm pointing westwards at its extremity is largely built upon the ancient mole, and is awaiting the installation of a light on the mole-head.

Berth. It is almost impossible to berth stern to the quay because a rocky reef 3 ft underwater runs parallel to it some 7 yds off for about half its length. Possibly a yacht not exceeding 6 ft draught could berth at the short arm at the mole's extremity. There are plans to dredge the eastern part of the harbour to 8 ft and to 16 ft on its south side. Quays are also planned along the shore; also the ancient south mole is to be built up. Until this is done, however, the place must be considered only as a summer boat harbour.

Facilities. Hotels, tavernas, restaurants, cafés, discotheques, a few shops, mostly tourist. Buses on the main road. Also taxis.

The village extends northwards from the main Heraklion-Ayios Nikolaos road and along the shore towards the peninsula on the other side of which is a large conspicuous, white complex of buildings known as a Holiday Village.

Towards the N. end of the village there is a much restored base of a Roman fountain with an interesting mosaic showing the catching of various kinds of fish. Rectangular Roman fish-tanks can be seen cut into the rock below the church on the promontory.

The village population is just over 700, many of them being employed in the brick factory.

There is also good temporary anchorage under the lee of Cape Khersonisos.

Island of Dhia (Standia), an off-lying island, is 6 miles N.N.E. of Heraklion. It is hilly and barren. Of the two coves in Ormos Mesarios, that lying to the N.E. affords useful anchorage in northerly winds. Sometimes used by fishermen.

Heraklion (Iraklion). The principal town in Crete with a well-sheltered commercial port and useful centre for visiting Knossos. The population has grown to 209,000.

Approach and Berth. The entrance is easy to find by day or night. Having rounded the extremity of the mile-long breakwater, a yacht should proceed up harbour into the Venetian basin which may be very congested. Berth off the eastern mole, bows N.W. in 3 fathoms. Mud bottom. Well-sheltered with only a limited surge in northerly gales. The castle provides excellent shelter from a strong Meltemi, whose average direction is N. to N.W.
Note. The lights at the entrance to the Venetian harbour are frequently out of order.

Officials. A Port of Entry with Customs, Immigration and Harbour Authorities close by. Weather forecasts may be obtained from the Pilot Office.

Facilities. Fuel, water, electricity, telephone at yacht berth. Ice from the factory near the Harbour Master's Office. Hotels and pensions of every category, restaurants, tavernas, and famous *souvlaki, bougatza* and *loucoumades* places. Provisions of all kinds from the market at the top of the main street leading up from the port (Odos 25 August). A great many tourist shops. Six flights daily to Athens, four a week to Rhodes, an occasional unscheduled one to Mykonos. Daily ferries to Piraeus every night. Buses to everywhere in the island.

From Heraklion one should certainly visit the Museum (open 0800 to sunset,

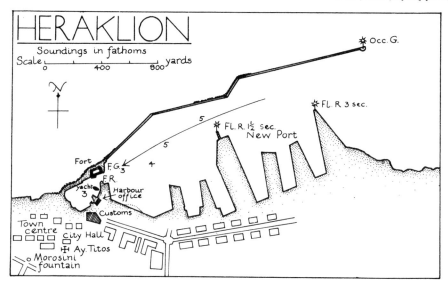

but closed on Sundays, afternoons of Mondays and public holidays). Knossos for the Minos palace – 5 km away – buses every 10 min from the bottom of the main street leading up from the harbour, or from opposite the Piraeus steamers. There is also Phaestos for the Minoan palace; a day excursion to the village of Anoyia, 53 km W. of Heraklion, famous for its weaving, and a night excursion to the village of Axos, 8 km further for Greek dancing and bouzoukia.

History. Heraklion was famous in Venetian times for the dramatic siege by the Turks. Despite help from many Christian countries of Europe, the Venetians after 22 years of siege finally surrendered to the Turks in 1669.

Bali. An anchorage in a small cove 14 miles E. of Rethimnon often used by local fishermen.

Approach. The small fishing hamlet can be seen squeezed between the sharp twin peaks on the E. side of the bay; the more northerly peak can be distinguished by a small white church and school on top.

Anchorage. Off the narrow beach there are convenient depths on sand and small stones. The bottom shelves gradually but space is restricted, and should a medium-sized yacht find insufficient room to swing, she can anchor in the bay opposite where the holding is similar. Though open to the N.E., the anchorage is reasonably sheltered from the northerly summer winds but in winter gales are severe and the local fishing craft haul out on a small ramp.

Rethimnon is an interesting small Venetian port with a recently built outer harbour.

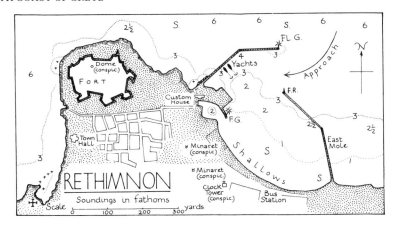

Approach and Berth. By day the Venetian fort on the west side of the harbour is conspicuous, but by night the harbour lights are difficult to pick out against those of the town. The new north breakwater extends for a quarter of a mile in a N.E. direction. There are depths of about 15 ft by the outer N.W. arm where a yacht should berth. There is sometimes a swell. The harbour is open to the E. and S.E. Gales or strong north winds bring in a heavy swell, whilst a north gale causes the seas to surmount the breakwater. Small yachts sometimes enter the crowded inner basin – the former Venetian port. They berth stern to the south quay in depths of about 6 ft, but the place is continually silting and it should be approached with caution. The quay has been resurfaced with marble slabs and is therefore a good clean place for washing sails.

Officials. Harbour Master and Customs by the inner basin.

Facilities. Water on the N.E. arm of the quay from a hydrant. Adequate provisions in the old town, excellent local fruit and vegetables, good wine, hotels and pensions; excellent fish tavernas by the old harbour. A small museum. Frequent buses to Hania, Heraklion and villages in the province depart from a bus station in the new eastern part of the town.

There is a small zoo in the park, the only place where you can see an Agrimi (*capra aegagrus*), the Cretan ibex, at close quarters. This fine animal is protected, and exists only in the remote mountains above the Samaria Gorge and in the off-lying islands of Ayii Theodori and Dhia.

History. At the time of the Turkish attack in the mid-17th century, Rethimnon, considered to be the strongest-defended town in Crete, fell in three days.

Souda Bay, although providing the best shelter in Crete, is not a port where yachts are welcome. The approaches and the naval dockyard are part of the Greek Navy's southern base and limits of prohibited areas are strictly enforced. Photography is forbidden.

Approach. The main shipping passage towards the port at the head of the bay is not buoyed except for some floats marking the closed area between Cape Souda and Souda Island.

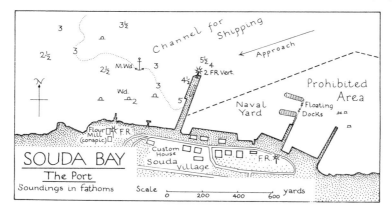

Considerable development of the dockyard has taken place including floating docks off the naval yard. Special care should be taken to avoid the dockyard area shown in plan as well as the coast of the Akrotiri Peninsula.

Berth. Either anchor N.W. of jetty or berth off it. Instructions will be given vocally from a pilot boat or by hailer from the jetty. Unless delayed by bad weather or in need of urgent repair, a yacht is discouraged from remaining here longer than necessary.

Officials. Harbour Master and Customs. Souda is not a Port of Entry.

Facilities. Adequate fresh supplies in the village. Bus service to Hania where most things can be got.

Souda Bay War Cemetery lies beyond the N.W. corner of the bay, 3 miles west of Hania and north of the main road. It affords a lovely view across the bay to the distant hills, and surrounded by trees and flowering shrubs, it contains the graves of 1,498 men who fell in this gallant defence.

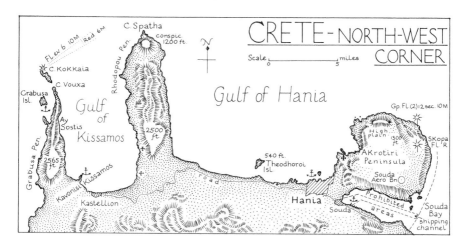

Hania (Khania or **Chania),** smaller than Heraklion, was the capital of Crete and is an attractive old town to visit. Its small though picturesque Venetian harbour has poor accommodation for a yacht and can only accept vessels not exceeding 10-ft draught.

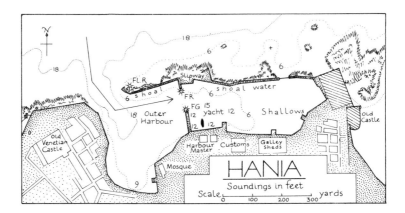

Approach and Berth. Chart 1698, plan. During fresh northerly winds entry should not be attempted. The molehead should be given a generous offing, and a yacht should proceed into the inner harbour and berth stern to the S. quay by the harbour office in depths of about 12 ft. The bottom being largely flat rock, holding is very uncertain and it may be necessary to berth alongside. With fresh onshore winds a swell enters the port. Prevailing wind in summer N.N.W. to N.

Officials. As for Port of Entry.

Facilities. Water and fuel available at the quay. The slipway, not recommended, can haul out vessels of over 60 ft and up to 100 tons displ.; a trawler fitting-out yard. Also a 5-ton and a 3-ton crane. Provision shops in the town, restaurants at the quayside, banks, hotels, tavernas and a hospital. Ice from a factory near the market. Bus services to Souda, Rethimnon and Heraklion from nearby bus station; from west bus station a service operates to Palaiohora, Kissamos and Samaria: also to Ayia Triada monastery on the Akrotiri Peninsula, thence by foot to Gouberneto and stalactite caves of St John the Hermit.

Hania's population has grown to 120,000. The town is less overrun by tourists than many places. Its small museum in a Venetian building is near the port and worth a visit. The best of the Venetian buildings stood on the hill east of the harbour and were destroyed in the Second World War. There is local industry in tanning, metalwork and wine. The countryside is well cultivated.

Kavonisi Kissamos. The new harbour lies on an isolated strip of coast 3 km N.W. of Kastelli village at the head of the Kissamos Gulf. The low rocky projections of Kavonisi extending for nearly $\frac{1}{2}$ mile in a N.E. direction has been

22 Island of Ios: the anchorage

23 Santorini: the summit
of Thira

24 Santorini: looking down
at the small quay from
the village of Thira
800 ft above

used to advantage in protecting the new harbour from the W. to N. quadrant while two moles are being built to provide shelter on the eastern side. Construction of a road and a broad quay has been completed and half of the 200-yd mole was finished early 1977; this is being continued in a S.E. direction and a temporary green light marks its extremity.

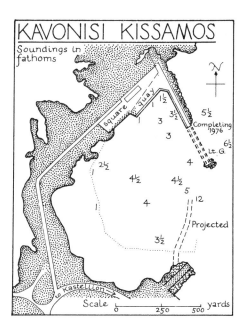

Approach and Berth. The breakwater and high ground overlooking the harbour and a small white church west of it can be identified from seawards. The entrance has depths of 4 fathoms and behind the mole the harbour has been dredged to 3 fathoms towards the root. Strong N. winds bring in a swell which can make the harbour untenable. Silting also takes place.

Facilities. Nothing as yet, except a telephone; buses run to Kastelli, 3 km. The mail steamer calls and is met by taxis. At Kastelli there are provision shops, hotels, restaurants, workshops and a small museum. Bus service to Hania. Weekly ferry to Yithion.

Island of Grabusa is isolated, with an insecure anchorage, beneath steep cliffs, on the N.W. of Crete. Still used occasionally by coasting craft, it has been neglected since the last century when British frigates used to anchor here in the course of stamping out piracy.* In the two years prior to the subjugation of Grabusa, the pirates' base, a total of 155 ships were plundered and their cargoes

---

* In February 1828 H.M.S. *Cambria*, a brig, when in pursuit of pirates missed stays and struck the reef, becoming a total loss. Some fittings from her rigging have recently been recovered from the bottom.

disposed of; 28 of them wore the British flag. For a whole year no currants reached Britain. The Venetian fortification still remain, but the only inhabitants are a few shepherds.

With northerly winds there is good shelter, but should the wind shift to W. or S.W. one should clear out. Grabusa can be reached by caïque from Kissamos.

Pondikonisi, a tall off-lying islet (unlit), lies almost 5 miles W. of Grabusa. The N.W. cape of Crete, also an islet, forms the S.E. side of the Anti-Kithera Channel.

9
The Cyclades

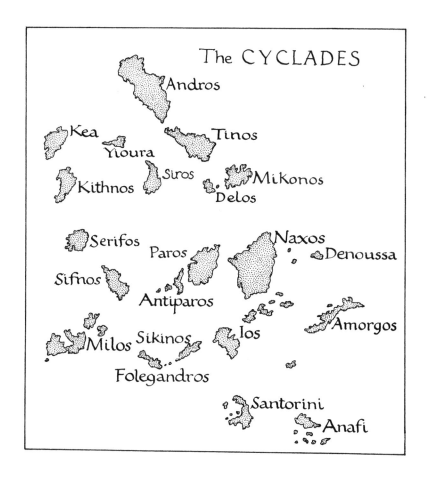

AMORGOS
 Katapola: The Port
 Kalotaritissa Cove
 Katakambos (Akrotiri Bay)
 Nikouria Anchorage
 Ayia Anna

ANDROS
 Gavrion
 Batsi Bay
 Paliopolis
 Port Andros (Kastro)

DELOS
 The Pier
 Furni Bay

IOS
 The Port
 Manganari Bay

KEA (KEOS or ZEA)
 Ayios Nikolaos
 Vourkari Bay
 Livadhi Bay
 Pisa Bay
 Kavia Bay
 Polais Bay

KITHNOS (THERMIA)
 Merika Bay
 Episkopi
 Apokrousis
 Fikiada
 Loutra
 Ayios Stefanos

MIKONOS (MYKONOS)
 The Port
 Ormos Ornos

MILOS
 Adamas

NAXOS
 The Port
 Kouroupa Point
 Cape Prokopis
 Cape Moutsouna
 Kalando Bay
 Apollona Bay
 Koufonisi (Koufo Islands)
 Skinoussa Island
 Myrsini Bay
 Iraklia Island

PAROS
 Paroikia
 Naoussa
Antiparos
 Despotico

SERIFOS
 Koutala Bay
 Livadhi Bay

SIFNOS
 Kastro
 Faros
 Plati Yialos
 Fikiada
 Vathy
 Kamares Bay
 Vourlithia
 Ayios Georgios

SIROS (SYRA)
 Port Siros
 Ormos Megas Yialos
 Foinikos

THIRA (SANTORINI)
The Port
South Anchorage

TINOS
The Port
Kolimbithra
Panormos

THE LESSER ISLANDS

ANAFI GROUP

DONOUSSA
Dhendro Bay
Roussa Anchorage

'DRY ISLANDS':

SIKINOS

FOLEGANDROS
Karavostasi
Vathy Bay

KIMOLOS
Psathi Bay

KINAROS
Pnigo Creek

LEVITHA ISLANDS
Levitha Inlet

YIOURA (GHIAROS)

9

The Cyclades

Ah! lonely isles, fragments of earth, that with his thunder
The wild Aegean girdles, like a belt about you thrown . . .
Antipater of Thessaloniki trans. F. L. LUCAS

INTRODUCTION

The Cyclades are still the most Greek part of Greece. On the tops of the tall hills one sees the abandoned terraces and some olive trees. Looking down to the clear blue water of some small cove one may see moored a couple of fishing boats. But the inhabitants today are mostly the old, for nearly all the young men have been attracted by the more remunerative life of the mainland towns, and summer tourists have taken their place.

According to *Sailing Directions* there are nineteen islands encircling Delos, once a holy city and centre of the Confederacy. Some of these islands are small or unimportant and nearly all are largely barren, for they lack water and vegetation and produce little in excess of their actual needs. In ancient days, the best of the marble used in statuary and architecture was hewn in some of these islands and minerals also were obtained. Today there is a small export of cattle, honey, oil, olives and wine, and the standard of living is simple. The life-line of these islanders is the frequent steamer to Piraeus as well as the ubiquitous caïque which plies among the islands. Though poor, they are a friendly people with great poise and dignity.

The character of each differs from that of its neighbour although they have a common pattern, the heterogeneous styles in architecture betraying the variety of their previous rulers. The houses are mostly built in the form of a cube and painted a dazzling white, with a flat roof, in contrast to the eastern islands such as Samos, Khios, and parts of Mitilini, whose villages are in the Turkish style, with red tile roofs and projecting balconies. In Santorini, Tinos, Naxos and other islands of the Cyclades there is often interesting Venetian influence still remaining – not surprising, after three or four centuries under the rule of Venice. This great empire occupied these islands mostly to provide safety for their ships trading to Constantinople and the East. They named the Aegean 'The

Archipelago'; a title inherited by the seamen of the British and French Levant companies. The British sailors referred to it always as 'The Arches'.

The principal town, or Chora, is usually known by the same name as the island. The Chora was often in a high position on a hill, originally built (for defence against pirates) with the stronger outer walls of the house side by side and without openings. Sometimes the houses were grouped closely together outside the castle, which in case of attack became a refuge for the inhabitants. Very occasionally the village of the port has also been the capital, and examples of this kind are Mikonos and Paros; but nearly always the ever-latent fear of piracy drove the people of these Aegean islands to the safer alternative of establishing their Chora inland. To augment this natural form of self-preservation, the landowners sometimes built fortified towers, and though these have largely disappeared, traces of them could be found recently in Andros, Khios, Kithnos and Amorgos. Most islands have one or more monasteries sometimes deserted or in a poor state of repair.

Only a strong navy could suppress piracy and it was not until a final effort was made by British frigates in the early part of the 19th century that these islanders, after many centuries of fear and suffering, at last felt their safety assured. This had its influence on the ports, for from then onward the life of the port began to overshadow that of the inland Chora.

The great excitement in the port is the arrival of the Piraeus steamer whose approach is heralded well in advance by the port authority. People appear from nowhere and immediately assemble on the quay, the departing travellers encumbered with boxes, suitcases, baskets, children and chickens. This event may take place at any time during the day or night and, as everyone knows the steamer will not wait, they jostle, unable to suppress their excitement at the prospect of a glimpse of the outside world. At most of the better-developed islands there are berthing-quays where the steamer may lie snugly alongside; but at some places she anchors outside the harbour and the intending passengers must pile into boats which, when closely packed, then proceed to the waiting ship. As some of these people cannot afford any sheltered accommodation on board they huddle together at night on deck which, during the cold winter weather, must be the height of discomfort.

Passengers, who have disembarked from the steamer, may find the whole family waiting on the quay to welcome them back from Athens. If the arrival is in the day-time they all pause at the cake-shop – for the men a glass of ouzo and *mezes* (cheese, olives, gherkins) or *dolmades* (meat and rice in vine leaves) or *garides* (prawns) – for the women probably *baklava* and for the children *loukoumi* (Turkish Delight) from Syra or Andros. All will like fruit. Then there is coffee, served in the Turkish manner with a glass of cold water.

In every island a number of the young men migrate to America, Canada and Australia. A surprisingly large proportion return to their native island in their old age in order to spend the last years of their lives among the quiet, simple surroundings of their boyhood. For the visitor they are often a great help in elucidating unknown facts about the people and the place, and thus contribute to the understanding of the local people.

Island of Amorgos (Chart 1663)

Long and narrow with tall bare mountains rising to over 2,000 ft and precipitous cliffs, it is primitive and not too spoilt. The small capital is reached from the little port at the head of Katapola Bay. If approaching the island from the S.E. the monastery of Khozoviotissa (not shown on chart) is most conspicuous.

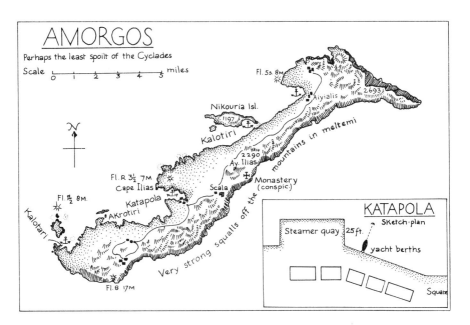

Katapola: The Port

Approach and Berth. When in the vicinity of Katapola Bay one should head for the S.E. corner.

The port has been improved by the construction of a 180-ft steamer quay at the outer end of the angular section of the old quay, thus offering further protection at the yacht station. There are 15-ft depths along the east side of the quay; ample bollards are provided. A yacht should berth under the lee of the quay with anchor N. Beware of shallow in corner E.S.E.

Facilities. Water from a hydrant on the quay opposite the small square, diesel from a shop nearby. Water containers may be filled from a fountain a little further along the quay. Provisions of all kinds. Excellent fish. Two small hotels, four tavernas on the quay, one on the opposite side of the bay; several cafés. Piraeus steamer calls three times a week, Rhodes ferry twice. Bus morning and evening to the Chora.

There is no anchorage on the steep rugged S.E. coast of the island, but on the N.W. coast, normally the weather shore, are four somewhat deserted places suitable in fair weather for a small to medium size yacht: Nikouria, the best, can be uncomfortable in W. weather.

Kalotarıtissa Cove, immediately E. of the cape on the extreme S.W. end of Amorgos, is very small but provides complete protection from all directions. Good holding on a level sandy bottom and ample swinging room, but a depth of only about 10 ft inside. The entrance is straightforward. The shores are deserted, but the cove is used temporarily by fishermen and could be of interest to a small yacht. (It is unnamed on the chart but has a small settlement at its head.)

Katakambos, about 2.7 miles E.N.E. of the west point of Amorgos, is a cove about ½ mile long between high hills, partially protected by the island of Petalidha, which lies across its mouth. There are no dangers in the approach and the shores appear to be steep-to. On the eastern shore there is a small concrete pier projecting about 45 ft into the bay, with 7–8 ft depths at its outer end. It is safe to anchor in about 2 fathoms on a sandy bottom off the pier, but towards the beach it shoals quickly. Viewed from the pier the cove appears landlocked and though considered a good anchorage locally, Meltemi winds often send in a surge. Except for two small churches the shores are deserted.

Nikouria, the best anchorage, lies in a bight between the tall islet and the shore. Anchorage is on a sandy bottom in 3-fathom depths. Protection in prevailing north-west winds is adequate, but gusts come off the high land; only with a westerly does a swell come in. The shores are deserted. Note the channel leading eastward has at least a depth of 10 ft.

Aiyiali bay provides a small port for the hamlet of Aiyiali. It lies in an attractive setting affording adequate protection for a yacht behind a short quay with a short breakwater extension; in prevailing north-westerly weather the sea may sometimes be disturbed. There are depths of at least 2 fathoms close to the quay and ample room to manoeuvre and avoid the clumps of floating mooring lines of the local fishermen. One can also anchor off the village in calm weather in depths of about 20 ft on a bottom of sand and grass. In 1980 a short breakwater was built for the Piraeus steamer.

Facilities. Tavernas, cafés, shops, two hotels. The Piraeus and Rhodes ferry calls.

From Katapola a road ascends to the Chora – a typical Cycladic village of white houses dominated by a ruined Venetian keep on the mountain spur. Several paths lead up from the head of the bay – 1 hr walk. If one approaches by bus a number of very small churches with barrel roofs are to be seen near the roadside.

The visit to Khozoviotissa Monastery – one hour's walk down a track from the Chora – is the main object of a call here. This small 9th-century monastery partly built into caverns is supported by its massive white buttresses projecting upon a vertical cliff-face. Far below, the waves of the blue Aegean can be seen beating against the rocks. When the traveller, Bent, came here in the latter part of the last century he had to enter by a drawbridge 'with fortifications against pirates'. He described the whole setting as being 'truly awful'. Unoccupied for some years, the monastery was inhabited recently by five monks.

A century ago the island of Amorgos had a population of nearly 4,000; it has since been slowly dwindling and is now less than half. The neglected terraces on the seaward slopes are witness to the declining agriculture. Although many young men leave to seek a more profitable living elsewhere the export of goat hides for shoes continues and a small fishing fleet is maintained. The tourist boom has helped to maintain the economy of the island.

Island of Andros

One of the largest and most northerly of the Cyclades, Andros has a mountain ridge with peaks rising to over 3,000 ft. Though from the coast the rising slopes appear barren much of the interior is green and wooded; the small town and villages support a population of 10,500.

The south-west of Andros is mainly bare and monotonous, and of interest from seaward only for the remarkable walls which divide the barren properties – slabs of slate standing on end separated by horizontal layers of stone. Low woolly clouds lying on the high mountain ridge are an indication of strong north winds. Towards the N.W. end of this coast is:

Gavrion, a spacious port, well-sheltered, with a small hamlet on the waterfront.

Approach and Anchorage. Chart 1833, plan. There is no difficulty making up for the harbour entrance though caution is necessary at night to avoid the Vovi shoal. In seeking shelter during the Meltemi strong gusts are experienced when beating into the harbour and once inside it is best to anchor off the village in 3 fathoms. At the seaward end of the quay which has recently been extended to accommodate the ferry, there is sufficient depth for a yacht to lie stern-to with the anchor to the north or south. A yacht drawing less than 10 ft can anchor beyond the jetty, much used by car-ferries loaded with lorries of local mineral water. Harbour works repaired 1981.

Facilities. Fresh supplies are obtainable. There are one or two hotels, bars and modest restaurants. Regular steamer communication with the mainland by ferry from Rafina and to Tinos and Syros. An undependable water supply at the quay.

The 3 miles of coast between Gavrion and Batsi has some small bays with excellent sandy bathing beaches. These are now being exploited by the Tourist Organisation; hotels and restaurants are springing up everywhere.

Batsi Bay, 3 miles S.E. of Gavrion, has recently become popular as a summer resort for Athenians.

Approach. Passing S.E. of Megalo Islet the entrance to the bay, with its small white houses, opens up. A flashing light is now established on the rocky point on the west side of the entrance.

Anchorage and Berth. Anchor on the N. side of the bay in convenient depths on a sandy bottom. Alternatively there is just sufficient room for a medium-sized yacht to berth stern to the quay projecting from the S. end of the village.

The quay extends only for 70 yds in a N.W. direction and has depths of 10 ft 2 yds off. Shelter in summer is good but during southerly gales the harbour is untenable, although the mole was recently extended.

Facilities. Water hydrant is available at the quay by arrangement with the Harbour Master. Fuel can be obtained in cans from Shell. Restaurant, tavernas and provision shops are on the waterfront. A bus service runs to Gavrion and Korthion twice daily and to Andros six times.

Batsi is a relatively new place lying in an attractive setting. Hitherto the island was known only for its ship-owning families, but now with the quick connection to Athens an increasing number of people come here in summer. The shores of the bay are surprisingly green with lemon trees and mulberries; there are a number of fresh-water springs.

About 4 miles S.E. of Batsi are a few scattered ruins of the ancient capital **Paliopolis**. Modern villas sprinkled on either side of an attractive steep green valley make the place easy to distinguish from seaward; but the anchorage is very open and the holding insecure. Of the ancient moles shown on Captain Graves's chart of 1844 only 2 or 3 yds of the S. mole now remain above water. A few architectural remains can be seen standing above some lines of cypresses – portions of ancient walls and an arch. The site is best visited by bus from Batsi.

Port Andros (Kastro) on the N.E. side of the island has become important on account of the main village adjoining it. The harbour with its short breakwater affords only adequate protection, with good holding in N.E. winds but it is quite impossible to get in or out.

The little town is the most attractive on the island and is well worth a visit. The old houses stretch along the peninsula either side of a paved marble street ending in a square facing the ruins of the Venetian castle. Here is the Maritime Museum and the monument to the Unknown Sailor setting out with his duffel bag over his shoulder. One of the many decorated medieval dovecotes is by the fish-market. Provisions of all kinds can be obtained in the town and there are pleasant open-air tavernas.

Island of Delos

The extensive ruins of Delos, former head of the Delian Confederacy, are of great interest. Barren, low-lying and uninhabited (except for the museum caretakers) the island is visited daily by hundreds of tourists. They come in cruise ships or from Piraeus by steamer to Mikonos and thence by caïque to Delos; having seen the ruins they are ferried back in the afternoon to their steamers. Facilities at Delos are poor. Yachts may not stay overnight.

> **Anchorages.** Chart 1647. The main channel is inadvisable on account of the foul nature of the bottom. There is a choice of two places providing other yachts are not also here:
>
> **S.E. side of the pier.** A small yacht not exceeding 7-ft draught can berth stern to a very small jetty and there are 9-ft depths at the concrete end of the pier. Ferry-caïques also use this pier.
>
> **Fourni Bay.** Anchoring overnight or landing at any time is prohibited.

The north wind whistles through this strait all day reaching a strength of Force 6 or 7 during Meltemi conditions. Should the wind shift to south good shelter may be found on the island of Rhenea in a cove on the southern end of Skinos Bay.

By the main site of the ruined temples is the museum and a small hotel with a shop selling local handicrafts. A guide may be hired. All round are drums of columns, plinths of broken colonnades and foundations of vanished temples all broken off at a low level; only the terrace of lions in white Naxian marble (7th century B.C.) stands out, forming an impressive approach to the temple as one comes from the port. Appearing considerably less robust than lions of today, their lean bodies may perhaps have been sculptor's licence; apart from these the rest of the ruins are Hellenistic. Close by is the dried-up sacred lake and the bases of columns which once formed the Temple of Apollo.

Winding up the hillside is a narrow cobbled street leading to the theatre, on either side are the stone walls of once elegant houses with little niches to take the lanterns which lit the street.

The restored private houses are in much better state than the remains of the temples themselves; here are terracotta stoves, marble tables, and well-heads, some inner courtyards with colonnaded verandas, portions of paintings and

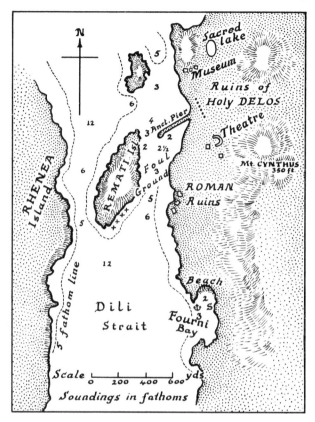

stuccos (resembling those at Pompeii) and some remarkably complete and interesting mosaic pavements.

Brief History. Early legends tell of Delos rising from the sea to become the refuge of the pregnant Latona and so the birthplace of Apollo and Artemis. As a holy shrine it was respected in later years by some of its conquerors; Polycrates of Samos is said to have secured the Holy Island to its neighbour Rhenea with a chain. During the Peloponnesan War Athens removed all tombs to Rhenea and forbade birth or death in Delos, thus completing the purification begun by Peristrates. Delos took no part in the Persian War, but fear of the Phoenicians led to the establishment of the Delian Confederacy, almost immediately dominated by Athens. It was independent in Macedonian times but later again placed under Athens by Rome. It is perhaps best known for the yearly Theoria, or pilgrimage, and the choir of Delian maidens.

In the early Roman era this island was made into a free port, and though destroyed later by Mithridates's admirals it became, according to Strabo, a great centre of commerce, 'thousands of slaves changing masters in a day'; they were provided by pirates to satisfy the needs of Rome, and both the kings of Egypt and of Syria co-operated in this trade.

In the later centuries Delos was plundered many times. Randolph, writing in 1687, stated 'The ruins are carried away by all ships who come to anchor there, so as part are in England,

France, Holland and mostly Venice.' Those making the Grand Tour a century later, would, as a matter of course, help themselves to what they could remove.

French archaeologists claim to have excavated a slipway longer than any found in Piraeus. Perhaps this discovery may lend support to an observation by Pausanias – 'I have yet to hear that any man has built a larger vessel than the one at Delos which is banked for 9 banks of oars.'

A stone stairway ascends to the top of Mount Cynthus, and from here one has the clearest impression of the island. In the cool of the evening, when the north wind abates, a peaceful quiet descends upon the island and one can see the ruins reflecting something of their strange, eventful history. Most impressive of all is to land when the moon is full; shining brilliantly on the white marble lions, they appear quite ghostlike in an eerie stillness broken only by the occasional bark from a shepherd's dog.

> *Les fêtes et les gloires étaient passées; le silence*
> *était égal sur la terre et sur la mer; plus*
> *d'acclamations, plus de chants, plus de pompes sur le rivage*
> CHATEAUBRIAND : *Itinéraires*

Island of Ios

This barren, though inviting island of gentle slopes, has three or four sheltered inlets as well as the attractive Ios Bay. Unfortunately tourism has destroyed the port, but the population remains at about 1,270.

The Port

Approach and Berth. Chart 1832, plan. Ios Bay can be entered by night as well as by day. There is good holding and shelter 150 yds from landing quay in 4 fathoms (see plan). The small port recently built in the N.E. corner has a quay on the N. side where the steamer berths; small yachts berth inside.

Facilities. Many hotel-restaurants and tavernas (where ice is sometimes obtainable) and several shops both at quayside and in the chora which can be reached by bus. Water hydrant and fuel on the quay. The Piraeus steamer calls two to three times a week, and a few caïques from neighbouring islands are often in port.

The small village, 20 min walk up the hill, is attractive with its flagstone paving, the edge of each stone being carefully outlined in white. Among the little white houses are one or two where provisions can be bought. There is nothing of antiquity on the island save the site of one of the many tombs of Homer, but both village and country have much charm.

Known to the Turks as 'Little Malta' on account of the good shelter, this bay was once used by some of Britain's anti-piracy ships for careening.

Historical Interest. A memorable incident occurred in 1692 when His Majesty's hired ship, the galley *Arcana*, sank as she was being careened. Mr Roberts,* who had saved himself but lost

---

* Mr. Roberts' *Adventures among the Corsairs of the Levant* (1699).

all his possessions, described how he was captured by Corsairs and made to work for them on board as gunner for many months, suffering great hardship. He writes '... twelve rogues ... laid hold of me, and carrying me on board on the starboard side, when I no sooner ascended but came a fellow and clapped a chain on my leg, and no one spoke to me one word.'

Manganari Bay on the south coast is another suitable anchorage but rather exposed to gusts of wind during Meltemi. Two small hotels have recently been built here.

Island of Kea (Keos or Zea)

A mountainous island supporting nearly 4,000 people, it is of little importance today. Its shape and contours are remarkable especially when seen from the air; there is a high central ridge (1,800 ft) with deep-cut, barren valleys which fall symmetrically away on either coast down to the sea.

The island is separated from its neighbours by the channels of Kea on the N.W. and Kithnos on the S.E. The Kea channel is especially important as it lies

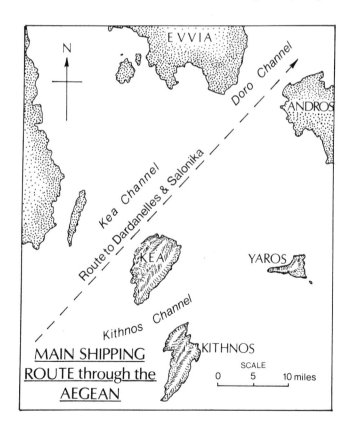

on the route to the Dardanelles and Salonika. The current here runs to the S.W. being much influenced in strength by the Meltemi wind. Though the current in the Kithnos channel runs more swiftly, there is sometimes a counter current running close inshore.

> In the First World War during the Gallipoli campaign and in Macedonia, German U-boats and mines took a heavy toll of British transports. On the forenoon of 21 November 1916 Britain's largest passenger ship *Britannic* (48,000 tons), whilst employed and painted as a hospital ship, was proceeding empty to Salonika to fetch wounded. Passing through Zea channel a violent underwater explosion shook the ship and she began to sink. Three naval patrol vessels rushed to the rescue and saved all but twenty-three of the crew. It was never proved whether the sinking was due to U-boat or mine.

Ayios Nikolaos (Chart 1833) is Kea's only good harbour. This spacious bay, once used as an important coaling depot, has two arms:

The northern one, Vourkari Bay, with a good anchorage under all conditions, has convenient depths off the hamlet where a small yacht may berth off the quay.

The southern arm, Livadhi Bay, with a quay off Korissia hamlet, is protected by a mole whose extension was breached in July 1981; this necessitates the use of Vourkari Bay until repairs are completed. A marina is projected.

From Korissia a motor-road ascends to Kea village, the island capital, standing 1,000 ft above the bay. This is an interesting example of a mountain village with narrow white-washed paths separating little white houses which seem to stand almost on top of one another. The medieval village was built on the site of the early Greek city Iulis, among whose ruins some of the Arundel marbles were recovered.

Passing through the village and walking in an easterly direction for about 20 min one comes to a colossal lion, 20 ft in length, hewn from the rock-face and standing on the side of a valley. Its presence may lend support to the legend that the island was once inhabited by nymphs who were frightened away by a lion and fled the island.

The most impressive feature of the steep mountainous countryside is the ubiquitous terracing. Hardly a slope is without it, yet today nearly all is neglected, for only the older men remain in the island, the young men go abroad seeking more profitable occupations elsewhere. Even the valona oaks no longer contribute to the acorn exports (for tanning) and the vineyards are mostly uncared for.

The following temporary anchorages on the west coast may be found convenient in summer weather:

Pisa Bay where a landing may be made to ascend the torrent bed to Ayia

Marina, a small church beside a remarkable three-storey medieval tower, now largely fallen apart. The anchorage is exposed to S. and the holding uncertain, but at the pier in the S.W. corner of the bay a yacht may usually find a berth.

Kavia Bay provides good holding and shelter from N. & E. at the head of the bay where some fishing boats are kept. There is nothing here of interest. A large hotel is on the seaward side of headland.

Polais Bay, on the S.E. coast, is much exposed to the swell, but it attracts keen underwater fishermen who sometimes land large fish. The remains of the ancient town of Karthea can be found close by, together with a few inscriptions.

Island of Kithnos

Formerly Thermia, a largely barren island of some 1,600 people, it is of no particular interest, though it has a number of inlets suitable for summer anchorages.

On the *West Coast* are:

Merika Bay, the port for the mail steamer which now berths alongside. It has previously been poorly sheltered and without attraction, but since the completion of harbour works in 1976 the situation is much improved (Chart 1825). S. side of S. jetty reserved for fishermen.

> **Facilities.** Excellent restaurant. Fresh fish. Buses to Driopis and Kanala.

A new hotel has been built in the port, and a motor-road connects with Kithnos, the principal village, where adequate provisions are obtainable.

North of Merika are three other anchorages shown on Chart 1825. Of these **Episkopi** is similar to Merika as regards shelter. **Apokrousis**, a deserted bay further north, is much better sheltered; it has only a couple of villas.

Fikiada, also a deserted bay, but smaller than the others, affords almost all-round shelter. There is no land communication here; only one summer villa stands by the shore with a short pier. Recognised from seaward by prominent church on headland.

> **Anchorage.** See plan; let go on a sandy patch as convenient. Bottom is coarse sand with long weed through which a plough anchor does not always cut and dig itself in.

On the *East Coast* are:

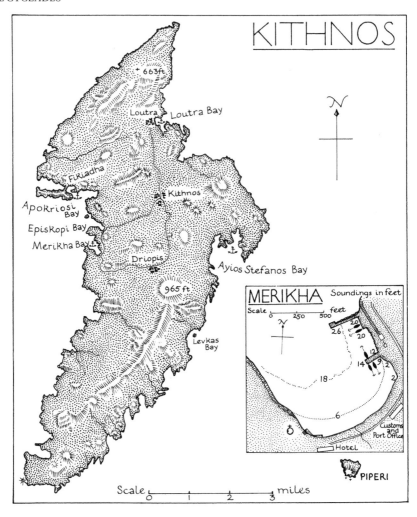

Loutra, an uninteresting anchorage with partial shelter, off a former 'Cure Resort', on the N.E. side of the island (Chart 1825, plan).

> **Approach and Anchorage.** The white hydro and small houses are visible some distance to seaward. The most convenient anchorage is in the S.E. creek where half-way along are depths of 3 fathoms on a sandy bottom (also some weed and small stones). There are one or two bollards for warps on the northern shore. A heavy mooring-chain runs along the bottom from the white bollard to the opposite shore. Shelter is reasonably good.

> **Facilities.** Limited provisions may be bought locally and there are one or two bars and a restaurant in the small hamlet. The Piraeus steamer calls once a week in the summer months. Kithnos village is 40 min walk along a road.

Though not many visitors come to this place, the old thermal baths establishment, built for Greece's first king, Otto of Bavaria, is still kept open.

An ore-tip and a mooring buoy in the exposed bay are relics of a mining concern no longer in operation.

From Loutra a track leads northwards towards C. Kefalo. Before reaching the cape itself one sees on the western shore, standing on a steep rocky projection 400 ft high, the ruins of a Venetian castle with its square tower defending the gateway. Most of the masonry has been quarried for building drystone walls in the vicinity; nevertheless, this medieval ruin is impressive.

Ayios Stefanos is well sheltered, being slightly open to S.E. but always tenable as an anchorage. (See plan, Chart 1825.) Several small houses stand by the beach, and a couple of fishing boats usually base themselves here.

Caution: The rocky shoal two cables south of the entrance point can usually be recognized by the discoloured water.

History. This island, one of the Duchy of Sanudo in medieval times, was ruled for 300 years by the Gozzadini family until it fell to the Turks in 1617. Their castle was in the extreme north, approached by a track from Loutra and their coat of arms is to be found on the façade of the church at the Chora.

Kithnos has little to offer and is mostly bare scrub. One wonders how, during the Second World War, a small party of the Long Range Desert Group managed to land on the east coast and remain hidden on the mountainside reporting on enemy shipping, while the occupying German garrison was unable to detect their presence.

Island of Mikonos (Mykonos)

This largely barren island, lying close northward of Delos, has become a tourist resort with modern hotels. Population 4,000. Its port serves as a base for tourists arriving in steamers from Piraeus, who are then ferried by the local caïques to Delos.

The Port

The North Mole has been extended, but the new part has been destroyed and is now under water. The red buoy marks the limit of the obstruction.

Anchorage. Yachts sometimes berth among the caïques in the S.W. corner, which is conveniently close to shops and restaurants; however the Meltemi can make the southern part of the harbour most uncomfortable. More sheltered, but noisy and dusty berths, also suitable for bathing are:

(a) Off the inner wider portion of the North Mole, with anchor S.S.E.

(b) Stern to the new quay which runs S.S.E. from the root of the North Mole (see plan).

Facilities. Water and fuel. Fresh provisions, good restaurants, tavernas, some modern hotels. There are daily steamers to Piraeus, Tinos, twice weekly to Rafina and frequent air service to Athens. In the season it is very crowded with holiday-makers of all classes and with visitors off anchored cruise ships.

White houses line the harbour with the small town rising on the slopes behind. Along the ridge above the slopes are the white-painted windmills.

Though the countryside is almost barren and without interest, the town is charming with its dazzling white houses – sometimes of two or three storeys – with doors and shutters in green, and little churches with blue domes. The narrow winding streets are pleasant to wander through, having the occasional attraction of a small square, a Venetian well-head, or an outside stairway. The Museum of Antiquities on the seafront contains objects brought from Delos and Rhenea.

There is practically no history attached to the island. Strabo mentions that the islanders become bald at an early age and Pliny writes that the children were often born without hair. Today they appear to be quite normal.

The local industry is cotton-weaving and clothing, such as shirts, skirts, and belts, attractively displayed for sale to tourists in many boutiques.

Ormos Ornos, a bay on the south side of the island, is sometimes used as a yacht anchorage, the depths being convenient, and shelter good. During the strong Meltemi gusts it is recommended to make use of the mooring buoy in the N. corner of the bay. Tourists have begun to appreciate its attraction as a bathing resort; one can, however, find two unfrequented bays lying further eastward; the first, Psarou, is the more secure. These have pleasant anchorages on a sandy bottom, but are open to the south. There are tavernas at each of them.

For yachts making eastward, it may be useful to anchor for the night in the small bay in the S.E. corner (N37° 26.25, E25° 25.5) close to fishermen's houses. The rocks marked on the chart are easily identified and the anchorage has almost all-round shelter. The holding is sand on rock.

Island of Milos

A volcanic island with mountains forming a circle round a huge bay, with its port which is sometimes covered by cement dust.

The Port (Adamas)

Approach and Berth. Chart 1832 makes pilotage easy, and lights having now been established on Lakida Point and Bombarda, entry by night presents no difficulty. Two jetties not shown on the chart have now been built out extending southwards from the shore at Adamas. The westernmost is used by the mail steamer and small freighters which berth alongside. A yacht may berth at the extremity of the eastern pier in depths of 2 fathoms or anchor off. The bay being large would not afford much shelter to a small yacht in the event of a blow from the southern quadrant; but it is one of the best harbours among the islands for small steamers. The holding on the sandy bottom is good, but cement dust covers everything.

Port Facilities. The unattractive port of Adamas is of recent development; it has a modern hotel and a few shops and a modest restaurant. Limited fresh provisions are available. Water and fuel available. Ice can be bought. The Piraeus steamers call.

Half-an-hour's drive takes one to the Chora, attractively built upon the hill over Hellenic remains, with a Greek theatre. Within 200 yds of this theatre the famous Venus – now in the Louvre – was found in 1820. A Venetian castle stands on the summit. The village, which is interesting and not too spoilt, affords fine views over the surrounding fjords and nearby islands.

The island's population of nearly 4,500 is mostly occupied in mining sulphur, bensonite, barium, etc. There are some villages connected by roads. The lower slopes of the mountains are largely covered with scrub, and there is some cultivation.

Early History. The old capital of the island, dating probably from Neolithic times, lay on high ground north of the island and has recently been excavated. According to Thucydides the indigenous population was exterminated by invading Athenians in 416 B.C.

During the centuries of Turkish domination, the island enjoyed much prosperity, and so long as it paid tribute to the Pasha no force was ever used to prevent its harbour from being used as a great base for pirates. It was here they brought their prizes for disposal and consequently the port grew rich as a mercantile transhipment centre.

(See adjacent island of Kimolos (Psathi Bay), p. 265.)

Island of Naxos

With its 14,000 inhabitants it is the largest and most mountainous island of the Cyclades. '*La plus grande et la plus belle*,' says the *Guide Bleu*. Because of its agriculture and the activity in the harbour it gives the impression of having a brisk trade. The quayside is usually animated with café life, restaurants and tavernas, buses and taxis, steamers coming and going, and caïques loading and unloading. Much of the countryside is green with some running streams.

The Port

Approach and Berth. Chart 1832. The harbour is easy to find day or night, but in strong northerly winds the main breakwater is inadequate and seas surmount its low wall, setting up a surge within. The inner mole has been extended with quays to enable the Piraeus steamers to berth. A yacht station has been established on the S. side of the inner mole at which yachts may anchor with bow facing S., stern to quay. Not comfortable in N. winds.

Facilities. Shops, tavernas, cafés and small hotels on the waterfront; more hotels in the town. Water on the W. side of steamer quay near the barrier. Fuel in the village. An archaeological museum in the Kastro, a Byzantine museum. Taxis for driving to country villages. Mail steamers call daily. Discothèques can be noisy.

Above the port are the few interesting remains of the old Venetian town standing on the side of the hill. Much of it is built inside the Venetian castle and is being gradually restored. The population (1978) is 2,900 and declining, in spite of ever-increasing tourism, much of it run by Athenians.

Extending round the quay is an old winding street crossed by arches; Venetian doorways, pediments and occasional coats of arms can be found.

In the country there is more cultivated land than in any of the Cyclades. Because of a generous rainfall one sees citrus fruits, olives, almonds, many kinds of vegetables, as well as oleanders and flowers. The marble quarries have been worked since earliest times and it is still one of the exports today.

A number of country drives suggest themselves. One passes by attractive mountain villages, one or two deserted; but there are half a dozen fortified monasteries and some defended 'towered' mansions (country houses of Venetian landlords known as *pirgoi*) and some churches. Towers and water-mills are to be found in the fertile valleys with their running water. One interesting trip is to visit the colossal Apollo (14 ft tall), cut in marble some 2,000 years ago, at the northern end of the island S.E. of Cape Stavros. It was intended for Delos and

Gng the

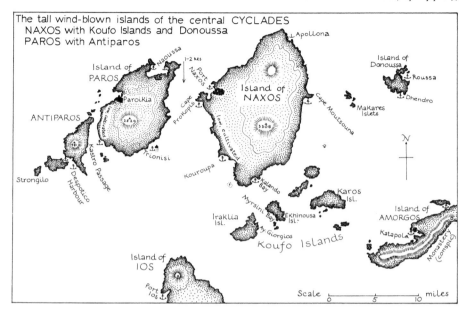

The tall wind-blown islands of the central CYCLADES
NAXOS with Koufo Islands and Donoussa
PAROS with Antiparos

would have been taken on rollers down to Apollona Bay, and thence by sea. At the last moment it was decided that the quality of the marble was poor, and so the statue was abandoned without ever being detached from its bed. The white marble is still used by sculptors, but emery and lemons are more profitable exports.

Early History. In very early days Naxos was famous for its wine and it was here that Dionysus (Bacchus) is reputed to have found Ariadne (daughter of the Cretan king) after her desertion by Theseus. The Venetians made good use of the island early in the 13th century when Marco Sanudo, taking advantage of the declining Byzantine Empire, captured it. The descendants of this great adventurer, who set themselves up as Dukes of Naxos, ruled this island and others of the Cyclades for 350 years until overwhelmed by the Turks in 1566, but even then Venetian influence continued and there is a Roman Catholic archbishop today.

The island was restored to Greece after the liberation in 1829.

Other anchorages off Naxos. Chart 1663. (See plan above.)

On the West Coast (where, along its northern shores, pilotage should be treated with caution) are two anchorages referred to in *Sailing Directions*. They can be useful to a yacht working up the Naxos Strait against strong winds, impeding sea and consequent adverse current:

Kouroupa Point. Lying 2 cables eastward of the cape is a delightful sandy bay with excellent holding in 3 fathoms. A hotel at the head of the bay makes a good distinguishing mark. Unfortunately tourism has crept in and the beach has become a resort.

Cape Prokopis, nearer the port, also affords a good lee.

Both the above anchorages are under the lee of low-lying land which allows the wind to blow at constant strength.

On the East Coast is a lee under

Cape Moutsouna. In a bay on the south side is fair anchorage near a jetty used by lighters when shipments of emery are being taken away.

Kalando Bay, near the south point of the island, is rather open and susceptible to a reflected swell as well as mountain gusts. Good holding (fine weed on sand) in 3-fathom depths. The shores are deserted.

Apollona Bay, on the N.E. Coast with its hamlet of about 260 people, can hardly be recommended as an anchorage. If wishing to visit the great Apollo by sea, a yacht should choose calm weather. The anchorage is in 3 fathoms on a sandy bottom 80 yds S.E. of the hamlet where a quay provides slight protection from the prevailing wind. The Apollo statue lies 200 yds inland in the old quarry. Under usual summer conditions it is preferable to drive here by the new road from Port Naxos.

Koufonisi, the small Koufo Islands. Lying close S.E. of Naxos only one is large enough to support a village community:

Skinousa (Ekhinousa Island), relatively low-lying, has a narrow inlet, Myrsini, on the south side affording good shelter in the prevailing summer winds.

Myrsini Bay is actually a creek with a small stone quay from which the village spreads out.

Approach. The entrance can be distinguished by a small light tower (Lt. Fl. W. 4) on the west side of the creek.

Berth. The inlet runs N.N.E. and near its head a small bay opens on the eastern side. On the northern side of this bay is a shallow quay where small fishing boats moor. On the southern side is a quay to which a yacht can go stern-to with depths of 7–8 ft at its western end; towards the other inland end the depths diminish rapidly. Sea-bed is irregular; boulders and sandy patches.

Facilities. Fruit,bread and vegetables can be bought only at the hamlet – 15 min walk.

Life on this small island is simple, but the standard of the people is the same as in the larger communities. Some of the Kalymnian sponge-boats base themselves here in summer.

Iraklia Island has an inlet, unnamed on the new chart but once called Ayios Giorgios, on the N.E. corner. It can be recognized by a few white houses lining the waterfront.

> **Anchorage** is at the head of the creek in 3–5 fathoms on a sandy bottom with room for a medium-sized yacht to swing. A swell sometimes rolls in. This anchorage is not as sheltered as Myrsini Bay.

A road leads to a village on the hill and there are a few farmsteads on the slopes.

Island of Paros

Half the size of Naxos, Paros has a population of about 7,000 who live in the three main villages of Paroikia, Naoussa and Marmora and in scattered farmsteads. The mountains being lower and the contours more gentle, shelter under the lee of Paros during strong north winds is less blustery than at Naxos.

Paroikia, the principal port, consists of two quays and a pleasant village where supplies and provisions can be obtained.

> **Berth and Anchorage.** Chart 1832 and plan. Berth at the quay inside the new port. In strong

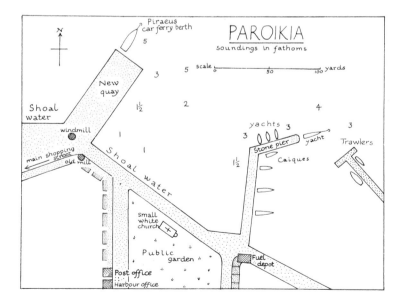

north winds it is recommended to anchor at the head of the bay where there is also good holding and better shelter. Apart from the natural shelter provided by the bay it is very exposed for a yacht to berth off the town quays. Other considerations are the change of weather and the busy traffic with small steamers, ferries and caïques constantly arriving and leaving, and the noisy music.

Officials. The Harbour Office beside the Post Office faces the public gardens.

Facilities. In the village is a wide choice of modern shops, small summer hotels, restaurants and tavernas. Water and fuel by truck from Naoussa. A local retsina and a red wine are produced, both quite palatable. Ice at the factory. One or two engineering shops, banks and taxis in the village. Car ferry from Piraeus calls daily and connects with Naxos. A caïque ferry runs to Antiparos.

The village (3,000 inhabitants) has much charm. The narrow winding streets with little white houses are attractive. Many of the older ones retain their frontage but are being converted into modern shops or flats – all are scrupulously clean being whitewashed every year and even the flagstones of the streets are outlined in white as in other of the Cyclades.

The principal object of interest here is the Katapoliani or Ekatopiliani (Church of the Hundred Gates). The church is, in fact, three churches in one, the main structure being of Byzantine conception with an early basilica (partly built of columns from a Greek temple) and a baptistry. It is all of much interest and should be visited as well as the small museum close by.

In the village is the tower of the Venetian Kastro – a medieval structure of long marble blocks, drums of columns and plinths collected from early Greek temples and fitted together to form a tower.

About 5 miles eastward of the village and reached by taxi are the ancient marble quarries. The seam of transparent white marble which formed the medium for Praxiteles' work and for the Parian Chronicle (describing ancient history from 1382 to 355 B.C., now at Oxford among the Arundel Collection) is no longer worked. After being quarried for long periods during the early centuries the place was abandoned until the last century when some of this marble was required in 1844 to form part of Napoleon's tomb. The quarry, once more abandoned, can be visited by scrambling down a steep gully, but as much of the tunnelling is underground a torch is necessary.

Recent archaeological excavations have revealed Mycenaean defences.

Naoussa is a substantial village in the centre of a broad inlet. A very shallow caïque port (5–6 ft) lies close by, but two sheltered anchorages suitable for yachts are under each headland of the approach. The shores are largely deserted.

Anchorage. Chart 1832. Anchorages suitable for a yacht are in the N.W. and N.E. corners of this large bay. Though protected from sea and wind there is sometimes the reflection of a swell during the Meltemi.

History. This place used to be severely afflicted with malaria. Once a main base for the Russian fleet under Alexis Orloff after 1770, it had large shore installations and gun defences on the western headland; but after a few years the base had to be hurriedly abandoned on account of the declining state of health among the sailors.

There is also good shelter towards the southern shore of Paros both close westward of Trionisi and in the southern approach to the shallow pass between Paros and Antiparos Islands. Chart 1832.

Island of Antiparos is a flat little island with the hamlet of Kastro and a famous grotto. Its interest for a yacht lies mainly in the 14-ft passage between Paros and Antiparos, and the harbour of **Despotico**.

Approach. Chart 1832, made from recent Greek surveys, shows that the two shallow channels between Paros and Antiparos have changed considerably since Commander Graves's survey in 1842. His original '14-foot passage' now called the Pass of Kastro is shown as having a minimum depth of only 8 ft whereas the N.E.–S.W. passage is reputed to have 13 ft. A yacht would naturally choose the deeper water, but examination of the sea-bed showed the bottom to be irregular, at one point with a depth of only 9 ft over a reef. Although the water is very clear the passage should not be attempted except in calm weather and even then a deep draught yacht is recommended not to accept the risk.

Anchorage. The harbour of Despotico is frequented by caïques and has the reputation of being a good all-weather port. It has convenient depths and good holding. (Formerly, in the 16th and 17th centuries, it was the laying-up port for all the pirate vessels, including Genoese, French and Maltese galleys.)

A road leads to Kastro for basic provisions.

The grotto, which lies $1\frac{1}{2}$ miles from the sea and 4 from the village, is now electrically lit in order to attract the tourists who visit the island from Paros. It is recorded that in 1673 the French Ambassador to the Porte came here with 500 followers, and celebrated the Christmas Mass. He afterwards removed several of the statues which had been hidden in the grotto and took them to Paris: some of them may be seen in the Louvre today.

Island of Thira (Santorini)

Appearing in the distance as a peakless cone, it is, in fact, an ancient volcano forming a circular island which has been split in two by a tremendous eruption; probably the same great upheaval, with attendant earthquakes and tidal waves, that scientists consider to have destroyed the Minoan palaces of Crete in Mycenaean times. There has been a number of severe eruptions since those days,

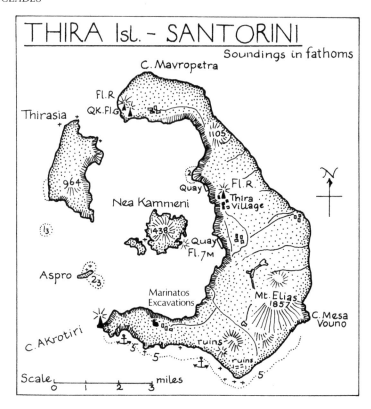

THIRA Isl. - SANTORINI

Soundings in fathoms

C. Mavropetra

Fl.R

QK.Fl.G

Thirasia

1105

964

Quay

Fl.R.

Nea Kammeni

Thira Village

13

1438

Quay

Fl.7M

Aspro

23

Marinatos Excavations

Mt. Elias 1857

C. Mesa Vouno

C. Akrotiri

ruins

5

5

ruins

5

Scale

miles

0   1   2   3

one alluded to by Strabo in the 2nd century B.C. when 'flames rushed forth from the sea for a space of four days, causing the whole of it to boil and be on fire'. The tall Mt Prophet Elias, nearly 2,000 ft, is crowned by a remarkable white monastery and a radar station well worth a visit for the splendid view.

Entering the wide, sheltered strait among the islands, a broad ribbon of white houses appears on the skyline above the sheer, brown cliffs. This is Thira, the capital.

To the southward is the lava islet of Nea Caemene where caïques are often to be seen moored to the rocks in the sulphurous water above the little crater which still spews out its sulphur fumes through the sea-bed beneath. Taking advantage of this natural benefit provided gratuitously by the sea-bed, vessels used to remain here for a day or two after which their bottoms are foul no longer.

The Port

Berth. Chart 2043. The small quay beneath the main village of Thira is easily distinguished by day. Though there are depths of 6–10 ft, the sea-bed falls away very steeply. The big mooring buoy for yachts close to the quay was reported sunk in 1982. In the event of a swell or unsettled conditions a yacht should proceed to the south of the island and anchor where indicated in the plan.

A new quay 200 yds long has been built at **Athinio**, 2 miles south of Thira anchorage. The daily ferry goes alongside and is met by taxis and a bus. Steamers to Piraeus, Heraklion and Ios.

Facilities. On the main quay there are now two small tavernas where basic provisions can be bought, but normal fresh provisions must be got at Thira and brought down by mule. The owners of these beasts, whose numbers appear to be inexhaustible, make a lucrative trade carrying tourists up and down between the landing and Thira.

When berthing off the quay it is an awe-inspiring sight to find oneself lying beside the crater-wall of a gigantic volcano. Beneath the water is a drop of 1,200 ft, and opposite are the islets – the remains of the volcano's shattered walls.

The mule-track zigzags up the 700-ft precipitous slope. The sides of the cliff, once the interior of the crater, are sometimes ash-red and even black; often corrugated as if with pillars, interspersed here and there are troglodyte dwellings.

The long narrow village of Thira with a population of 1,400 clings to the top of the ridge. Its two streets lined with white houses, and often spanned by arches, are attractive. There is a cathedral and several churches, and the peal of bells is sometimes heard. (See plates 23 and 24.)

The view from the top is magnificent, for one appears to be standing almost directly above the quay with probably one or two yachts and caïques moored beneath. This high plateau is agreeably peaceful after the disturbing impression left by the nether regions of the port. Across the deep blue water are the steep, brown cliffs rising vertically from the depths, and in the distance can be seen other islands of the archipelago.

One of Santorini's difficulties is shortage of water. Though rainwater is collected and run into the numerous cisterns at Thira, supplies are insufficient, and during the summer months a tanker from Piraeus must sometimes augment them.

The tourist trade contributes considerably to the resources of this island, there being a number of excursions to places of archaeological interest. In addition, there is an export of pumice and wine, tomatoes, barley and beans all of which help to support the island's 345,800 inhabitants.

Early History. It was about the time of the Exodus of the Israelites when the Bronze Age was at its height that both Santorin and Minoan civilization in Crete disappeared almost overnight.

At Akrotiri in the south of the island one can see in the cliffs the successive stratas of lava and pozzolena. Excavations near here reveal a number of fragmentary stone walls sunk deep in a landscape of volcanic dust. Pieces of wood cut before the disaster have been recovered and revealed by radio carbon dating to be about 1410 B.C. In the early 1970s the Greek archaeologist Marinatos excavated some remarkable frescoes showing seven Mycenaean sailing vessels probably about 70 ft overall with sails furled, one with a single squaresail bent to 2 yds; others paddled by a dozen or more men. These vessels have long overhangs and are each steered by a helmsman on the starboard side. These are now in the National Museum in Athens. Inland excavations at ancient Thira and Thyrasia reveal, under the pumice dust, houses of prehistoric inhabitants with walls still standing. Pottery bears a similar style to the Mycenaean designs.

All these places can be visited by taxi from Thira village, the Marinatos excavation being about a mile inland from C. Akrotiri.

The powder of pumice has been located in thick layers on the seabed in a S.E. direction from the island. It was blown by the Meltemi across to eastern Crete whose inhabitants were forced to abandon the whole area for a considerable period. Archaeologists have proclaimed since 1880 that the great upheaval took place about 1500 B.C.; certain scientists now have reason to believe that it took place considerably earlier.

Island of Serifos

Mountainous and barren, it has two large bays on the south coast:

Koutala Bay, a former ore port both for the ancients as well as the modern Greeks, is an unattractive anchorage largely because of the disused ore tips and the iron mines which disfigure the whole countryside.

Anchorage. Chart 1833 shows clearly the choice of where to anchor. The large mooring buoys shown on the plan have now been removed.

The only dwellings are those connected with the old iron-ore workings.

Livadhi Bay provides good shelter in agreeable surroundings at the foot of the mountain village of Livadhi – a picturesque approach (Chart 1833).

The new mole extending 100 yds eastwards from Ak. Poundi is marked by a small light structure at its extremity. (The light formerly on the cape has been moved 100 yds east.)

Berth. Yachts sometimes berth inshore of the ferry on S. side off end of jetty or anchor in the bay which is rather deep until it shelves towards the shore. The holding of soft mud may grip a CQR anchor, but during strong gusts with northerly winds a fisherman's anchor usually drags. Small yachts can berth stern-to just inshore of the steps on the new mole, but depths are only 6 ft and shoal rapidly. There is sometimes space to berth stern-to at the smaller inner quay (about 8 ft depth), otherwise anchor in the bay which is rather deep until it shelves towards the shore. The port is usually very crowded in summer.

Facilities have recently been improved; most of the fruit and vegetables from nearby market garden, brown bread from Chora. Fresh water from a nearby tap, summer hotels and some restaurants. Frequent buses.

The village of Livadhi clings to the hill immediately above the port; its little houses of dazzling white standing out prominently against the barren hillside can be seen many miles away. The ascent up a mule track is a steep, but rewarding experience taking at least $1\frac{1}{2}$ hrs to the top and back. One taverna.

The harbour, which is very shut-in by the surrounding mountains, can be remarkably hot in summer, but the sandy shore attracts visitors, and villas are springing up.

The abandoned iron-ore workings to be seen on many hillsides of the island were started by the Romans and continued throughout the Middle Ages until recent years. When the Venetian conquerors came their seamen complained of their 'compass needles being disturbed by the iron ore'. Today there is very little employment and the population of the island is declining; at Livadhi it is only about 200.

Island of Sifnos

This appears from seaward as mountainous and barren; but inland it is fertile with two main inland villages, Apollonia and Artemona. On the coast are a number of inviting anchorages suitable for yachts connected by local ferry boats based at Kamares. Tourism is developing, but the population remains at 2,000.

On East Coast:

Kastro, the most beautiful, is a shallow cove overlooked by a Venetian citadel with its high white walls and old houses clinging to the top of a conical hill. Unfortunately there is no proper harbour, and only in settled weather can a yacht anchor under the lee of Cape Eftamartiroi or in the entrance to the cove (see plan, Chart 1825). A road leads up to Apollonia, the principal village, standing on the plateau above. It has recently been given a new look.

Faros. A charming inlet affording sheltered anchorage for a medium-sized yacht, but many villas are growing up by the shore.

> **Anchorage.** Chart 1825. Let go in 5 fathoms 100 yds off the centre of the hamlet; sandy bottom. The anchorage is open, only through a narrow sector, to south.

> **Facilities.** A good taverna. A café and small houses line the shore. A motor road leads over the hills to Apollonia. A few fishing boats work from the port.

Plati Yialos. See Chart 1825. This is an open bay in attractive surroundings and a suitable anchorage for a large yacht. It has a reputation for violent squalls which sometimes sweep down from the mountains with strong N. winds. Hotels and many little houses are spread round the shores of the bay. A road leads up to Apollonia.

Note. After a strong northerly blow the passage across to Antiparos should not be attempted by small vessels on account of dangerous breaking seas.

On West Coast:

Fikiada, a deserted inlet with good shelter.

> **Anchorage.** Chart 1825. Proceed near the head of the creek and let go in 3 to 4 fathoms on a sandy bottom with patches of weed. Room for medium-sized yachts to swing. Open to W.S.W.

There are no facilities or dwellings at Fikiada; only the attractive little white domed church of Ayios Georgios standing on a rocky slope, completely cut off, on the north side of the entrance.

Vathy. An attractive well-sheltered anchorage in the midst of mountainous surroundings. A number of little white houses spread themselves along the shore.

Anchorage. Chart 1825. Let go where indicated on the plan; sandy bottom with fine weed and shelter nearly all round. Room for three or four medium-size yachts.

Facilities. A modern hotel taverna, café and basic provisions.

Vathy is the best harbour in the island and is always practical even in bad weather. Here is the beautiful church of Taxiarchis. A poor road (not for vehicles) leads to Apollonia.

Kamares Bay, the mail-steamer port, is both the least attractive and least sheltered of all, but the new pier and protecting mole have improved matters.

Anchorage. Chart 1833. Anchor in convenient depths at the head of the bay or berth off the new 75-yd pier with depths of 20 ft alongside. Bottom appears to be hard sand into which anchors do not readily dig in; holding is most unreliable. The bay is exposed to W. and a swell usually rolls in. The thrice-weekly steamer goes alongside.

Facilities. A few local shops can provide provisions. Fuel and water are available. A bus runs (to a schedule) to Apollonia. Summer hotels and villas have recently been built along the shore.

Other anchorages off Sifnos:

The following two inlets lying towards the northern tip of the island have suitable anchorages for small yachts:

Vourlithia. A deserted creek with convenient anchorage in 3 to 5 fathoms near its head. The bottom is sandy and the creek is open between W. and S.W. The mountainous sides rise rather steeply and in strong winds gusts could be expected.

Ayios Georgios has anchorage at the head of a sheltered creek for a small to medium-sized yacht.

Anchorage. Let go in 3 fathoms where the small houses begin. Run out a warp to the small quay (3-ft depths). Bottom is hard sand and one cannot be sure that a plough anchor will easily dig in. Excellent shelter, almost all round. The sides of the creek not being high strong winds should not cause discomforting gusts.

The houses of the small hamlet are mostly abandoned and only half a dozen are still occupied. The local people are all old, occupied with pottery, fishing and grazing goats. Communication is by boat with Kamares and track to Artemon village.

Though of little importance today, in ancient times Sifnos was rich on account of its gold mines, and witness of this period is the splendid marble treasury still to be seen nearly intact at Delphi.

Island of Siros (Syra)

Siros, the town, is capital of the Cyclades, with a population of nearly 13,000 little more than half of whom are Catholic; unlike the villages, where they are practically all Catholic.

Ermoupolis. The two main churches, the Catholic founded by Genoese and Venetians and the Greek Orthodox, are each perched on a hill above the town which has an impressive arcaded 19th-century square, clock tower and small opera house – the most striking and well-shaded city centre of the Aegean and so un-Greek like in appearance. In the port are two floating docks, a new shipyard, repair quays, floating cranes (10–28 tons), two merchant navy training schools.

Tourists know Siros for its manufacture of Loukoumi (Turkish Delight).

The Port

Approach and Berth. Chart 1833. Yachts should berth stern-to some 250 yds further W. of Hotel Hermes. There are two ferry-boat berths further along, one being at the end of the quay. Caïques and trawlers berth further west.

The harbour, normally quiet in the summer months, is poorly protected from east winds which bring in a heavy swell and may make conditions at the furthest quay intolerable for a yacht.

Officials. A Port of Entry; the usual quota of officials.

Facilities. Most things can be obtained at the market leading to the quayside including water and fuel. There are a number of new hotels and tavernas. A bus runs in summer to Foinikos, a much developed resort with a fine bathing beach. At the shipyard a yacht can be slipped on a skid cradle. The Piraeus steamer calls daily.

A British War Cemetery lies W. of the town by a road running N. beside the sea. There are also two cemeteries by St George's church where 111 men were buried, many being survivors of the transport *Arcadian*.

Other anchorages off Siros recommended for a temporary stay are:

Ormos Megas Yialos. This T-headed bay has good holding on a sandy bottom in the N.W. corner in convenient depths of 2–3 fathoms. The headland called Akri Grammatika is composed of marble slabs on which sheltering mariners during past centuries have scratched their names and dates.

Foinikos lies on the S.W. corner of Krasi Bay and is a pleasant place to bring up. The summer resort of Posidionia lies on the E. side of the bay.

Approach. Chart 1825, plan. A high rocky point marks the N. entrance, and the low-lying Psakhonis islet must be passed with care. The many recently built villas are conspicuous.

Berth. Medium-size and large yachts should anchor in the N.E. corner of the bay, open to S.W.

Shallow draught yachts have been recommended to moor on the S. side of a broad quay in depths of 7–8 ft. Shelter here in N. winds is good and no swell enters the bay.

Facilities. At the hamlet fresh provisions are obtainable. A taverna. Water available at the old North quay; bus service runs to the town of Siros.

History. The British interest in Syra began after the founding of the Levant company in the reign of Queen Elizabeth, but its real prosperity was during the last century in the early days of steam.

After gaining her freedom from the Turks in 1829, Syra found herself in a fortunate situation. Her commodious port lay in a strategic position on the trade route between the Black Sea, Levant and western ports. In those days steamers could proceed only limited distances without bunkering, and Syra's geographical position was in the precise locality to suit most routes. Thus the packet service, Egypt-Constantinople, Austro-Lloyd from Piraeus, Trieste and Brindisi, and the French Messageries ships, Bibby Line, etc., all called here for bunkering; it became in consequence a market for British coal. With its growing commercial importance consular representation was established; in addition to the British Consul there were nine consulates of other nations, a British church and chaplain and Lloyd's agent. Several Greek vessels classed at Lloyd's in the 1850s were trading to England probably as a result of the repeal of the Corn Laws and the opening of the Black Sea grain trade.

Siros has never been devastated by foreign invaders nor persecuted by the Turks as has happened to other islands. It was fortunate in having had a Capuchin mission which for centuries had the protection of France, and the Turks never molested them. It seems that this happy state of security attracted refugees who had fled from other islands, and thus at the time of the boom in shipping the manpower was available to help develop the resources of the port.

At the beginning of this century when oil began to take the place of coal, the importance of Syros declined but today there is again much activity in the port, mostly repair work and training schools.

Here, as in so many of these islands, the interest is entirely in the port, for the countryside is unwelcoming. The bleak mountains of Siros with their lower slopes now so barren and tree-less bear no resemblance to their description nearly three thousand years ago by Homer:

> *'Of soil divine,*
> *a good land teeming with fertility,*
> *Rich with green pastures, feeding flocks and kine*
> *A fair land with streams, a land of corn and wine.'*
>
> ODYSSEY XV

Island of Tinos

The island is remarkable as being the 'Lourdes of Greece'. A well-sheltered port with an interesting town (pop. 8,000) in mountainous surroundings.

Since 1822, when the miraculous icon of the Panaghia was discovered, pilgrims from Greece have flocked to Tinos every year to attend the great feast of

Our Lady on 15 August. Tinos has thus become a place of pilgrimage and the local inhabitants have prospered as a result.

The Port

Approach and Berth. Chart 1833 plan. Secure stern to the northern quay with anchor towards entrance. (Eastwards of the second bollard from the west it has been dredged.) A new quay has been built south of the main quay and the mole extended.

Facilities. Water, said to be the purest in Greece, is supplied by a tap close by. Plenty of provisions are available close to the quay; there are many hotels, restaurants and tavernas with good local wine. The two filling stations for fuel on the quay do not supply out of bond. Ice can be bought in the early morning only off Plateia Taxiarchon. The local weaving industry has some good examples in a shop leading up the hill. Mail steamers leave for Piraeus two or three times daily.

The harbour is large and the quayside usually animated with caïques loading and unloading, and many Greek visitors frequent the tavernas and restaurants.

From the quay, walking towards the hill, one soon approaches the large marble Greek Orthodox church. Although of no architectural merit, the forecourt is attractive, as well as the courtyard of the convent whose glaring white walls are softened by the shadows of the dark cypresses.

In Tinos church, a votive offering

Inside the church is the icon itself with typical Byzantine silver-work almost covering the painting of 'the great and gracious Lady'. Pilgrims are often wheeled in and the priests may be seen reciting their supplications, at the same time treating the pilgrims in no gentle manner as they twist them about, apparently to draw the Virgin's attention to that part of their anatomy they are beseeching her to cure. Hung from the roof of the church are many models often in silver – the votive offerings given by those who have been saved from a violent death by the intervention of the Virgin. Perhaps one of the more curious is that of a caïque which had been holed and was about to sink, but was saved by the timely arrival of a benign fish, which swam into the hole and so sealed it from the inrushing water. The hull, the sails and even the fish are skilfully and realistically worked in silver.

In the little crypt are two chapels, one marking the site of the discovery of the icon, and the other a memorial to the dead sailors of the Greek cruiser *Elli*. On 15 August 1940, when Greece was at peace with all nations, their cruiser *Elli* had been sent to attend the usual celebrations of Our Lady of Tinos and lay at anchor outside the port. She had dressed the ship in honour of the occasion and many of her ship's company were ashore. An Italian submarine operating under orders from Rome fired a torpedo, sinking *Elli* and many of the crew – an outrage the Greeks cannot easily forget.

The shores of the S.W. coast rise to a chain of mountains (more than 2,000 ft), their monotony being relieved by a number of mountain villages whose little white houses form a pleasant contrast to the bare, sombre mountainsides. These villages, conspicuous for their medieval dovecotes, have spring water at heights of 1,000 ft. A number of Jersey herds are grazed, the cattle being shipped to Piraeus sometimes in caïques.

Earlier History. Tinos came under Venetian rule in 1390 and was governed by Venice until 1715 when it was captured by the Turks. It was the last island to fall, although for nearly 200 years one island after another had been taken.

A low woolly cloud lying on the ridge of this island and on Andros is a sign of strong north winds. They sweep down the mountainside usually in violent gusts, and on the north-east or the weather side of the island the anchorages become quite untenable all the summer months. The two bays at the northern end of the island referred to in *Sailing Directions*, **Kolimbithra** with its deserted monastery and **Panormos** where the marble is shipped, can be most uncomfortable anchorages in summer.

THE LESSER ISLANDS

Anafi (Anaphi) Islands are a group of relatively flat and largely barren islands with very few inhabitants who live mainly in the village on the south of the main island which is hilly. Life is primitive, there being no running water or electricity. Here is an open anchorage where the mail boat calls. but there is no harbour – only a boat camber. Occasionally the island is overrun by a plague of partridges which cause havoc among the sparsely cultivated fields of the farmers.

Island of Donoussa (Dhenousa), a small but relatively tall island with a hamlet in the south, has two anchorages:

Dhendro Bay (Chart 1663), on the south coast, is distinguished by a blue-domed church standing in the middle of a small hamlet. The anchorage is on a sandy bottom in 5 fathoms open to the south, or off a quay in 6 ft. but the northerly swell curls round. About 100 people live on the island which in addition to the hamlet has a few scattered farmsteads. There are no roads and the island is primitive. A few caïques, used for fishing, are often berthed off a small quay. The weakly steamer anchors off.

Roussa (Chart 1663) lying on the E. coast is partly sheltered by the islet of Skilonisi. The best anchorage is off the beach, for the sea-bed near the islet rises too steeply. Dhendro Bay anchorage is the better.

> **History.** At the beginning of the First World War, Donoussa was the secret rendezvous for the German battle cruiser *Goeben* then being pursued by the British forces whilst escaping towards the Dardanelles. She urgently needed fuel and here a German collier was directed to await her arrival. Having topped up with coal *Goeben* steamed at full speed for the Dardanelles and, successfully eluding her pursuers, reached Constantinople; her presence exerted considerable influence in forcing Turkey into the war as an ally of Germany.

Sikinos and Folegandros, known as the *Dry Islands*, are mountainous, barren and steep-to. Both have open sandy bays and in summer they afford comfortable anchorage.

Island of Sikinos. One should make for Ormos Scala on the south coast of the island (Chart 1663).

> **Anchorage.** There is 2 fathoms close in and room to swing; the bottom is fine sand, A landing quay is on the western side of the small bay. The Meltemi produces a few strong gusts; it is entirely open to south.

> **Facilities.** A small taverna and one or two small houses are on the quay, and there is a freshwater well 200 yds inland. Provisions must be obtained from the main village on the hill.

The Chora lies on the mountain edge on the opposite side of the island – a village of 300 people, largely employed in cultivating the terraced vineyards and cornfields which cannot be seen from seaward. It is less than an hour's walk ascending an easy mule road to reach the village and is worth the effort. The local

Orthodox church is another hour onward; this was built around the former temple of Apollo whose Ionic columns still stand.

Island of Folegandros has no port, but a weekly steamer calls.

Anchorages
(a) **Karavostasi,** with the island village adjoining, may be approached with aid of Chart 1832. A short pier has been built on the S. side of the peninsula extending in a southerly direction; there is no light. The weekly ferry anchors close off. A stony road leads up to the Chora.
(b) **Vathy Bay** has convenient depths on a sandy bottom; but being rather open a swell creeps round the bay during northerly winds.

The island, with a population of only 500 people, offers nothing of particular interest, though a walk to the Chora is rewarding. The coastline is remarkable for its tall steep-to cliffs. Though cultivation cannot be seen from the sea, a number of terraces in the valleys leading up to the Chora are still farmed.

The remaining islands of the Cyclades are seldom visited:

Island of Kimolos is a barren-looking island close north of Milos with one or two sheltered anchorages. Barely a thousand inhabitants live here, mostly in the village.

Psathi Bay has occasionally been used by yachts who report favourably on its attraction. At the landing place is a taverna; the Chora lies on the hill above – an easy climb from the anchorages.

Island of Kinaros, is very small and uninhabited. Its usefulness to a yacht is the narrow, steep-sided inlet:

Pnigo Creek affording perfect protection for a medium-sized yacht. A beach lies at the head of this creek and is sometimes used by small caïques.

Approach. The creek is about 700 yds in length and without hazard until reaching a small patch of rocks on the western shore near the head of the creek. A shelf with depths beginning at 7 fathoms and slowly decreasing begins about half-way.

Anchorage. There are 3-fathom depths between a distance of 50 ft to 8 ft off the beach. Bottom is sand on rock. A warp must be run out ashore.

Levitha Islands consists of a chain of small islands lying about E.N.E. from the north of Amorgos.

Levitha Inlet is in the middle of the southern shore of the main island. It extends in an easterly direction, being rather narrow at its head and rocky at the sides. Although it provides all-round shelter the sea-bed consists mostly of flat rock and stones on which no anchor can hold. One or more warps are essential.

There are no permanent inhabitants; only one or two patches of cultivation and spring grazing.

Island of Yiaros, small and barren without a harbour, is sometimes used, as it was by the Romans, as a penitentiary for prisoners. Navigation is prohibited within 2 miles of the coast (Chart 1630).

Index

Main references are in bold; numbers in italic refer to maps, plans or drawings